THE REAGAN REVOLUTION?

THE REAGAN REVOLUTION?

B. B. Kymlicka and Jean V. Matthews
Editors

The Dorsey Press

Chicago, Illinois 60604

Acquisitions editor: Leo Weigman
Production editor: Mary Lou Murphy
Copyediting coordinator: Jane Lightell
Production manager: Charles J. Hess
Designer: Diana Yost
Compositior: The Saybrook Press, Inc.
Typeface: 10/12 Palatino
Printer: Malloy Lithographing, Inc.

ISBN-0-256-06135-1 (hardbound)
ISBN-0-256-06237-4 (paperbound)

Library of Congress Catalog Card No. 87−71556

Printed in the United States of America

1 2 3 4 5 6 7 8 9 0 B 5 4 3 2 1 0 9 8

Preface

There was something rather startling about the widespread talk in the early 1980s of a "Reagan Revolution" in the United States. The language of renewal is fairly common in American politics, but the language of revolution is not. Ronald Reagan and his team of supporters and advisors came to Washington in 1980 with the self-proclaimed intention of reversing the liberal trend of public policy that had dominated since the New Deal. Government was not the solution, they declared, but the problem, and the new administration aimed not just at curbing the growth of the positive state, but at overturning the liberal mind-set. Talk of "revolution" was somewhat uneasy for Reaganites who proudly espoused conservatism, but it is not unusual for revolutionaries to demand a return to earlier and purer days—to call for a restoration of authentic traditions that have been perverted. It was soon clear that this administration was not just a staid conservative regime. Though the attack on big government was the core of Reagan's "New Departure," much of the excitement and interest generated by the new administration was due to its plethora of social issues and its conscious philosophical attack on liberalism, which made it possible to believe that what occurred was not just a change of policy but a real revolution. This feeling was increased by perceptions of a general crisis of liberalism throughout much of the Western world. Canada and England both elected conservative governments; the Left was first defeated in Germany and then in France. Were we witnessing the end of an era in liberal capitalist democracies? Would there be a turn away from that ever-growing state that was so much a part of twentieth century life in the Western world?

These deeper questions lay behind the Centre for American Studies at the University of Western Ontario's decision to devote its annual lecture series and conference in 1986 to debating the question of the "Reagan Revolution." Enough time had elapsed to judge whether or not President Reagan had succeeded in "revolutionizing" American public policy and what the implications of the Reagan phenomenon might be. We asked individuals from different disciplines and backgrounds to offer their perspectives on several general questions: Had there, in fact, been a Reagan Revolution? If so, what did it include? If not, why had the administration failed to achieve its goals?

Most of the essays in this volume originated in our lecture series and the 1986 conference, although all have been revised and updated. The original audience for these presentations was a cross section of students and faculty for the public lectures, and for the conference, the audience was a select group of fifty academics studying the United States from various fields. Conference speakers had to step back from the minutiae and technical preoccupations of their disciplines, place their expertise in a wider context, and reflect on broader meanings of the past seven years' events in order to engage a general and critical audience. The strength of this approach continues in this volume with an interdisciplinary and cross disciplinary focus. Some of these papers are broadly philosophical, prescriptive, or openly critical, yet in every case the topic has engendered a lively and pointed response that readers will find both stimulating and thought provoking.

The book begins with an introduction by political scientist B. B. Kymlicka, who highlights themes addressed in succeeding sections. From the perspective of a student of parliamentary systems he assesses the unique powers and problems of the American presidency as an institution. This is followed by a piece from one of President Reagan's speech writers, Dana Rohrabacher, which both states the philosophy of the administration and reveals its characteristic style. The third section consists of three broadly reflective pieces on the meaning of the Reagan administration from the viewpoints of a historian, Richard Polenberg, a political scientist, James McNiven, and a sociologist, Alan Wolfe. The next four sections deal with the four primary areas where revolutionary changes may be manifested: James Tobin and William Niskanen on economics; John Chubb on politics; Peter Gottschalk and Kent Weaver on social policy; and Sayre Stevens and John Holmes on foreign policy. Finally, political scientist Bert Rockman concludes the book with a balanced assessment of where changes have been fundamental or superficial.

The Iran–Contra revelations of early 1987 diverted public attention from the more fundamental aims and achievements of the Reagan administration, and they cast doubt on whether the remaining two years of his presidency would produce further substantive changes. Nevertheless, in the first six years of office, Ronald Reagan succeeded in bringing a new climate of opinion to Washington and in shifting the terms and assumptions of American politics. We hope that this book will stimulate readers to think about both the specifics of the Reagan

Revolution and the deeper philosophical problems involved in choices of economic and social policy,—ultimately questions of political vision.

We wish to express our appreciation to the following individuals and groups for supporting the Centre for American Studies and the conference and lecture series on which this book is based: Denis Smith, Dean of the Faculty of Social Science at the University of Western Ontario; the Department of Economics; and the Academic Development Fund of the University of Western Ontario; the Social Sciences and Humanities Research Council of Canada; Western's American alumni association; and the United States Embassy in Ottawa. We also wish to thank David H. Flaherty, Director of the Centre for American Studies, for his unfailing encouragement, aid, and advice throughout this project. We are indebted to Leo Wiegman, of the Dorsey Press, for steering this project through its journey to the printer. Our thanks, too, to the Administrative Secretary of the Centre for American Studies, Linda Hill, for her tireless and invaluable help; to Frances Kyle for her assistance; and to Penelope Lister for her work on this book and in organizing the 1986 conference.

B. B. Kymlicka, *Department of Political Science*
Jean Matthews, *Department of History*

Profiles of Contributors

John E. Chubb. Senior Fellow, The Brookings Institution, Washington, D.C. Ph.D. in Political Science, University of Minnesota, 1979. Author of *The New Direction in American Politics*, ed., with P. E. Peterson, The Brookings Institution, 1985; *Interest Groups and the Bureaucracy: The Politics of Energy*, Stanford University Press, 1983; "The Political Economy of Federalism," *American Political Science Review*, December 1985; "Excessive Regulation: The Case of Federal Aid to Education," *Political Science Quarterly* 100, no. 2 (Summer 1985); "Federalism and the Bias for Centralization," in *The New Direction in American Politics*, ch. 10.

Peter T. Gottschalk. Associate Professor, Bowdoin College, Maine. Ph.D. in Economics, University of Pennsylvania, 1973. Author of "Do Rising Tides Lift All Boats?—The Impact of Secular and Cyclical Changes on Poverty," with Sheldon Danziger, *American Economic Review*, (May 1986) "The Impact of Budget Cuts and Economic Conditions on Poverty," with Sheldon Danziger, *Journal of Policy Analysis and Management*, Summer 1985; "Reagan, Recession and Poverty," with Sheldon Danziger and Eugene Smolensky, *National Tax Journal*, 1985; "A Framework for Evaluating the Impact of Economic Growth and Transfers on Poverty," with Sheldon Danziger, *American Economic Review*, (March 1985.)

John W. Holmes. Counsellor, Canadian Institute of International Affairs, and Professor of International Relations, University of Toronto, Toronto, Canada. LL.D., University of Western Ontario, 1973. Author of *Life with Uncle: The Canadian-American Relationship*, University of Toronto Press, 1981; *The Shaping of Peace: Canada and the Search for World Order, 1943–1957*, University of Toronto Press, 1979–82; *Canada: A Middle-Aged Power*, McClelland and Stewart, 1976; *Canada and the United States: Political and Security Issues*, Canadian Institute of International Affairs, 1970; *The Better Part of Valour*, McClelland and Stewart, 1970.

B. B. Kymlicka. Professor, Department of Political Science, University of Western Ontario, London, Ontario, Canada. Director of Research, Commission on Relations between Universities and Government, 1968–1969. Director of Research and Secretary, Commission on Post-Secondary Education in Ontario, 1969–1973. Dean, Faculty of Social Science, University of Western Ontario,

1976–1982. Ph.D., Columbia University, 1966. Recent publications include contributions to *Systems of Higher Education: Canada*, I.C.E.D., 1978; *Ontario Universities*, Ontario Economic Council, 1985.

James D. McNiven. Deputy Minister for Development, Government of Nova Scotia, Halifax, Nova Scotia, Canada. Senior Research Fellow for American Studies, Centre for American Studies, 1985–1986. Ph.D., University of Michigan, 1972. Author of "Canadian Trade Options from a Regional Perspective," in David Conklin and Thomas Courchene (eds.), *Canadian Trade at a Crossroads: Options for New International Agreements*, Ontario Economic Council, 1985; "Regional Development in the Next Decade," *Canadian Journal of Regional Sciences 9*, no. 1 (Spring 1986); "The Efficiency/Equity Tradeoff: The Macdonald Report and Regional Development," in William Coffee and M. Polese (eds.), *Recent Trends and Future Directions in Canadian Regional Development*, (forthcoming); "Triregional Economic Linkage: Overview and Agenda," in William Shipman (ed.), *Trade and Investment across the Northeast Boundary*, I.R.P.P., 1986.

William A. Niskanen. Chairman, Cato Institute, Washington, D.C. Ph.D., University of Chicago, 1962. Author of *Bureaucracy and Representative Government*, Aldine Atherton, 1971; *Structural Reform of the Federal Budget Process*, American Enterprise Institute, 1973; "Economic and Fiscal Effects on the Popular Vote for the President," *Public Policy and Public Choice*, 1979; "The Prospect of Liberal Democracy," *Fiscal Responsibility in Constitutional Democracy*, 1978.

Richard Polenberg. Professor of History, Cornell University, Ithaca, New York. Ph.D., Columbia University., 1964 Author of *The American Century: A History of the United States since the 1890s*, John Wiley & Sons, 1975; 2nd ed., 1979; *One Nation Divisible: Class, Race and Ethnicity in the United States Since 1938*, Viking Press, 1980; *Reorganizing Roosevelt's Government: The Controversy over Executive Reorganization, 1936–1939*, Harvard University Press, 1966; *War and Society: The United States, 1941–1945*, Lippincott, 1972.

Bert A. Rockman. Professor of Political Science, University of Pittsburgh, Pittsburgh, Pennsylvania. Ph.D., University of Michigan, 1974. Author of *Bureaucrats and Politicians in Western Democracies*, with Joel D. Aberbach, Harvard University Press, 1981; *The Leadership Question: The Presidency and the American System*, Praeger Publishers, 1982; "The Modern Presidency and Theories of Accountability: Old Wine and Old Bottles," *Congress and the Presidency*, Fall 1986.

Dana Rohrabacher. Speech Writer to President Reagan, Washington, D.C. M.A., University of Southern California. Mr. Rohrabacher is a journalist by profession, having worked as a reporter and editorial writer in Los Angeles for a number of years. He was a reporter for City News Service in Los Angeles and an editorial writer for the "Orange County Register," California's fourth largest newspaper. He has also written several film scripts.

Sayre Stevens. President, National Security Research Group, Systems Planning Corp., Arlington, Virginia. Ph.D., University of Washington, 1965. Author of "The Soviet BMD Program," in Ashton B. Carter and David N. Schwartz, *Ballistic Missile Defense*, Brookings Institution, 1984; "The Soviet Factor in SDI," *Orbis 29* (Winter 1986).

James Tobin. Stirling Professor of Economics, Yale University, New Haven, Connecticut. Ph.D., Harvard University, 1939. Author of *The New Economics: One Decade Older*, Princeton University Press, 1974; *Welfare Programs: An Economic Appraisal*, American Enterprize Institute, 1968; *Asset Accumulation and Economic Activity: Reflections on Contemporary Macroeconomic Theory*, Blackwell, 1980; *Macroeconomics, Prices and Quantities: Essays in Memory of Arthur M. Okun*, Brookings Institution, 1983; *Essays in Economics, Theory and Policy*, MIT Press, 1982.

R. Kent Weaver. Research Associate, Government Studies Program, The Brookings Institution, Washington, D.C. Ph.D. in Political Science, Harvard University, 1982. Author of *The Politics of Industrial Change: Railway Policy in North America*, Brookings Institution, 1985; "Are Parliamentary Systems Better?" *The Brookings Review*, 3, no. 4 (Summer 1985); "Controlling Entitlement," in *The New Direction in American Politics*, Chubb and Peterson (eds.), 1985; "Government Enterprize in Competitive Markets," in Economic Council of Canada (ed.), *Government Enterprize: Roles and Rationales*, The Council, 1984; "Review Essay: Governments in Business," *Policy Studies Review* 4, no. 1 (August 1984).

Alan Wolfe. Professor of Sociology, Queen's College, The City University of New York. Editor of *The Nation*. Author of *America's Impasse: The Rise and Fall of the Politics of Growth*, Pantheon Books, 1981; *The Limits of Legitimacy: Political Contraindications of Capitalism*, Free Press, 1977; *The Seamy Side of Democracy: Repression in America*, 2nd. ed., Longman, 1978.

Contents

Part I

THE AMERICAN PRESIDENCY: AN OVERVIEW

Chapter One

Introduction

B. B. KYMLICKA

It appeared to be the opinion of the Convention that [the executive] should be a character respected by the Nations as well as the federal Empire. To this end . . . as much power should be given to him as could be . . . guarding against all possibility of his ascending in a tract of years or Ages to Despotism and absolute monarchy.
ABRAHAM BALDWIN OF GEORGIA, 1787.[1]

The American presidency is the most important political office in the Western world—and probably in the whole world. Questions about that office and its incumbent, therefore, are of vital interest both to Americans and to citizens of many countries. But the U.S. presidency holds our attention not only because of its political importance; it arouses our curiosity because it reflects the intrinsic characteristics of the U.S. system of government.

Americans often assume that the way they define democracy and their ideas about how it should be reflected in the institutions of their government is "normal"—or, at least, most natural and certainly the most desirable form of government. This is not surprising. The U.S. Constitution has survived over 200 years encompassing changes (including a civil war) that have destroyed many other countries. Americans have discovered a recipe for a democratic and constitutional form of government that balances the necessary rigidity with appropriate flexibility and that achieves the desirable balance of power between separate branches of government. Moreover, not only has this

---

[1]Quoted in Max Farrand, *The Framing of the Constitution of the United States* (New Haven, Conn.: Yale University Press, 1976), p. 162.

form of government survived; it has flourished. The United States of America has become, certainly since World War II, an imperial power—an imperial democracy.

The longevity and success (together, perhaps, with a certain provincialism that permeates the United States) hide from Americans both the uniqueness of their successful government and the possible shortcomings of the system. The office of the presidency is one focus of such curiosity, not necessarily because it is more mysterious than other branches of government (the marvelous workings of Congress are harder to explain), but because the president is "the" government that foreign governments deal with and because he is the commander in chief—and thus the lord of every citizen's future. When, therefore, a candidate for the presidency such as Ronald Reagan comes forth, who is determined to bring about a "revolution" within the American government, we want to find out what happens when he is elected.

In one sense, it is nonsense to talk about the "Reagan Revolution." Revolutions in most definitions mean dramatic and, in social terms, violent upheavals. With the typical hype that characterizes modern mass democracies, the term has been applied to Ronald Reagan because he promised a "New Beginning" during his election campaigns of 1980 and 1984, which his supporters called the Reagan Revolution. What that slogan meant was never very clear. Revolutions, because they inevitably extract heavy costs, are justified by lofty appeals to some ideal future, some distant utopia. Ronald Reagan's revolutionary ideal was a curious mixture of the old and the new. It was optimistic—and presumably future oriented; but it was also very conservative in that it sought to build upon values of an imaginary American past from the freedoms of the frontier to the firm convictions of the religious. The vague justifications of the Reagan Revolution were not revolutionary; they were reassuring and promised to bring America back into the military, political, economic, and moral leadership of the world.

The assumption underlying these appeals was the perceived decline of the United States: the Soviet Union was gaining on the First Republic; there was a military "window of vulnerability"; the U.S. economic and political situation at home and in the world was deplorable and in decline. Reagan argued that all of this was due to corruption of the American moral fiber and to the loss of American self esteem and optimism in the future. The Great Democracy needed reassurance and a moral resurgence.[2]

---

[2]Wrote the neoconservative Podhoretz: "We had, Reagan suggested, lost or forgotten the principles through which we had become the most productive, the most prosperous, the strongest and most respected nation on earth." Norman Podhoretz, "The New American Majority," *Commentary*, January 1981, p. 28.

But if the electoral appeal was vague, was it possible that the Reagan administration's policies would flesh out these vague promises and create a revolution in America? There is, indeed, a consensus among observers that Reagan came to power with a more detailed set of policy proposals than any recent president. Were these new policies revolutionary? It is here that the term seems most inappropriate. Even when seen in their original, pristine forms, these proposals didn't spell out "revolution"; they did, however, intend a dramatic redirection of U.S. domestic policies. They also *implied*, but did not state, a drastic restructuring of American government. Indeed, the former couldn't have been accomplished without the latter—as David Stockman, the able director of the Office of Management and Budget, later concluded:

> The true Reagan Revolution never had a chance. It defied all of the overwhelming forces, interests, and impulses of American democracy. Our Madison government of checks and balances, three branches, two legislative houses, and infinitely splintered power is conservative, not radical. It hugs powerfully to the history behind it. It shuffles into the future one step at a time. It cannot leap into revolutions without falling flat on its face.

Stockman continued:

> The Reagan Revolution was radical, imprudent, and arrogant. It defied the settled consensus of professional politicians and economists on its two central assumptions. It mistakenly presumed that a handful of ideologues were right and all the politicians were wrong about what the American people wanted from government. And it erroneously assumed that the damaged, disabled, inflation-swollen U.S. economy inherited from the Carter Administration could be instantly healed when history and most of the professional economists said it couldn't be.[3]

When Stockman writes "democratic," he means "constitutional" as the way the U.S. government is structured. One virtue of the U.S. Constitution—demonstrated all too often in recent years—is that it prevents the domination of or the subversion of U.S. government by the executive branch. What is puzzling, and what needs explanation, is the recurrent attempt by the executive branch to dominate or subvert its equivalent branches.

One possible reason is that the United States has the only Western democratic government that unites the head of state and the chief executive officer in one person. It combines, to use Walter Bagehot's expression, both the "dignified" and the "efficient" parts of government in one office, the president. By the former, Bagehot meant the kind of government institutions or persons "which excite and pre-

---

[3]David A. Stockman, *The Triumph of Politics* (New York: Harper & Row, 1986), pp. 9, 395.

serve the reverence of the population" and, by the latter, "those by which, in fact [the government] works and rules."[4] In the United Kingdom, as well as in Canada, the "dignified" part belongs to the Crown: the monarch or her representative in Canada, the governor-general, expresses the idealized personification of the state; she stands for the United Kingdom and Canada. Nobody blames or associates the Queen or the governor-general with any particular policies or a particular political party. Policies are associated with the prime minister and the cabinet, the "efficient" aspect of government.

The distinction between the dignified and efficient aspects of government is interesting and important, especially in democracies. It separates the responsibility for running the government, with its corresponding accountability to the people, from the symbolic continuation and very existence of the state. In countries where there is a separation, the failure of the governing party, and the prime minister, does not herald the end of the world; it causes a change of leaders. Thus, in a most famous case, in May 1940, when the British Conservatives decided that the leadership of Neville Chamberlain was no longer acceptable, given that his appeasement policy did not work, they picked Winston Churchill as his successor. Countries that do not have monarchs to perform the dignified function find it useful to create an office to fill that role (usually called the president, as opposed to a prime minister).

The Americans, for historical reasons, have not separated these aspects; they are combined in the presidency. When an American president is elected, he becomes the beneficiary of the democratic mandate, and inherits the mantle of a king. The comparison of the president to royalty is easy for American commentators. Thus, when Howard Baker was appointed as chief of staff to Reagan, *The Wall Street Journal* called it "the Baker Regency."[5] Many other commentators have termed both his predecessor, Donald Regan, and Baker as prime ministers. Nothing could be more far-fetched—unless one con-

---

[4]Walter Bagehot, *The English Constitution* (London: Thomas Nelson and Sons), p. 74. Bagehot also believed that "the acute framers of the [American] Constitution, even after the keenest attention, did not perceive the Prime Minister to be the principal Executive of the British Constitution." He also stated, "Inevitably, therefore, the American Convention believed the king, from whom they had suffered, to be the real executive" (p. 132).

[5]*The Wall Street Journal*, March 2, 1987. The whole editorial is predicated on an explicit analogy with royalty: "The aging king, though still acclaimed by the people, had developed powerful foes within the court. Not least, he had capped the taxes and rents the nobility could collect from his subjects. One day, the king slips. No immediate harm comes to the kingdom, but the embarrassment is acute, for the king has broken a pledge."

siders the prime ministers of much earlier centuries in the United Kingdom.

This fusion of the head of state and the chief executive officer provides the American leader with the "teflon" coating. He stands both for a particular partisan position and for "America." This very powerful combination has become even more potent since the invention of mass media—especially television.

It is hard to attack the president—it is almost like attacking the United States as a whole. Indeed, the constitutional provision that must be followed to remove the occupant of the White House is a civilized and ritualized form of regicide.

One can also see the glorification of the presidency in the role of his "significant other"; where else among democratic countries is the wife of the political leader characterized as the *First Lady*? Who knows the names of the spouses of the prime ministers of Australia, Japan, or Canada? Who cares what the husband of the British Iron Lady, Mrs. Thatcher, does?[6]

Yet, even the universal tendency to worship temporal leaders does not explain the extreme reluctance of Americans to judge their president as they judge ordinary mortals. Lies and phony presentation of issues are called "inoperative statements" or explained as "misspoken" words. It is not accidental that American politics has contributed these expressions to the English language and that these expressions have been used by people who defend American presidents. It is as if Americans conceived of their chief executive not so much as a politician but more as a "great moralist" who does not speak in ordinary language but engages in pronouncements. It is part of Reagan's strength that he speaks in generalities: he exhorts the nation; he celebrates the resurrection of the American spirit; he preaches the righteous sermon.[7] It is hard to apply the ordinary yardsticks of veracity, logic, or fact to such pronouncements, for so doing would be inappropriate. But if it is all magic—movie or otherwise—how do we cope with the real issues? It is one thing for the natives of Papua to believe in the cargo cult; it is quite another item when an imperial democracy turns to magic as a solution to its economic, social, and military problems.

---

[6]In Canada, the Mulroney government tried for a time to emulate the Americans by presenting Mrs. Mila Mulroney as the "First Lady" of Canada, but it did not sit well with Canadians and was abandoned. For an interesting survey of this attempt, see Robert Fulford, "Imagining Mila," *Saturday Night*, April 1987, pp. 23–29.

[7]Typically, perhaps, in invoking the sermons of the Puritans, he improves on it. Thus, the call is not only to "build the city on the hill," but to make it a "golden" city.

It is ironic that when former president Jimmy Carter tried to bring an element of realism to the nation, it turned on him.[8] Reagan, as the "great communicator," in a set piece that came to be known as "The Speech," lambasted Carter for belittling America and for not having faith in the country.

To observers outside the United States, the spectacle of Reaganism is of more than passing interest. The United States, whether it has lost its global hegemony or not, is still the most powerful country in the world; it is certainly the most important neighbor for Canada.[9] The question a worried friend keeps on asking is: How well does U.S. government serve not only its own people, but the rest of us as well? How will this great imperial democracy come to terms with its role in world affairs and its domestic politics? These are not new questions; they only have new contexts. For the United States, the context is the increased influence of Congress on foreign policies, the influence of domestic parochial interests on Congress, and the inability of the administration to formulate, justify, and implement sensible foreign policies.

Yet, the need for strong leadership in the American system is acknowledged by all. Symptomatic of the need is the proposition that "the President is the only one we have; we have to rally around him." (Or, in the Democratic version, "we have to help him.")[10] Even such great liberals as Senator Daniel Moynihan of New York (with the authoritative air that only an ex-professor can muster) say that "Ronald Reagan does not lie."[11] Members of Congress, especially the Democrats (still afraid of Reagan's public relations ability), tried at first to absolve the president from any wrongdoing in the Iranian/Nicaraguan fiasco during the early weeks of its public disclosure.

---

[8]For the background and analysis of the "Crisis of Confidence" speech by Carter, see Robert A. Strong, "Recapturing Leadership: the Carter Administration and the Crisis of Confidence," *Presidential Studies Quarterly* 16, no. 4 (Fall 1986), pp. 636–50.

[9]For an introduction to this topic, see D. H. Flaherty and William R. McKercher, eds., *Southern Exposure: Canadian Perspectives on the United States* (Toronto: McGraw-Hill Ryerson, 1986).

[10]Even the defeated 1984 Democratic presidential candidate, Walter Mondale, could not bring himself to denigrate the president after the Iranian affair was exposed by the Tower Commission. He felt vindicated because "now Americans see it and the collapse of the President in the polls is precisely for those reasons I talked about—a President who wasn't in charge, a President who was isolated, absent from policy making." But, he also said, . . . "a weak President is something that weakens us all." Bernard Weinraub, "Walter Mondale on Not Saying 'I Told You So,' " *New York Times*, March 4, 1987.

[11]On the *CBS Morning News*, November 26, 1986.

The teflon protection of the American president is a durable and thick coating. The difficulty comes when the coating wears off and the base metal appears for all to see—such as when the Iranian affair became public knowledge. It is at this point that politicians and commentators call for rescuing the presidency from "the mounting pressure of an outraged citizenry."[12] Indeed, so dire is the need for helping the president that the same author who fears the "outraged citizenry" advocates that "Americans must learn to believe again, both as a simple fact and as an indestructible myth in the stability of their political system."[13]

Whatever the real meaning of this grand dictum (and it is hard to fathom the curious amalgam of "simple fact" and "indestructible myth"), the purport is clear: It is not only the individual act of the president that is questioned; the very system is under stress. What in the system is at fault?

One explanation is that the combination of efficient and dignified aspects of government is fortified by other influences. The president (and the vice-presidential running mate) are the *only* politicians elected nationally. Unlike all other politicians who represent only local or regional interests (no wonder their view is that "all politics is local," as former Speaker of the House Thomas (Tip) O'Neill put it), the president has a national constituency. This gives the president a legitimacy that is lacking in all other politicians.

The temptation springing from this qualitatively different democratic mandate is strengthened by a constitutional amendment limiting the president to two terms of office. Again, one can sympathize with the profound American distrust of the "man on horseback." Paradoxically, it is because the U.S. president is such a mixture of royal adulation and democratic legitimacy that the desire to limit his tenure of office appears desirable. Yet, it also leads to the opposite temptation, especially if and when the second term is won by a "landslide" endorsement. As recent evidence shows, it is when the president has convincingly won his second term, and when the restraints imposed by accountability through the fear of another election disappear, that the chief executive tries to subvert settled conventions of U.S. politics, and in so doing, the president may commit crimes.

It is possible to enlarge on this lack of accountability. Apart from reelection, there is no "responsible" government accountability— in the parliamentary sense—in U.S. government. The president does not have to face the Congress day in and day out and exchange words with the leader of the opposition at two swords' length. In-

---

[12]A. Weinstein, *New York Times*, November 30, 1986.

[13]Ibid.

deed, he does not have to brave the questions of the opposition at all. He can evade any hostile questioning altogether either by not submitting himself to it or doing so under conditions that are most favorable to him. From outright neglect of the mass media to staged "photo opportunities," the president can manipulate both the conditions and the timing of his public appearances. Even if he agrees to a press conference—the closest Americans come to submitting their leader to direct questioning—there is, apart from the obvious limitations of time and audience control by the president, the enormous disparity of legitimacy and status.[14] How dare the press question the president in an impolite way? They are not his equals—as the prime minister is vis-à-vis the leader of the opposition—but his loyal subjects, as they acknowledge by standing up when he arrives and leaves.

There is more to the feeling of awe than a mere manipulation of the media. The U.S. Constitution places enormous pressure on the president.[15] He really is the only executive of the United States. Only the president can decide all the issues that the government faces. This necessitates a knowledgeable and strong staff. Most political issues are not black and white—no matter how strongly the opposing views may be held. It is important that the president is confronted with the strength of various opposing arguments and how strongly they are held.

This picture of White House decision making, however, presupposes the role of the president as a Solomon, choosing wisely among the various alternatives presented to him. What happens in real life may be more complicated. The president may hold some strong opinions himself; indeed, he may be a victim of strong prejudices. Who, within the administration and within the White House, will stand up to him? Who will tell him that his views are untenable, unrealistic, dangerous—or whatever? The Tower Commission faulted the secretaries of state and defense for failing to defend their views on the Iranian arms deal to the president. But, as Stockman reports on his experience with Ronald Reagan: "It is difficult politely to correct the President of the United States when he has blatantly contradicted himself."[16]

---

[14]By the middle of March 1987, President Reagan had not held a press conference for 115 days—longer than any other president except Richard Nixon during the Watergate episode.

[15]"(Our) entire governmental system revolves around the concept of a Presidency in which all the reins that control national action are in the hands of one man. Legitimate power can be exercised only through his office," stated George E. Reedy, who has served as press secretary to President Johnson and who wrote three books on the presidency, in *New York Times*, March 6, 1987.

[16]Stockman, *The Triumph of Politics*, p. 357.

It is difficult in that nobody but the president has an independent power base. Some aides feel a moral obligation to serve the president by being truthful, but the White House, as George Shultz observed, is "an idiosyncratic place, more like a court—and I'm not speaking of the Reagan Presidency, but any Presidency. It's organized around and for the President, whoever that President is."[17]

Presidents have also learned to appreciate the power of the mass media—especially television—and the opportunity it gives them to dominate the political scene. The importance of television begins even before the president takes office. Walter Mondale was probably the last nonphotogenic presidential candidate—from now on the ability to master television and to project the right personality image on that medium will be essential for any candidate. Here, Reagan illustrates another problem with the U.S. political system. The road to the White House now starts far ahead of the election. To compete in the campaign marathon, aspirants have to devote much of their time to the actual campaign by collecting a lot of money and creating their own organizations. The proliferation of primaries and the decline in the importance of the party organization and party bosses has made it easier for what may be called the "privatization" of the political process. Ronald Reagan, like Jimmy Carter, owed less to his political party than to his own coalition; the party owed him for providing leadership.

The difficulty stems from the separation of the *electoral* and *governmental* aspects of U.S. politics. There are people who fear that the confluence of modern media technology and the lack of party articulation may turn the race for the White House into a competition in which the required qualities for a successful leader of the nation and the Western alliance may be overshadowed by the demands of electoral appeal. There is little doubt that Ronald Reagan ran good electoral campaigns; it is more doubtful whether he also possessed the necessary qualities to govern. How does one reconcile the electoral support for Ronald Reagan and his undoubted mastery of the media

---

[17]R. Steel, "Shultz's Way," *New York Times Magazine*, January 11, 1987, pp. 19–20. Others have made similar points. A good illustration of the worship of the U.S. president is provided in an article by John S. D. Eisenhower in the *New York Times* of January 16, 1987: "We Americans have built our President into a sort of demigod. . . . The President lives and breathes behind great white columns, guarded by hordes of Secret Servicemen and White House police officers. When he attends official functions, he pauses grandly at the entrance, as the Marine Band bursts out with the pompous "Hail to the Chief." Lifelong friends no longer call him by his name: it is always 'Mr. President.'. . . That condition would not be so serious were it not for the fact that the hubris spreads like a disease to the President's associates, both family and staff. The trend seems to be for staff officers to consider themselves powers in their own right."

with the following appraisal offered by *Time* magazine after the Tower
Commission Report was released in March 1987:

> Reagan stands exposed as a President willfully ignorant of what his
> aides were doing, myopically unaware of the glaring contradictions be-
> tween his public and secret policies, complacently dependent on advisers
> who never once, from start to finish, presented him with any systematic
> analysis of aims, means, risks and alternatives. And, in the end, as a
> President unable to recall when, how or even whether he had reached
> the key decision that started the whole arms-to-Iran affair.

And:

> The picture of an inattentive, out-of-touch President may have been
> limned before, but never so authoritatively. . . . [This] is the same Reagan
> who has never admitted, probably even to himself, that his tax and
> spending programs were bound to result in gargantuan budget deficits.[18]

One shrewd observer of the presidency, Professor James David
Barber, explains this contradiction in terms of presidential "character." Through his studies, Barber has developed categories of character that allow him to speculate on how well White House incumbents
will do:

> Such rough predictions do not require psychoanalysis or other myste-
> rious methods. What they do require is an insistence that we bring to
> bear *Presidential* criteria when we pick a President, based on straightfor-
> ward understanding of what a President has to do and how similar char-
> acters in that office have met their challenges. The Reagan debacle, from
> the 'effectiveness' which gave us history's biggest deficit to the collapse
> of American political integrity in the world scene, ought to underline that
> need.

> In short . . . we have wound up again and again with Presidents who
> have mastered campaigning but brought into the very center of the Gov-
> ernment a fatally flawed set of political habits. One wonders all over
> again: When will we ever learn to evaluate Presidents, not after they
> have nearly done us in but before they win the job?[19]

Professor Barber is right. In democracies, the ultimate responsibil-

---

[18]*Time*, March 9, 1987, pp. 16–17.

[19]James David Barber, "How to Pick Our Presidents," *New York Times*,
March 8, 1987. Russell Baker put it more succinctly: "Presidents like Mr. Reagan were bound to result from the game-show campaigning which evolved
after politics became television, forcing politicians to entertain or die. Once
Presidential campaigns ceased to be about running the country and became
competitions for television ratings, the chances of getting anybody competent
into the White House diminished." *New York Times*, March 10, 1987.

ity for the selection of leaders rests with the people. Indeed, it is often necessary to remind ourselves that in a democracy we have the kind of government we deserve. But surely one can also ask through what instruments and what process the people select leaders. It may be misleading, unfair, and perhaps not useful to blame "ourselves" for ignoring the necessary presidential qualities. What is involved here is not only the tendency of modern mass democracies to engage in image manipulation but also the institutional process through which we select our leaders. There is something to be said for an institutional reform of how presidential candidates are picked.

Another aspect of this electoral/administration dichotomy is the increasing tendency of presidential candidates to promise more and more—and for the American public to expect more and more from their leaders. There is an insatiable demand for attributing to the government—even by those who run against it—powers that in more sober moments nobody expects it to have. Yet, the candidates promise and promise. Thus, even Reagan promised that he would bring better living standards and greater prestige to the United States. The amazing thing about Reagan wasn't that he made these promises but that he implied that they could be achieved without any sacrifice.

There is nothing new in democratic politicians promising more and more. What is perhaps new and disturbing is when the politicians, especially U.S. presidents, begin to believe that they can actually deliver on these promises. Without the checks that the system is built on, this temptation to make the promises true, combined with the desire to leave a mark on history, can lead directly to welcoming the kind of attitude displayed by Lt. Col. Oliver L. North: "Can do."

Finally, once elected, the U.S. president is faced with a system that is also unique among Western democratic nations: He brings with him thousands of followers who will make up the top echelons of the administration. It used to be argued that this was an advantage of the U.S. system; it allowed the incoming president to pick the best brains in the country who supported his policies. The permanent civil servants—invariably called "bureaucrats" in the parlance of incoming managers—were viewed as deadwood, as obstacles to a quick and efficient implementation of the "new policies" and devoid of any new ideas. From John F. Kennedy to Ronald Reagan, the White House complained about the dull-witted and uncooperative bureaucrats.[20]

---

[20]"It was a constant puzzle to Kennedy that the State Department remained so formless and impenetrable. He would say, 'Damn it, Bundy and I get more done in one day in the White House than they do in six months in the State Department.' " Arthur M. Schlesinger, Jr., *A Thousand Days* (Boston: Houghton Mifflin, 1965), p. 406. On the attitude of the new frontiersmen to the state department, see Chapter 16; on the attitudes within the Reagan

There is some justification for the perennial complaints about bureaucrats. At the same time, there are many good reasons why they resist new proposals; they have seen and tried many ideas and they have accumulated a treasury of experience that every sensible politician should value. All recent presidents, and especially presidents who did not know Washington, have ignored the accumulated wisdom of permanent officials—and all have paid a price. "It's as if there was no memory," observed Donald F. Rumsfeld about the Iran fiasco.

Of course, if the intention is *to start* a revolution, then it may be necessary to have a wholesale replacement of personnel. That, after all, is what Lenin preached and practiced (almost).[21] But if the continuation of settled policies or an honest and critical review of new ones is desirable, then the U.S. system of "a government of strangers" (to borrow from an evocative study of this phenomenon by Hugh Heclo[22]) presents some problems. There are no simple answers. The Reagan administration, however, presents an example of what happens when dramatic, if not revolutionary, changes are attempted within the U.S. system of government.

How do we evaluate the impact of a president? An obvious way is to inquire about his policies. In the case of Ronald Reagan, it is generally conceded that he came to power with the determination to

---

White House, see the *Tower Commission Report*, p. 45: "On May 17, Lt. Col. North 'strongly urged' that VADM Poindexter include Secretary Shultz and Secretary Weinberger along with Director Casey in a 'quiet' meeting with the President and Mr. McFarlane to review the proposed trip. VADM Poindexter responded, 'I don't want a meeting with RR, Shultz and Weinberger.' "

[21]One such enthusiast in the Reagan administration was supply-side econonomist Paul Craig Roberts. Writing about his breakfast in the White House with the president on March 30, 1981, he observes: "Presidents seldom know more than a few of their appointees and have no idea who they are relying on. The lack of contact between a president and his government was dramatized by the watchful eye that the Secret Service kept over the roomful of people bearing presidential commissions. In a brief address to the group the President again exhorted his government to put policy before politics. A man sitting next to me asked if I was new to government. It was his third administration, he explained. All of a sudden the pleasure of breakfasting at the White House gave way to a sinking feeling that the Reagan revolution was running on retreads. I felt lonely and wondered if the President did." Paul Craig Roberts, *The Supply-Side Revolution* (Cambridge, Mass.: Harvard University Press, 1984), p. 125. Roberts served as assistant secretary in the Treasury Department.

[22]Hugh Heclo, *A Government of Strangers* (Washington, D.C.: The Brookings Institution, 1977).

reverse the direction of policies established by his predecessors. The purpose of these reversals was fairly simple: to roll back the state, to cut taxes, and to reestablish the military preeminence of the United States in world politics. The first two goals were obviously connected;[23] the latter wasn't, and it led to inevitable contradictions that the president resolved by putting what he called national security ahead of any budget consideration.[24]

Translating these goals into specific policies, however, posed a number of problems. First, the president apparently had the impression that there was a lot of "waste" in government,[25] and that the costs of government could be cut back if this waste was eliminated. The budget makers in the Office of Management and Budget had a difficult time convincing him that the elimination of waste would not be sufficient for government to balance the budget, cut taxes, and increase defense expenditures.

---

[23]In the eyes of some people, the connection was conspiratorial. Writing in the *New York Times*, July 21, 1985, Senator Moynihan claimed: "The policy was the Administration's deliberate decision to create deficits for strategic, political purposes. . . . The Reagan Administration came to office with, at most, marginal interest in balancing the budget—contrary to rhetoric, there was no great budget problem at the time—but with a very real interest in dismantling a fair amount of the social legislation of the preceding 50 years. . . .Thus the plan: reduce revenues. Create a deficit. Use the budget process to eliminate programs. . . . A hidden strategy? Not really. On February 5, 1981, 16 days in office, the President, in his first television address to the nation, said: 'there were always those who told us that taxes couldn't be cut until spending was reduced. Well, you know, we can lecture our children about extravagance until we run out of voice and breath. Or we can cure their extravagance simply by reducing their allowance.' " Senator Moynihan claimed in the article that this plan was dreamed up by some high-powered intellectuals who came to Washington with Reagan. According to a report in *Time* magazine of July 22, 1985, p. 20, Moynihan had Stockman in mind.

[24]Reports Stockman: " 'Defense,' [the President] had said repeatedly, 'is not a budget issue. You spend what you need.' " *The Triumph of Politics*, p. 283.

[25]Stockman recalls that the president was fond of drawing upon anecdotes as a source of wisdom. One of his favorite stories concerned the time in California when people in one department had to fold records before they could be kept in filing cabinets. "One of our people [the president said] found out you didn't have to do this. We just ordered new metal cabinets which were twice as wide, so records would fit without folding. It saved thousands of work hours." Stockman observed: "I would hear the filing cabinet story many times over the next four years. *It was the single lens through which the President viewed the federal budget. I would try many times to dissuade him from that point of view, never with success.*"(emphasis added) Stockman, *The Triumph of Politics*, p. 346.

Secondly, and perhaps more importantly, the president thought that the undesirable consequences of many New Deal, New Frontier, and Great Society programs outweighed their good intentions. Some presidential advisers, and possibly the president himself, also believed that the very existence of these programs was destroying the kind of America they wished to create—or recreate. Moreover, the president also wished to "free" American business from the deadening hand of allegedly excessive governmental regulation. There is no better defense of that view, together with its rhetoric, than what is presented in a following chapter by Dana Rohrabacher, one of the president's speechwriters.

There is disagreement among observers about what Reagan accomplished in this area. The essays by Gottschalk and Weaver in this book do not document any great upheavals in social policies; rather, they demonstrate that the beginnings of reducing these programs had already started under President Carter. They also show how difficult it is to rearrange governmental priorities—either because of the institutionalized nature of the programs or because the American public, through its representation in the Congress, does not approve of dramatic changes. It is possible that what Reagan did accomplish was to test the lower limits of what modern democratic governments can do.[26] Perhaps it took a president with primitive understanding and an easy disregard for fiscal realities to undertake this task.

The failure to reduce social programs sufficiently to compensate for the increases in defense and a stubborn insistence on tax cuts can be explained in two ways: either by a woeful ignorance of political and economic realities or by a zealous adherence to an economic theory that was not a theory but instead a dressed-up ideology. Tobin and Niskanen discuss the economic consequences of the Reagan administration in Part IV. Their assessments leave the reader with an uncomfortable feeling. Indeed, as Niskanen points out, our

---

[26]One of the main advisers to the president was Richard Darman, who published the following assessment on the prospects of rolling back the state just before he joined the administration:

> The interest in limiting the growth of government must also be tempered by realism. The growth of government may be slowed or even stabilized, but it is virtually certain not to be reversed. Aggregate U.S. governmental expenditures taken as a percentage of gross national product remain below the levels of most developed societies, and the opportunities for shrinking are few.

Richard G. Darman and Laurence E. Lynn, Jr., "The Business-Government Problem: Inherent Difficulties and Emerging Solutions," in *Business and Public Policy*, ed. John T. Dunlop (Boston: Graduate School of Business Administration, Harvard University, 1980), p. 58.

understanding of what actually happened on Reagan's "watch" is incomplete.

Yet, the idea of "rolling back the state" had a wide appeal. Even liberals began to acknowledge that the welfare state built up by Democrats and Republicans since the 1930s was not working as intended. The very political philosophy of the welfare state was seriously questioned and often abandoned. There was an ideological vacuum on the Left, and some of its former adherents emerged as thinkers on the "neoconservative" Right.[27] The Left was bereft of any sensible—and certainly any electorally salable—alternative. Alan Wolfe's essay explores some of the issues that the Left is facing and how it interprets the Reagan era.

Was the ideological bankruptcy of the Left and people's weariness with the welfare state responsible for the electoral defeat of the Democrats? Did the election of Reagan and the direction in which he promised to take America reflect the wishes of the electorate? What does the Reagan election demonstrate? Did it complete one of those long-term tidal waves of political change from one political party to another? Or is there something occurring that makes the assumption of mere historical repetition inappropriate and misleading? Political parties may retain the same labels, but who they represent and what policies they stand for may change. The demographic changes in the United States alone—the population shift from the Northeast to the Southwest and the South—were bound to produce political changes, along with the alterations in the very structure of the society and the economy.

It is sometimes argued that these changes will manifest themselves in the sixth realignment of political parties—a long-term shift in the dominance of one party over the other.[28] The arrival of Reagan—or, if others are to be believed, the arrival of Nixon—heralded the breakup of the Democratic party as the majoritarian party of government with a replacement of Republicans. Because of changes in American society and in the U.S. government, this interpretation is be-

---

[27]On the link of these neoconservatives to the Reagan administration, see Sidney Blumenthal, *The Rise of the Counter-Establishment* (New York: Times Books, 1986).

[28]A brief and good summary of the origins and history of the idea of realignment can be found in Arthur M. Schlesinger, Jr., *The Cycles of American History* (Boston: Houghton Mifflin, 1986), pp. 34ff. See also Walter Dean Burnham, "The 1980 Earthquake: Realignment, Reaction or What?" in *The Hidden Election*, ed. Thomas Ferguson and Joel Rogers (New York: Pantheon Books, 1981); and James L. Sundquist, *Dynamics of the Party System*, rev. ed. (Washington, D.C.: The Brookings Institution, 1983).

ing questioned and modified. The essay by John Chubb explores these topics.

Presidents may be considered "great" when they manage not only to initiate new policies but to have these policies institutionalized—that is, to have them established as part of the accepted political landscape and even embodied in separate organizations or institutions. The most obvious illustration of this "institutionalization" was the creation of the Department of Education (DOE) by President Carter and the failure of the Reagan administration to abolish it. In many ways, erasing the DOE should have been easy. It stood as a symbol of federal intervention in areas belonging to individual states, and it was one of Reagan's targets during the 1980 campaign.[29] Yet, neither the "New Federalism"—the fourth "New Federalism" in recent years—that was to move responsibilities for many federal programs to the states, nor the hostility of the Reagan administration toward the DOE, managed to eliminate it.

While the DOE still exists, federal *support* of education has undergone changes mainly because of the administration's pursuit of the New Federalism. But even these efforts to change educational funding have met institutionalized resistance symbolized by the existence of the DOE and fortified by the vested interests of Congressional leaders and other local politicians and bureaucrats.

There are, finally, two other ways to look at the presidency. One way is to identify it as a personification of "America," and to describe the country through it. Because of its fusion of the royal and democratic attributes, the U.S. presidency lends itself to such a personalization. Indeed, the presidency is often used as a synonym or metaphor for the society as a whole.

A good illustration of this approach to the study of the presidency or, more accurately, of the president as a symbol of the United States, is Garry Wills's *Reagan's America*. As the title indicates, this book is supposed to be a study of America; it is, in fact, a study of Ronald Reagan. Wills maintains that it is through an understanding of the president that we can understand the United States. At its best, such a search for the "meaning" of Reagan can lead to interesting new perspectives on the mood and values of U.S. society; at its worst, it

---

[29]Reagan's attack on the DOE also foreshadowed later events. Reagan said that the department, newly created by President Carter, "Is 'planning all manner of things to limit and restrict institutions of this [St. Joseph College] kind because their faith is totally in public education only.' No one in the press or the Reagan entourage had the foggiest idea of what the candidate was talking about. Whether Reagan did, either, was doubtful, but it was late in the day and the candidate was unavailable for questioning." Lou Cannon, *Reagan* (New York: Perigee Books, 1982), p. 278.

sinks into cheap rhetorical devices and metaphors that by explaining too much, explain very little.[30]

Wills speculates about the "nature" of the American society without explaining why or how that "nature" is peculiarly American. Yet, his effort is typically American in so far as his answer to "What kind of a nation are we?" is an exercise in introspection on values: the essential part of our fate is deposited within us, in the values we hold—a doctrine surprisingly not that different from the attitude of President Reagan and his supporters.

The other approach to understanding the president is through the study of history. But a historical approach does not come easy to an optimistic society such as the United States—a society that has, so far, believed more in its ability to shape its future than to learn from its past.[31] It has seemed easier to speculate about the "nature" of the American society with little or no historical references.

An illustration of an instructive historical study is the essay by Richard Polenberg in Chapter 3. It compares and contrasts two presidents, Franklin D. Roosevelt and Ronald Reagan. This historical perspective allows us to appreciate the changes that American government and society have undergone since the 1930s and 1940s.

A different kind of historical approach asks, "How did we get here?" and "Are there some broader forces at work that would help us understand the present?" There are historians and social philosophers who speculate about these questions, people who deal with large brushes on wide canvases. Arthur M. Schlesinger, Jr., however, combines that approach with an abiding interest in what role the American government, and especially the presidency, has played in U.S. history. His most recent book, *The Cycles of American History*, is a magisterial review of the various sources and interpretations of U.S. history.[32] To Schlesinger, U.S. history is "a carpet" that has many

---

[30]This rhetorical device is called "antisagoge" and a good illustration of it is the following quotation from *Reagan's America*:

> The geriatric "juvenile lead" even as President, Ronald Reagan is old and young—an actor, but he is authentic. A professional, he is always the amateur. He is the great American synecdoche, not only a part of our past but a large part of our multiple pasts. That is what makes many of the questions asked about him so pointless. Is he bright, shallow, complex, simple, instinctively shrewd, plain dumb? He is all these things and more.

Gary Wills, *Reagan's America* (Garden City, N.Y.: Doubleday, 1987), p. 4.

[31]"History is bunk," as Henry Ford put it—and Americans think it worthwhile to record in their books of sayings.

[32]Arthur M. Schlesinger, Jr., *The Cycles of American History* (Boston: Houghton Mifflin, 1986).

figures, but only two strands or themes: "I will call one theme the tradition and the other the counter-tradition. . . . "These themes have many forms but they alternate in cycles and are "self-generating."[33]

To skeptics, this may seem somewhat unsatisfactory, even unhistorical. The only strings that bind this bountiful sheaf of historical reviews, this "carpet," are threads of cycles and dialectical alternations of the ethos of messianism and the ethos of realism. Schlesinger neither shows how these threads bind the historical developments together nor why they developed as they did when viewed as a whole. Perhaps the sheer encyclopedic intellect and the ecumenical spirit that permeates the book (though the ecumenism is not wholly catholic: Schlesinger has some pet heretics) prevent the author from arriving at a better explanation than this: "The roots of this cyclical self-sufficiency doubtless lie deep in the natural life of humanity." (p. 27)

It is possible that the Reagan administration, viewed from the perspective of a historian, will not be anything more or less than the nadir of the liberal or the zenith of the conservative wave of American history. But the Reagan administration came to power while the United States faced issues it had not dealt with before. One issue is international in character: the development of economic interdependence among the trading nations of the world. Although still the most powerful, the United States has lost its overwhelming economic predominance. It has also become much more dependent on international trade.

What should be the state's role in international trade and in the domestic adjustments to changes caused by its development? The issues and problems stemming from this development are many, but chief among them is the relationship of trade to politics. In a crucial way, this isn't only a question of providing assistance to displaced workers or protecting the industry against unfair imports; the central question is the role of the state in the economy.

Similarly, by the 1970s, it was clear that the kind of social programs devised since the 1930s were redundant, misdirected, or, due to changing circumstances, counterproductive. Even the liberals, who were responsible for the creation of the so-called welfare state, felt either uneasy about many of its manifestations or they became outright critical of it. Again, the basic question here concerns the role of the state: What should the responsibility of the individual citizen be and what can and should be done by the state as an expression of our collective responsibility, our social citizenship?

When liberals called for the use of the state as an instrument of intervention, they did so in the name of a social ideal—an ideal that

---

[33]Ibid., pp. 3, 19, 23, 26, 27.

reflected a vision of a better society: more equal, more prosperous, and presumably more free. These socially desirable ends justified the means. When Reagan attacked the state, wishing to roll it back, to cut back both its positive (support) and negative (regulation) activities, he was expressing the disappointment of many people with how it had worked out. But the rolling back of the state became a slogan of its own: Reagan administration programs, as reflected in the campaign and official pronouncements, were devoid of any vision, any ends towards which Reagan wished to lead the nation. Exhortations to build a golden city on the hill were never elaborated upon or explained. It was as if the rolling back of the state had become an end in itself.

And that is the issue: What is the role of the state in a modern society that is becoming more interdependent both domestically and on actions of other states? What is the *necessary* role of the state in such a society? Reagan raised the issue; it remains unresolved both as to purpose and means.

Finally, the Reagan administration, in attempting a dramatic reversal of policies, tested the stability as well as the flexibility of the U.S. constitutional system. It may be that, in retrospect, it was this testing that will be remembered most; it revealed both the weaknesses and the strengths of the system; the strengths prevailed. The Founding Fathers did not really like revolutions.

SUGGESTIONS FOR FURTHER READING

de Tocqueville, Alexis. *Democracy in America* (1834), ed. Phillips Bradley. New York: Vintage Books, 1960.

Fisher, Louis. *Constitutional Conflicts between Congress and the President.* Princeton, N.J.: Princeton University Press, 1985.

Kessler, Frank P. *The Dilemmas of Presidential Leadership: Of Caretakers and Kings.* Englewood Cliffs, N.J.: Prentice Hall, 1982.

Schlesinger, Arthur M., Jr. *The Cycles of American History.* Boston: Houghton Mifflin, 1986.

David Stockman. *The Triumph of Politics.* New York: Harper & Row, 1986.

Part II

THE IDEOLOGY OF "THE REAGAN REVOLUTION"

What I'd really like to do is go down in history as the president who made Americans believe in themselves again.
RONALD REAGAN

The first essay in this collection, by Dana Rohrabacher, a speech writer for Ronald Reagan, is an excellent example of both the working philosophy behind the Reagan administration and the style with which that philosophy is publicly expressed and, one suspects, conceived by its adherents. It should be read both for what it tells us about the self-image of the administration, about its assumptions and political ideas, and also as an example of political rhetoric, that is, the art of persuasion. In this regard, the anecdotal quality of the style is striking. From the opening image of the closed ranks of the organized society and the chaotic marketplace of the free society, the ideas are encapsulated and conveyed in images and in stories—perhaps one should call them parables—like the tale of the Soviet potato farmer or the Christmas rush at the post office. As all great communicators have always known, the story is probably the best way to get a point across to a wide audience and to ensure that the point then sticks in people's minds; on the other hand, if the thinker *thinks* in anecdotes, this may lead to a dangerous oversimplification of what are, in reality, very complex matters.

Rohrabacher might say that the genius of Ronald Reagan was that he *could* simplify, he could cut through the oversophisticated thinking of late twentieth-century liberalism to pose a stark dichotomy between the grey stagnation produced by an overgrown government and the efflorescence of human energy and creativity let loose when the dead hand of the state is removed. This is the message of Rohrabacher's paper (this piece was written as a speech), in which the president saves the country, in the nick of time, from the slough of despondency where the excesses of too much government had plunged it. Rohrabacher is probably right in his concluding statement that Ronald Reagan "ignited a new spirit of optimism in the United States" and that this will ensure his reputation as a "truly historic figure." In this conclusion, Rohrabacher engagingly subsumes much of the academic thinking of the new conservatism in direct and simple language. The Laffer curve and supply-side economics become obvious common sense, the jaundiced reappraisal of welfare by Charles Murray and Thomas Sowell appears in the image of the welfare-damaged, native-born, ghetto black wallowing in despair and self-pity, while the illegal immigrant eagerly washes cars or dishes and works his way into the middle class. We see the revived spirit of volunteerism exemplified in Rohrabacher's own donation of his time to teach writing in a disadvantaged Washington, D.C. school. (And yet, even in the Reagan era there is a need for a government office of Private Initiative!) Finally, the Strategic Defense Initiative (SDI) is described, not in terms of technical mastery, but in moral terms, as the humane alternative to mutually assured destruction.

A liberal might object to this essay in that liberalism since the New Deal has been caricatured—that the Great Society was not 1984. But political speakers are not required to make the best case for their opponents. Their job is to make the best case for their own side, and this is what Rohrabacher has done in a winning and plausible way.

SUGGESTIONS FOR FURTHER READING

Friedman, Milton, and Rose Friedman. *Capitalism and Freedom*. Chicago: University of Chicago Press, 1962.

Friedman, Milton, and Rose Friedman. *Free to Choose: A Personal Statement*. New York: Harcourt Brace Jovanovich, 1980.

Nash, George H. *The Conservative Intellectual Movement in America since 1945*. New York: Basic Books, 1976.

Reagan, Ronald, and Richard G. Hubler. *Where's the Rest of Me?* New York: Duell, Sloan and Pearce, 1965.

Reagan, Ronald. *A Time for Choosing: The Speeches of Ronald Reagan, 1961–82*. Chicago: Regency, 1983.

Wills, Garry. *Reagan's America*. Garden City, N.Y.: Doubleday, 1987.

Chapter Two

The Goals and Ideals of the Reagan Administration

DANA ROHRABACHER

In the first half of this talk, I will examine the philosophical foundation of the administration. For the sake of discussion, we will call it the Reagan team world view. Obviously, there are differences within the administration, so let me just add that this is my view of the Reagan team world view.

I was a journalist before coming to the White House. The time spent as a journalist in the 1970s broadened my horizons as nothing else I have ever done. It helped equip me for my current job. It dramatically increased the scope of my vision. I find that those who are the strongest advocates of more and more government, people who are looking to political leadership for solutions, generally lack the ability to appreciate the enormous opportunity all around us, not just for self-advancement, but for problem solving in general.

Clearly, the Reagan philosophy emphasizes nonpolitical solutions to contemporary problems; it reverses a trend that started in the 1930s and accelerated in the 1960s. Those who look to the state generally believe that progress comes when the energy, talents, and creativity of a nation are harnessed, directed, and brought to bear on weighty problems. This is in stark contrast to the Reagan philosophy. The best road to progress, we believe, lies in freeing the energies of the people; such liberation will permit individuals to meet the challenges confronting society by coming at those challenges from the bottom up and from many directions.

The latter approach—based on individual choice rather than political planning—is, in my opinion, both moral and more likely to bring progress; yet, it is less salable than the former. It is next to impossible to prove, at any given moment, that an individual-directed society is stronger than a centrally controlled, politically directed society. To demonstrate this, visualize two communities that I will describe.

First, picture a place where all the inhabitants are in uniform. They are marching in step in platoons and regiments. Military music, blaring from loudspeakers, keeps everybody marching at a fast clip. Few people are talking to one another. There are huge, Greek, temple-like buildings in the distance and large, modern apartment complexes situated near what looks like a giant factory. This view is the epitome of organization and regimentation; it is a truly command-dominated society.

Now contrast that community with another place that could not be more different. Here, people scurry back and forth in what appears to be total chaos. Some people are standing around talking to one another; some of them are arguing. The competing voices blend with a mixture of sounds: cars honking, street vendors trying to attract customers, stereos blasting. Nonconformity is everywhere. A potpourri of structures line the street: some large, some small, some shabby and in disrepair, others still under construction.

Which one of these communities is the strongest and most likely to meet the challenges of time? In an age of television, it might appear to be the first one. That is because people marching in a row make a good picture. Immense government edifices, oozing with power, make good backdrops. Boasting officials, with authority to order the marching platoons and regiments, are almost bigger than life.

The strongest and most progressive society, however, the society most likely to meet new challenges and move ahead, is the one in which the people are more free and less directed by political authority. It may look like chaos, but each person in the second society knows exactly what he or she is doing. By itself, an individual's task may not seem impressive, but the sum total of this freewheeling activity is far more productive, a far greater force for change, than what is found with their regimented counterparts. Decisions in the second society are made instantaneously by each person, with maximum flexibility, with all the incentive and creativity generated when individuals realize that their destiny is in their own hands. It is freedom—not regimentation—that unleashes the power of the human spirit, the most valuable asset of any society.

This freedom is what motivated many people to come to America. It is to the credit of our forefathers and mothers that once they were here they steadfastly refused to be harnessed. Americans do not like to be told what to do. When all the rhetoric dies down, this talk about harnessing the resources and the energy of America, or any other country, is really about ordering people to do what they do not choose to do—whether those orders come from an elected authority, an appointed authority, or simply an individual who assumes authority.

The Reagan team world view ties American prosperity to the fact that people in the United States, by and large, have been free to make their own choices and that political power has been severely limited (if not totally absent). In his later years, George Bernard Shaw, while lecturing in the United States, lamented this fact. "When you come to examine the American Constitution," he said, "you find that it was not really a constitution, but a charter of anarchism. It was not an instrument of Government. It was a guarantee to the whole American Nation that it never should be governed at all. And that is exactly what the Americans wanted."

Shaw, a Fabian socialist and advocate of central planning, thought this was dreadful. Shaw believed people should be regimented—governed—to create a near perfect society. It was precisely when intellectuals of Shaw's ilk began to dominate Great Britain that it began to decline.

Nevertheless, Shaw's observations about the American Constitution are not totally without merit. Fundamentally, Americans have always believed that as long as people don't infringe on the rights of others, they should be free to govern themselves. Socialists are not necessarily opposed to this; but they are tied to the utopian idea that one central authority with enough power can plan away every problem perplexing our society.

Yet, if more government, central planning, and political direction were the way to a better future, then we would live in a far different world. People would be risking their lives, braving barbed wire and minefields, to get into the Soviet Union. The USSR would be a paradise created by central planners who are free of the corrupting influences of profit and private property. The reality is in stark contrast to this vision. The Soviet Union, rich in resources, with a well-educated and creative population, has little economic vitality. Government control and planning have turned what was once the breadbasket of Europe into a food-importing nation.

A friend of mine who deals in international commodities studied the crop situation in Turkey, across the border—just a line on the map—from the Soviet Union. During the last few decades, the Soviets have suffered an incredible number of crop failures not experienced by their neighbors a few miles away. My friend decided that there were only two explanations: Either the communist officials are lying, and their crop losses are due to a failure of their system and not perpetually bad weather, as they claim, or, there is a God and he hates communism.

President Reagan has a story he likes to tell about the commissar visiting the collective farm:

> The commissar grabs the first farmer he sees and asks how life is on the farm. The nervous plowman answers, "Perfect, I've never heard anyone complain about anything. Never."

The commissar then asks, "Well, what about the potato harvest?"

The farmer replies, "It is incredible. I've never seen so many potatoes. If you stacked them in one pile it would be so high it would reach the foot of God."

The commissar interrupts, "Wait a minute. This is the Soviet Union. There is no God."

"That's O.K.," says the farmer as he shrugs, "There are no potatoes either."

Some will argue, however, that government planning in the Soviet Union, with its totalitarian system, is different than it would be in a freer country. In a democracy, political leadership can be a significant force in solving problems. That would be nice to believe. Another story that would be nice to believe is the one about the tooth fairy.

I think that the illusion of political leadership—vigorous, sensitive, hardworking, and well-educated government officials—has been very harmful to the well-being of the American people. President Reagan is fond of saying that the progress we've enjoyed during his administration is due primarily to the efforts of the people: entrepreneurs, workers, individuals cooperating in profit-making and nonprofit enterprises. The president says, and I agree wholeheartedly, that all we've done since getting to Washington is to get government out of the way. The people did the rest. This is the kind of leadership that means something, and it is a far cry from the sloganeering and flimflam of the 1970s.

I submit that even a good man and courageous leader like President Reagan would be unable to make the United States a better country if he attempted to do it through bureaucratic solutions.

There are many reasons for this. One reason is the totally different attitude found in government. There is a story Lenard Reed loved to tell about the fellow who did some late Christmas shopping. He fought his way through the crowd in a department store, selected a present, and finally elbowed his way to the counter. While the clerk was taking his credit card he remarked, "What a mob." The clerk looked around and said, "It's the *best* day we've had all year." After transacting his business, the late shopper made his way across the street to the post office, an equally mobbed establishment. He finally made it to the front of the line with his package. As the postal clerk took his cash, he commented on the size of the crowd. The clerk looked around and said, "Yeah, it's the *worst* day we've had all year."

This is no slur on postal clerks or on government workers. They are usually fine, dedicated Americans. Yet, we must admit that a different attitude prevails in the private sector where profit and competition are important factors. Like it or not, those who emphasize government solutions are in favor of channeling authority and resources to people with less incentive to work and less flexibility in approaching a task. Total state planning, if put into practice in the United States, would turn

America into one big post office. We'd all be living our lives as if everything was always three days late.

Having worked on the inside of government now, I can tell you that there are understandable and predictable reasons for why political approaches to problems become bogged down, and why the costs are higher and the results less impressive than in the private sector. (These factors can be mathematically equated.) Even more damaging than the inherent inefficiency of bureaucratic approaches, however, is what happens to the spirit of a country.

One hundred fifty years ago, a young Frenchman named Alexis de Tocqueville toured our young country, chronicling his observations in *Democracy in America*—a book I would recommend to every student trying to understand the United States. De Tocqueville was nearly overwhelmed by the energy and vibrancy of our young republic and its people: "America is a land of wonders in which everything is in constant motion and every change seems an improvement," he wrote; "No natural boundary seems to be set to the efforts of man, and in his eyes what is not yet done is only what he has not yet attempted to do." Through good times and bad times, Americans have managed to maintain this sense of optimism and pride. However, our government gradually grew and power gradually became more centralized in Washington. What follows is admittedly a Reaganite analysis.

In the 1970s, it was clear that something had gone dramatically wrong. The sense of optimism and confidence was replaced with a pessimism totally out of line with the American character. We were, for the first time in our history, told by major political figures to lower our expectations and that some of our problems were unsolvable.

Our economy was on the edge of a catastrophe, and our standard of living, productivity, real take-home pay, and long-term investment were declining. State and local governments seemed paralyzed and we began hearing a refrain that America's best days were over.

As much as our political opponents would like us to believe otherwise, the paralysis of our country in 1980 was not brought on by the personality of President Reagan's predecessor, and it was not the product of some uncontrollable cycle. The problems we faced then, from which the United States is just now emerging, were the result of overly concentrated power and resources in the federal government.

Federal tax revenues, for example, doubled between 1976 and 1981. By 1980, working people were being taxed at rates that only a few years before had been reserved for the affluent. Federal social spending skyrocketed, yet economic progress for the less fortunate, our minority population in particular, which had risen in years prior to the Great Society, ground to a screeching halt. People blamed this on defense spending. In reality, defense spending shrank by about 20 percent, while social spending went through the roof.

By the end of the decade, the private sector, along with state and local government, found that they had neither the authority nor the resources to get the job done. Federal regulation of the private sector and state and local government added enormously to costs and complicated every project. Power was in the hands of far-away federal officials who had never been elected. Local officials, with their revenue bases assimilated, went to Washington to travel door-to-door begging for handouts. No major project, private or public, was considered feasible without federal backing.

Paralysis was spreading throughout the country, from the bottom up. At an individual level, social welfare spending, far from erasing the blot of poverty, made the situation worse. Aid to Families with Dependent Children and other federal programs exacerbated attempts to improve the well-being of people in need by making it possible—indeed, acceptable—for the less fortunate to remain living in wretched conditions as wards of the state. Even worse, politicians trying to exploit hatred between the races and encourage envy convinced—and they continue to do this—many young blacks to not even try to improve their lot; they claimed that racism will beat them down every time. This has done an incredible disservice to a whole generation of black Americans.

At the same time, all around the country, people from incredibly disadvantaged backgrounds, people from every race and ethnic group, were and still are getting jobs—sometimes earning meager wages, but earning enough to sustain themselves and maintain their dignity. These people have worked their way up into a decent life. This has happened on a colossal scale. Who are these people? They are the people most isolated from government, people who are afraid to have any contact with public officials or to accept a government subsidy. They are illegal aliens.

It is sad to see our own citizens, supposedly protected by government, totally dependent and with shattered self-esteem. It is tragic to hear healthy young people lamenting the lack of opportunity and unwilling to try, using racism as an excuse for not making an effort. All of this occurs while immigrants, many of them from West Africa and the Caribbean, earn a living driving or even washing taxis. Economist Walter Williams points out that these same black immigrants seem to be progressing up the social ladder into the middle class much faster than native-born blacks. This sad situation is also the legacy of liberalism in the 1970s.

The political leaders have meant well, but liberalism has created a new bondage for America's less fortunate. It has fostered a sense of resignation and hopelessness in people who need encouragement. Our poor citizens, indulging in self-pity, feel helpless. They are being left behind by foreigners who come to the United States, who gladly accept entry-level jobs and work their way up. Liberals, with good intentions, have paved the way to a welfare hell for far too many Americans.

The Reagan administration has put the emphasis on economic growth rather than on liberal redistribution schemes, and because of it, everyone is better off. For example, in 1984, the United States experienced one of the biggest declines in the number of people living in poverty in our history; 1.8 million Americans were lifted out of poverty. It is important to note that it takes time for the policies of a new administration to be put in place and time for them to affect society. It was in 1979, just as the tax-spend philosophy of the previous administration was coming on line, that poverty began to escalate. As our policies began coming on line in 1983, the increase in poverty halted. Last year, we actually reversed the trend.

Of course, social welfare is only one aspect of the paralysis that massive government brought to America. I am convinced, and much of the Reagan administration tax policy is based on this belief, that there is a level of taxation a country cannot rise above without knocking the legs out from under its economy. High taxes destroy any incentive to work, save, or invest. They siphon money into the bureaucracy that should be used to finance new job-creating and wealth-producing private enterprise.

Much of the economic stagnation that engulfed America in the last decade can be traced to overtaxation. When someone suggests solving a problem through political channels, no matter how good the cause, there will be a bill to pay, perhaps through higher taxes, perhaps through inflation, perhaps through economic stagnation. These solutions are far more expensive and less likely to work than their private-sector counterpart. Had the economy kept on as it was before President Reagan's election, the only kind of job open to many college graduates would be in fast food restaurants.[1] That is the price this generation would have paid for decades of liberal folly. Looking back, it is a bit frightening to think what life would be like in America had the inflation, economic trends, and state of mind of the 1970s continued into the 1980s.

Admittedly, much of what I say is hard to calculate. By the end of the last decade, for example, Americans were looking to the federal government as the first and only solution, rather than the last resort. How many, thinking it government's responsibility, did not get involved in community efforts to help the less fortunate? How many

---

[1]The charge is made that in this administration good paying jobs are disappearing and the new jobs created are dead-end, low-pay positions. This politically motivated charge is false. Journalist Warren Brookes has documented, and the Bureau of Labor Statistics backs him up, that a greater portion of the new jobs being created in the United States are in the higher paying, high-skill category. If there has been a shift, it has been a shift up, according to Brookes.

refused to volunteer or to lend a hand because of the prevalent attitude of letting government do it?

A major thrust of this administration has been to encourage people to get involved in problem solving, to help one another, to join with others to improve their community. A few days after his inauguration, President Reagan made this clear when he said, "Let us pledge to restore, in our time, the American spirit of voluntary service, or cooperation, or private and community initiative, a spirit that flows like a deep and mighty river through the history of our nation."

Consistent with this goal, the office of Private Sector Initiatives is an important part of the White House in this administration, thoroughly integrated into our overall effort. In December of 1981, the president established a forty-four member Task Force on Private Sector Initiatives to seek out more and better ways to activate private industry and individuals. Since day one, wherever he has gone, the president has sought out and raised examples of good citizenship and community spirit—commending those people involved and encouraging others to do the same.

We have had some success in redirecting people back to the activities in their own communities that really make a difference. For example, crime has been a ballooning threat to our people and a blot on our nation for two decades. To the astonishment of experts, serious crime has declined in the last two years (1983–84). More progress is needed along with tougher law enforcement like the death penalty and the elimination of the exclusionary rule and other nonsensical roadblocks to successful prosecution of the guilty. But presenting government as the ultimate answer would be totally nonproductive.

There are many nongovernment, nonpolitical approaches that have played a role in combatting the crime problem. Individual responsibility and common sense top the list. I am talking about burglar alarms, dogs, and more secure doors and windows. The growth of Neighborhood Watch programs has been significant as well. Private spending on Neighborhood Watch and similar programs had tripled between 1980 and 1984. I submit that an effective Neighborhood Watch program, using no government funds, is a more effective crime stopper than doubling the local police budget.

Education is another example. The amount of money spent on education by federal, state, and local governments skyrocketed out of sight in the last two decades. Yet, at the same time, evidence suggests that the quality of education provided to America's young people had declined. Test scores plummeted. Many of the educational challenges were outlined in the report issued by the President's Task Force on Excellence in Education.

The easy answer was throwing federal money at the problem. President Reagan's approach was different. He provided real leadership. Touring the country, he visited numerous schools and met with groups of educators and parents. The reform President Reagan proposed required commitment from the people. His solution was multifaceted: higher standards, more discipline, more emphasis on the basic skills, more parent and community involvement, and on top of the list, more local and parental control.

He launched the National Partnership in Education Program, calling on the private sector to help upgrade the quality of schooling. Part of this was an "adopt a school" concept, in which businesses were encouraged to help a particular school. The White House adopted Congress Heights elementary school, which is in a less-than-affluent area in Washington, D.C. We took this task seriously. I know, because for three months I spent two hours every Wednesday teaching fourth through sixth graders how to write.

In every state, people have been getting involved and demanding higher standards, more discipline from their schools, and volunteering to help as well. Amazingly, test scores have turned around and have headed up for the first time in decades.

The people of the United States have responded to the president and to their own instincts. More and more people are volunteering for charitable causes and community service. Individual giving shot up 11 percent in 1984.[2] Companies and corporations are joining in. For example, three weeks after the president asked the private sector to get involved in the missing children problem, the Trailways Bus Company and the International Association of Police Chiefs developed a program called "Operation Home Free," giving free rides home to runaways. In the first two months, hundreds of youngsters were returned to their families.

It is worth noting that during the 1982 recession, when corporate profits were down, corporate giving actually increased. We think that encouraging individual giving and personal involvement is better for all concerned: the giver, the receiver, and the spirit of our country.

The Reagan approach differs greatly from that of the past decade. When we got to Washington in 1980, federal spending was out of control; it was increasing at an annual rate of 17 percent. Had we done nothing about it, America would have been in serious trouble. One of the most distasteful tactics we have had to withstand has been the vicious name calling and personal attacks on the president and people who work for him by liberals who suggest that we are mean and uncaring.

Liberals talk as if advocating government programs is an act of

---

[2]Charitable giving went up 63 percent in the first 6 years of the Reagan administration. In a time of low inflation, this jump represents a giant step forward.

personal charity and that prescribing bureaucratic responsibility for every human problem reflects compassion. Charity, however, is not what you advocate be done with other people's tax dollars; instead, it is what you do with your own money. The strangest aspect of this concept is that many people who beat their chest and point a finger at us are often well-to-do. But the bizarre twist is that these affluent people often use tax loopholes—put into the tax law at their behest by liberal, welfare-state politicians—so, in reality, it is the middle class, and not the affluent, who pay for the programs they so fervently advocate.

People who advocate bigger government insist that they too believe in volunteerism. Yet, stressing government solutions incalculably undermines the incentive of private citizen involvement in worthwhile endeavors. For example, had turn-of-the-century politicians sold the American people on the notion that Boy Scouts and Girl Scouts should be a part of the government, we can imagine the results. Today there would be several massive structures in Washington stuffed with bureaucrats overseeing the Boy Scouts and Girl Scouts. In every city and hamlet there would be Boy Scout and Girl Scout centers, expensive government buildings with their own staffs. All the tents, camp-grounds, uniforms, handbooks, and snake-bite kits would be provided by taxpayers. We can only imagine the scandals of Boy Scout mess kits procured for $900 each. All scout leaders would be federal employees looking forward to retirement benefits. We are talking about billions of dollars.

Now, try to visualize someone like me, perhaps in a presidential campaign, suggesting that Boy Scouts and Girl Scouts, a multibillion dollar, tax-supported operation, could be financed without government support on a totally voluntary basis. We could get churches, business associations, and unions to sponsor local troops. It is unnecessary for each troop to have its own expensive government building for meetings. Instead, the scouts could get together in local halls, churches, and other gathering places in the community. People, mostly parents, would volunteer for the jobs now being handled by paid federal workers.

Who would ever take a man spouting crazy ideas like that seriously? It would be charged that I wanted to destroy scouting, that I was mean-spirited and hated children. My political opponents would receive large contributions from the political action committee of the federal Boy and Girl Scout Workers' Union. What I am describing is not so different from what is happening concerning many of the responsibilities assumed by government today. Much of what is done could be accomplished by volunteers or by profit-seeking entrepreneurs in the private sector.

But, at the very least, we in the Reagan administration believe that we should encourage private sector activities, and that we should discourage the growth of government. Of course, if government continues to take an increasing share of people's paychecks, which is what happened in the 1970s, there will be nothing left to contribute, invest, or anything else.

One of the president's major goals has been allowing the American people to keep more of what they earn. This is fair, and it puts decision making in their hands, which is more efficient and more reflective of a free society.

Our first effort was a 25 percent across-the-board reduction in income tax rates and an indexing of those rates to protect the people against inflation. The reductions were phased in over a three-year period, the last 10 percent took effect in July of 1983. The tax bill, like any piece of legislation, came out of the process different from when it went in. For example, the top income tax rates were dropped from 70 to 50 percent. The administration supported this amendment, but originally it was sponsored and pushed by Democrats, with the support of Democratic leadership in the House.

During the last campaign, our tax-rate reductions came under heavy attack; the opposition claimed these reductions were the root cause of the deficit. This charge ignores something every American knows: Our tax-rate reductions offset tax increases that were already built into the system. The average taxpayer stayed about the same. Government spending, even in domestic programs, continued to rise and federal revenues also continued to rise. The idea that we have shovelled money out of the Treasury and back into the pockets of the American people, thus stimulating the economy and creating a huge deficit in the process, is a myth.

Do not get me wrong. The American people are much better off than they would have been if their taxes continued to increase. The average American family of four with two wage earners, for example, would have paid $2,544 more in federal taxes.[3] These extra dollars have added much to the quality of life for working people. It also has meant much more for the economy than if we had let these dollars be taxed away and dumped in the federal feeding trough.

Reagan's tax policy is predicated on the now famous supply-side concept: when taxation reaches a certain level, increasing tax rates leads to less government revenue and decreasing tax rates increases the revenue. Economist Art Laffer charted it out on a napkin at lunch one day and it became known as the Laffer Curve. This commonsense notion was hotly debated, although it was clear even to the harshest critic that there is a level of taxation where people will simply stop working, creating, and producing, a level where people will quit reporting their money, a level where they will spend time, creativity, and resources to legally see that their income is not taxed.

---

[3]From 1982−84.

Today, supply-side economics is less controversial. First—and admittedly this is explained away by diehard Keynesians—by lowering the tax rates of the top bracket, we actually have been receiving more revenue from high-income taxpayers than if we had kept the rate high. The explanation for this is that at high levels of taxation it is more profitable for high-income people to hide money in tax shelters and invest in tax dodges. Even after legal and accounting fees are taken out, along with the profits of tax-shelter managers, tax avoidance schemes are profitable at high rates. The lower the tax rates, the less profitable tax avoidance becomes; thus, more money is brought into the system and taxed—even though it is taxed at a lower rate. Figures back up this proposition.

The second reason supply-siders are less controversial is that they have been almost the only economists whose predictions have come anywhere close to the mark. Art Laffer suggested early on that in 1983, once the last phase of tax rate reduction went into effect, the economy would skyrocket and inflation would stay low. Needless to say, almost every major figure in American economics, especially Wall Street economists, had dire predictions. The predictions of traditional liberal economists were gloom and doom at its worst. Inflation would take off, according to the preeminent names in economics, interest rates would go through the roof, business activity would fall, and unemployment would become a national tragedy. Obviously these dark predictions were miles off target. Only the supply siders, Art Laffer in particular, were accurate in their forecasts.

During the sharp recession suffered in 1982, which came as America began its transition from policies of the previous administration, there was tremendous pressure to raise taxes, increase spending and, in short, return to past policies. The president held his ground. Although we suffered moderate losses in the House in 1982, it is to the American people's credit that they basically stuck with the president during the economic crunch; they gave him the benefit of the doubt and time needed for his program to take hold.

In January 1983, as the supply-siders predicted, the economy took off. It has been one of the strongest economic expansions in this century. As of February 1987, the United States has had fifty months of growth and low inflation, one of the longest recoveries in postwar history. Interest rates have fallen from the high of 21½ percent when we took office to under 10 percent. Retail sales are up. Personal income is up. Over a million new businesses were incorporated in the last two years. Most of them are small operations; each one is an entrepreneurial dream of individuals. Overall unemployment is down to 6.9 percent. Today, more Americans are working than ever before in our history, and there is a higher proportion of the total work force employed than at any time.

There has been substantial investment in new technology by American firms and productivity is up. Our economy is, in fact, pulling the other world economies into better times. This is one reason for the trade deficit. As recovery begins to take hold throughout the Western world, which will happen faster if other Western nations would, as we did, lower their tax rates, the value of the dollar will begin to equalize with other currencies, and the trade deficit will ease.

In summary, President Reagan's policies have given America high growth and low inflation. Just by lowering inflation, he has dramatically improved the quality of life of the American people. They understand this, and they understand that when there was overwhelming pressure to reverse course, the president stuck to his principles. His strength and courage were rewarded by one of the greatest reelection victories in this century.

Where do we go from here? The deficit remains a problem to be confronted. The president feels that raising taxes will knock the legs from under economic growth and result in a larger deficit. The only alternative, then, is to cut government spending. Another priority is the president's proposal to overhaul and simplify the tax system. His position is clear: Taxes are too high and the system is too complicated. The president's program reduces the number of tax brackets from fourteen to only three: 15 percent, 25 percent, and 35 percent. Virtually everyone would pay a lower rate. At the same time, our program would close a multitude of loopholes and write-offs. This is a priority issue for the president. The professional Washingtonians are declaring the issues dead for this year, but the president will push hard in the coming months on this issue. If there is one lesson that political professionals should have learned in the last ten years, it is: do not underestimate Ronald Reagan's ability to mobilize the American people.[4]

Another area to watch in coming months is deregulation. One of the four parts of our economic recovery program was eliminating useless and counterproductive regulations that tied the hands of entrepreneurs, businesspeople, and state and local government. We saved our economy billions of dollars, which otherwise would have gone into filling out useless paperwork. Jim Miller, former head of the Federal Trade Commission—a champion deregulator, is taking over David Stockman's job as director of the Office of Management and Budget. This change could usher in a new round of deregulation.

The president faces a tough going on numerous issues including protectionism and immigration reform as well as major foreign policy issues. Invigorating the U.S. economy was one of Reagan's two preeminent campaign pledges in 1980. The other pledge was rebuilding

---

[4]This prophetic statement proved accurate. In 1986, Congress passed a major tax overhaul aimed at simplifying the system, making it more fair, and reducing tax rates.

America's military strength and seeing to the security interests of our country. Just as it is difficult in these good times to remember fully the days of killer inflation and economic gloom, the memory is also fading of the period after Vietnam and before Ronald Reagan when the United States was immobilized with self-doubt.

I fully acknowledge the United States is far from a perfect country. We have made mistakes. At times, we have not lived up to our principles. Yet, when put in perspective and compared to other nations, I am proud of my country. Certainly a number of the governments friendly to the United States are less than free and democratic. On this planet, there are few countries that are truly free and democratic. But where human freedom has existed in the last forty years, it has been secured by the military and political strength of the United States.

Try to visualize how different the world would be if, at the close of World War II, it had been the Soviet Union, instead of the United States, which had overwhelming military might and a nuclear monopoly. We all grew up in a world dominated by American military power. It is something that has been taken for granted by far too many well-meaning people.

During the 1970s, things began to change. The United States decreased its military spending by 20 to 25 percent in real terms. Our leaders energetically sought and reached agreements with the Soviet Union. Presidents Nixon, Ford, and Carter did their utmost to demonstrate a sincere desire for peace and goodwill. It was called detente. It perhaps reached its apex with a kiss planted on Brezhnev's cheek by an American president.

The Soviets took this opportunity to rush ahead with one of the most massive military buildups in peacetime history. While the American fleet shrunk from over 1,000 ships in 1969 to under 600 in 1980, the Soviets turned what had been little more than a coastal defense force into a powerful, battle-ready, two-ocean navy. While we neglected our military forces, they introduced new tanks and conventional weapons and built them by the tens of thousands. While the United States pulled back from developing new missiles and delivery systems—unilaterally cancelling the B-1 bomber—the Soviets deployed the Backfire bomber and introduced new missiles like the SS 20, which they menacingly perched facing Western Europe.

Had the trends continued, absolute military supremacy would have voluntarily been transferred to a repressive society that permits none of the freedoms we hold dear in Western democracies. Absolute military supremacy would have fallen into the hands of rulers who disdain the concepts of free speech, freedom of the press and religion and who ruthlessly stamp out moderating influences in their country.

I will not go into a detailed lecture on the Soviet Union or Marxism-Leninism; it is sufficient to say that I believe communism is a totalitarian philosophy that has brought deprivation and tyranny wherever it has gained control. This is not to suggest that all countries that are not communist are free but, clearly, those countries that are communist are not free. Communist countries are the only nations that erect walls to keep their people in.

The 1980 election marked the end of America's era of uncertainty; it marked an end of the Vietnam syndrome. As a candidate, he promised to rebuild our military strength, and President Ronald Reagan is doing just that.

Our goal is to maintain peace and protect freedom for ourselves and our friends and allies. We believe that people who hold power in dictatorial regimes do not respect weakness, and that the military strength of Western democracies is essential to maintaining peace.

We do not seek to dominate the planet militarily as we once did. Economically that is now impossible, and it is undesirable. Instead, we seek, in close cooperation with our allies, a military balance with our adversaries—a balance that will maximize the potential for peace. There is no reason for this balance to be at high levels; thus, we are negotiating in good faith with the Soviet Union for a reduction of both conventional and strategic forces. A mutual reduction of forces has been something President Reagan has long advocated, something he spoke of even before his election.

President Reagan and people who work for him do not relish using the resources of our country on weapons. We favor small government and believe that wealth should remain in the private sector to better the lives of the working people who produce it. People who portray us as happy about military spending are painting a false picture.

We do not believe the world is headed for another major war. In the long run, we believe that freedom will win without war. We believe that Marxism-Leninism will be just another sad chapter, like fascism and Nazism, in the history of totalitarian movements. Consistent with this assessment, the president believes that we should boldly proclaim the virtues of liberty and should not refrain from condemning the tyranny and aggression of our adversaries.

For this, the president has been labeled bellicose and belligerent. This charge is leveled at President Reagan at the same time that the Kremlin routinely blasts the United States with the vilest rhetoric and attempts to browbeat our allies in Western Europe with veiled threats. Unfortunately, there are many well-meaning people who give every benefit of doubt to the Soviets and, at the same time, criticize every flaw in Western democracies as if the exception is the rule.

Those of us in the West should admit we are far from perfect, but we have nothing to be ashamed of. Ignoring the dictatorial nature of communism or its vast military power is not going to make for a more peaceful world. Stretching rationality to the breaking point by suggesting that communist regimes are morally equal to Western democracies—and that what exists is nothing more than competition between two super powers—is not the way to peace.

President Reagan recently spoke to a reunion in Washington. "Time has proven," he said, "that those who gloss over the brutality of tyrants are not friends of peace or freedom." He added: "For truth to prevail we must have the courage to proclaim it." People in the audience knew those words were correct, for they were Jewish people, survivors of the holocaust, who immigrated to the United States after World War II.

Peace through strength has been said so often that it has the ring of a cliché, but that does not take away from the truth of its meaning. People who believe in it are no less dedicated to peace than people whose plan for peace is little more than granting the Soviets every wish in hopes that sincerity impresses them. President Reagan and people who work for him believe that strength and resolve can maintain peace and protect the freedom that exists on this planet.

There are two major ongoing Reagan foreign policy initiatives that I believe will dominate the agenda for at least the coming year. First, the weakness of the previous administration led the Soviets to miscalculate in Central America. The moment the Sandinistas took over Nicaragua, a breathtaking Soviet arms buildup began and a program for a communist takeover of Central America was set in motion. Had American policies not changed, Central America would today be a stronghold of Cuban—eastern European style—communist dictatorships.

When Reagan became president, it was said that the fall of El Salvador to communist insurgents was imminent. Slowly but surely the tide has turned. In El Salvador, a democratic government is growing stronger every day. The insurgents are beginning to defect. As they do, they confirm to the press what we said all along. The El Salavadorean insurgency has been supplied and directed from Managua—which acted as a surrogate for Moscow—since day one.

The dictatorial and communist nature of the Sandinista regime is becoming more evident every day. A genuine democratic resistance movement with broad popular support threatens to recapture the revolution and institute democracy, which was the original goal of most of the people who kicked out Somoza.

The United States obviously has not always lived up to its ideals in Central America. Today, we are on the side of democracy in that troubled region. At the end of the Reagan presidency, I believe a relatively free Central America—as compared to the brutal communist repression that would otherwise prevail there—will stand as a monument to Reagan's leadership—just as a free Greece today stands as a monument to the Marshall Plan and President Truman's determination to contain communist domination to Eastern Europe.

In the arena of nuclear weapons, the president's Strategic Defense

Initiative (SDI)—I call it a space shield, the media calls it Star Wars—is a turning point that will lead mankind to safer times.

The president is committed to moving forward with the research necessary to determine if such a system is feasible. The Soviets are screaming loudly and hypocritically about this research. Let no one forget that the Soviets have been involved in developing their own antimissile defense system for many years. I'm not suggesting that two wrongs make a right. Producing defensive systems that neutralize ICBMs and move away from the policy of mutually assured destruction is a right step, and a major step forward for mankind.

At one point in 1985, President Reagan met with his speechwriters and the subject of SDI came up. During our conversation, he mentioned the increasing escalation, brutality, and savagery of war during his lifetime. He told us that while he was in college, the airplane was just becoming a major weapon. He recalled that a debate took place in one of his classes. The question that divided his classmates: Would any American, with our high standards of morality, ever drop a bomb from an airplane on a city?

The president pointed out that only a decade later Americans were dropping thousands of bombs on the cities of Germany and Japan with little thought about morality. Technology has increased mankind's insensitivity to the horrors of war. SDI is the first step toward sanity. If we are to focus efforts of some of the best minds in Western democracies, let us do it by building technology that will be judged a success by how many lives it saves rather than how many people it can kill. This is a new way of thinking—a more moral use of our creativity and resources.

President Reagan's popularity is, in part, due to his ability to see beyond the problems of today. He is a man of vision. He is a man who believes that with freedom there is no problem mankind cannot overcome. He reignited a new spirit of optimism in the United States, especially among young people. The young people of today will look back on this man as a truly historic figure.

Part III

REFLECTIONS ON THE REAGAN REVOLUTION

Not only are the men of democracies not naturally desirous of revolutions, but they are afraid of them.
ALEXIS DE TOCQUEVILLE

The chapters in this section are reflections on the meaning of the Reagan phenomenon by a historian, a political scientist, and a sociologist. The historian, Richard Polenberg, sets the Reagan administration in a tradition of American public policy dating from the New Deal. The political scientist, James McNiven, tests the idea of a "Reagan Revolution" against concepts of revolution as a theoretical construct and sets it in relation to the emergence of new social and political forces. The sociologist, Alan Wolfe, approaches the question from an oblique angle: the weakness of a socialist Left in the United States, a weakness that he roots in the "premodern" quality of the American mentality. These three writers are not arguing directly against each other. Rather, they are offering different ways of comprehending the meaning of the changes summed up in the phrase "The Reagan Revolution."

Polenberg argues that the New Deal set a pattern for American policy in using federal government power for welfare that lasted through Democratic and Republican regimes alike until 1981. However, the era that began with the inauguration of FDR ended with the election of Ronald Reagan. There are interesting comparisons between the two presidents; in particular, both mastered the media and through radio, on the one hand, and television, on the other, entered into a special intimate relationship with the American people. Polenberg also assesses both as strong leaders who enhanced the power of the presidency. But this essay was written before "Iranscam," and the revelations of the Tower report showed just how shaky Reagan's control of

White House policy really was. Whatever his strengths and weaknesses as a president, however, Polenberg's main contention is that Ronald Reagan has effected a real revolution in American policy. He hasn't sought to roll back the New Deal, but he has deflected its trajectory. If the New Deal set in motion a particular way of dealing with social and economic problems that gathered scope and velocity in subsequent years, particularly in the 1960s and 1970s, then Reagan has at least managed to halt that momentum and effect a fundamental redirection of American policy. As many observers have pointed out, Reagan has altered the agenda of American politics and set new terms of debate. The change in the rhetoric and program of the Democratic party is perhaps the best testimony to this. American liberalism will eventually bounce back from the defeats of the 1980s, but it will be chastened and more hard nosed.

Like Polenberg, McNiven also sees Ronald Reagan as having reasserted the power of the presidency after a decade of eclipse, but his focus is less on Ronald Reagan as the creator of revolution than as the beneficiary of profound social changes created partly by developments in the world economy and partly by the particular outlook and problems of the baby boom generation. By the late 1970s, new classes, what McNiven calls the "new consumer" and the "new investor," no longer responded to the rhetoric of liberalism that had dominated American political life since the 1930s. These classes no longer felt that liberal policies met their specific needs. At the same time, they did not desire a wholesale abandonment of the liberal accomplishments of the last half century. One of the things that conservatives conserve, after all, is the basic structural change produced by previous revolutions. McNiven makes the provocative suggestion that just as FDR maintained that he had saved capitalism by restraining its excesses, Ronald Reagan may have saved the essentials of the welfare state by taking them off the political agenda and making them "part of the historical scenery."

Alan Wolfe's oblique angle of approach provides a rather different assessment of the meaning of the Reagan Revolution. In spite of its material wealth and technological innovativeness, Wolfe suggests that the United States, in its religiosity, parochialism, distrust of urbanism and cosmopolitanism, and distrust of the state, remains in striking ways less "modern" than the other developed industrial economies of the world. This is the real American "exceptionalism" and explains not only the failure of socialist or social democratic parties to gain any electoral support but also the relative backwardness of the United States in the state provision of social services such as health services, which are taken for granted elsewhere in the developed world. Should we regard the electoral triumph of 1980 and 1984 as products of the interests and aspirations of new social classes, in a classic revolutionary scenario, or, as Wolfe suggests, is the Reagan presidency an expression of the stubborn premodernity of American values? If the source of Ronald Reagan's electoral appeal lay in the fact that he embodied the revolt against modernity more perfectly than any other candidate and spoke to the profound distrust of modern values still strong among large segments of the American public, then perhaps we should see him as essentially a product of *counterrevolution*, a more benign Ayatollah Khomeini, reasserting the values of a traditional world against what had seemed the inevitable triumph of modernism.

SUGGESTIONS FOR FURTHER READING

Cannon, Lou. *Reagan*. New York: Putnam, 1982.

Dallek, Robert. *Ronald Reagan: the Politics of Symbolism*. Cambridge, Mass. Harvard University Press, 1984.

Howe, Irving. *Socialism and America*. New York: Harcourt Brace Jovanovich, 1985.

Neustadt, Richard E. *Presidential Power: The Politics of Leadership from FDR to Carter*. Rev. ed., New York: John Wiley & Sons, 1980.

Chapter Three

Roosevelt Revolution, Reagan Counterrevolution

RICHARD POLENBERG

Franklin Delano Roosevelt established a set of national priorities that lasted for thirty-five years after his death. His Democratic successors— Harry S Truman, John F. Kennedy, and Lyndon B. Johnson—adhered to those priorities, and so did Republicans Dwight Eisenhower, Richard Nixon, and Gerald Ford—however reluctant they were to admit it. But since 1981, there has been a drastic reordering of Roosevelt's priorities. Ronald Reagan has brought about a fundamental redirection of American politics.

There are several ironies in this. Reagan was born in 1911, the same year Roosevelt embarked on his political career by taking his seat in the New York State Senate in Albany. In 1932, when he was twenty-one years old, Reagan cast his first presidential vote for Roosevelt; subsequently, he cast his second, third, and fourth votes for him, too. Reagan's father, Jack, was a shoe salesman who had lost his job during the Depression. New Deal relief programs rescued the family, and Jack Reagan became the head of the local Works Progress Administration office in Illinois. After Roosevelt's death, Ronald Reagan remained a committed liberal, backing Harry Truman in 1948 and heading the Labor League of Hollywood Actors for Truman. Reagan even joined the Americans for Democratic Action. In his autobiography, *Where's the Rest of Me?*, Reagan described himself as a "very emotional New Dealer," and a "near hopeless hemophilic liberal" who bled for all the right social causes. In 1950, when a liberal Democrat, Helen Gahagan Douglas, was running for a United States Senate seat against Richard Nixon, her campaign manager did not want it known that Reagan was a supporter; he was reputed to be so far left of center that it was feared he would jeopardize her chances.

Reagan dates the beginning of his own political transformation from the late 1940s, when, he claims, he began to realize that the Hollywood film industry was infested with communists and that liberals failed to recognize the problem. To quote his autobiography again, "light was dawning in some obscure region in my head." He stopped being a near hopeless hemophilic liberal; it was as if he had overdosed on Vitamin K. By 1960, he had become an archconservative. Writing that year to Republican presidential candidate Richard M. Nixon, Reagan blasted John F. Kennedy's proposals to expand welfare programs: "Under the tousled boyish haircut is still old Karl Marx—first launched a century ago." In 1962, Reagan switched his affiliation to the Republicans, and two years later he supported Barry Goldwater's candidacy. By then, he was saying that the welfare state was "the most dangerous enemy ever known to man," that unemployment insurance was "a prepaid vacation plan for freeloaders," and that the graduated income tax had been invented by Karl Marx.

Yet, even after Reagan reversed political direction, he continued to identify himself with the Roosevelt legacy. In 1980, he cited Roosevelt three times in his speech accepting the nomination. He alluded to Roosevelt so frequently during the campaign that, on the day after the election, the *New York Times* ran an editorial entitled, "Franklin Delano Reagan." In 1981, the new president quoted Roosevelt at length in his inaugural address. Once in the White House, Reagan continued to talk about "the forgotten American," as Roosevelt did, and he used one of Roosevelt's favorite phrases: to promise "a rendezvous with destiny." In February 1986, in a freewheeling attack on social welfare programs before a joint session of Congress, Reagan said: "As Franklin Roosevelt warned fifty-one years ago standing before this chamber: He said, welfare is 'a narcotic, a subtle destroyer of the human spirit.' And we must now escape the spider's web of dependency."

Perhaps we have passed beyond the realm of irony and entered that of the surreal. President Reagan is quoting President Roosevelt— selectively, to be sure—in order to move the country in exactly the opposite direction. The Reagan administration has endeavored to redirect the course of American politics, and to a considerable extent it has succeeded. Let us see how, by examining Roosevelt's and Reagan's use of presidential power, their economic policies, and their attempts to institutionalize their programs.

Franklin Roosevelt is, by common consent, a president who exploited the full potential of his office. Theodore Roosevelt and Woodrow Wilson had employed executive power but not to the same degree. Franklin Roosevelt exerted a near-magnetic influence over Congress and the bureaucracy. More systematically than his predecessors, he used patronage to get congressmen to do what he wanted. Under FDR, it became standard practice for the executive branch to draft legislation and for Congress to react to the administration's initiative. Finding that government departments were often staffed by officials who were unsympathetic to New Deal objectives, Roosevelt bypassed these departments and set up emergency agencies to deal with labor, business, agriculture, and relief. In 1939, Roosevelt created the Executive Office of the President, which enabled him and later presidents to implement policies more effectively. Of course, no president always has his way. In his twelve years in office, Franklin Roosevelt lost his share of legislative and bureaucratic skirmishes; but he won even more than his share.

Roosevelt further enhanced presidential power by appealing directly to the voters. He used the radio, especially the fireside chat, to explain—rather, to advocate—his policies and build popular support for them. He did not make many such fireside chats because he did not want them to seem humdrum or routine; but the few fireside chats he made were extraordinarily effective. Sitting casually before the microphones, and speaking in soft, conversational tones, Roosevelt managed to give the impression that he was in his listeners' living rooms, that he understood their problems, and that he was doing his best to solve them. People sensed that they had a friend in the White House, and so even when one of Roosevelt's proposals was not especially well-liked he remained personally popular.

Roosevelt also used press conferences to get his point of view across to the people. Recognizing that most newspaper publishers opposed his programs—some publishers, he observed, deserved "neither hate nor praise, only pity for their unbalanced mentalities"—Roosevelt understood the importance of establishing a good working relationship with reporters. Since his press conferences were always held "off the record," the president could not be quoted directly without permission. Consequently, Roosevelt could engage in an uninhibited, freewheeling discussion. Reporters could ask whatever they wanted; previously, they had to submit written questions in advance and the president would choose which ones to answer. There were no such restrictions on spontaneity at Roosevelt's press conferences. In his first four years in office, he held 337 press conferences; after eight years, he had met with the press on no fewer than 711 occasions.

One of the reasons Roosevelt was so comfortable and effective in these meetings was that he had an extraordinarily detailed knowledge of governmental policy. Observers were always impressed with his grasp of what was happening in Washington, in the nation, and in the world. He had an uncanny command of the facts. Nothing seemed to escape his attention. When he wanted to explain a complicated proposal to reporters, he would tell them it was time for a "seminar," and for an hour or more he would hold their attention with a line-by-line analysis of that proposal. If he did not know everything there was to know about government, and, of course, no one could, he gave the impression he did.

For thirty years after Franklin Roosevelt's death in 1945, under Democrats and Republicans alike, there was a further expansion of presidential power. By the time Richard Nixon was reelected in 1972, people were talking about "King Richard" and the dangers of an "imperial presidency." What appeared to be a dramatic reversal then occurred as a reaction to Vietnam and Watergate. In 1974, Congress passed the War Powers Resolution restricting the president's ability to conduct certain kinds of military operations without obtaining legislative approval, and the Supreme Court decided that a claim of "executive privilege" did not mean that all presidential communications could be withheld from the courts. The Ford and Carter years witnessed an erosion of presidential authority. By 1980, Gerald Ford claimed that the presidency was no longer "imperial" but "imperilled," and Walter Mondale said, still more pungently, that the presidency had become "the fire hydrant of the nation."

By the mid-1980s, however, no one was making such statements, for Ronald Reagan had, by all accounts, refurbished executive authority. But his use of presidential power differs from Franklin Roosevelt's in important respects. Reagan does not have the same mastery of issues that Roosevelt did. Even disregarding the harsher comments of his critics—for example, that he is the "president with the seven-minute attention span"—it would be impossible to contend that Reagan knows about or cares about intricate details of economic policy. Nor can one envision the president leading an hour-long seminar for reporters as Roosevelt sometimes did. Reagan has been notoriously reluctant to hold press conferences, not so much because he is worried about making an offhand statement that will have harmful repercussions, but because he does not wish to expose his limited knowledge of controversial issues. Even one of his friendlier biographers, Lou Cannon, admits that the president's knowledge gap makes every press conference an "adventure into the unexplored regions of his mind." In his first four years in office, Reagan held 26 press conferences compared to Roosevelt's 337.

Nevertheless, Reagan has been a strong president. He has exerted an influence over Congress that, only a decade ago, seemed impossible for any president to exert. His administration has been highly effective in establishing legislative priorities and in showing a willingness to compromise when necessary (but only when necessary) to achieve its goals. The president has also put his own brand on the federal bureaucracy. Where Franklin Roosevelt dealt with conservative bureaucrats by creating emergency agencies and staffing them with dedicated New Dealers, Ronald Reagan has dealt with liberal bureaucrats by centralizing the budgetary process in the Office of Management and Budget and staffing it with diehard supply siders. Finally, Reagan has used television to appeal directly to the people in much the same way, and with much the same effect, as Roosevelt used radio. So it is not surprising that when voters are asked whether President Reagan has "strong qualities of leadership" that nearly three out of four answer "yes."

Just as the two presidents employed different techniques to enhance their power, they also used that authority for sharply contrasting purposes. During Franklin Roosevelt's twelve years in the White House, the government assumed increasing responsibility for the welfare of large numbers of jobless or impoverished people; the government also introduced a system of taxation that produced a modest redistribution of income from the rich to the poor. By Ronald Reagan's seventh year as president, the government had jettisoned many welfare programs, and it had implemented what can only be termed a Robin Hood-in-reverse tax program.

The fundamental assumption on which the New Deal was based should not be lost in the welter of alphabet agencies: that the great majority of those who were unemployed or impoverished were not personally to blame. They were not lazy; they were just unfortunate. They were not individual failures; they were social casualties. Whatever the potential risks involved in providing federal relief, the actual risks involved in not providing it were more severe. Roosevelt knew that a person who received federal assistance could become dependent on such handouts; but he also knew that a person who did not obtain aid would experience intense suffering. An astute politician, and a cautious one, Roosevelt did not go as far in this direction as many wanted, or even as far as he might have gone. But in providing federal relief—as in creating a social security system, in guaranteeing unemployment insurance, and in establishing a minimum wage—he recognized that the important thing was not how far a particular measure went, but the general direction in which it took the nation. The direction during the Roosevelt years was toward an assumption of new responsibilities by the federal government.

The redistribution of income that Roosevelt presided over occurred during World War II. The redistribution resulted partly from new tax laws, and it reflected the impact of full employment and wartime prosperity on the working class. From 1941−45, the incomes of the poorest fifth of American families increased by 10 percent, while the incomes of the wealthiest fifth increased by 20 percent. During those same years, the share of national income held by the wealthiest 5 percent of the people declined from 23.7 to 16.8 percent. Of course, wealthy individuals were considerably better off at the end of the war since 16.8 percent of the 1945 national income amounted to more than 23.7 percent of the

1941 national income. Relatively speaking, however, the final years of the Roosevelt administration had seen a modest redistribution of wealth in a downward direction.

Franklin Roosevelt created an agenda for American politics, and for thirty-five years, until 1980, politicians committed themselves to fulfilling it—Democrats eagerly, Republicans more grudgingly. The programs Roosevelt instituted were beneficial to many groups, and those groups provided built-in constituencies for maintaining the programs and for extending them. They were immediately institutionalized. The relevant political questions were not whether to increase social security benefits, provide more comprehensive unemployment insurance, or raise the minimum wage; the relevant questions were: By how much?

In 1935, Roosevelt was discussing the Social Security Act with his advisers. They warned him that payroll deductions amounted to a regressive system of taxation since all workers, no matter what their income, paid at the same rate. It would make more sense, they claimed, to have government fund the program. Roosevelt admitted that the bill was bad economics, but he insisted it was good politics. So long as social security rested on individuals' taxes, he said, "no damn politician can ever scrap my social security system." How could Roosevelt have known that somewhere in the Midwest, at that very moment, was a twenty-four-year-old radio announcer, Ronald Reagan, who would one day sit in the White House?

The Reagan administration has endeavored to turn the welfare state clock back, not to 1929 or even 1939, but to 1959. The administration had proposed, and obtained, much more stringent cuts in the Great Society programs of the 1960s than in the New Deal programs of the 1930s. The administration's budget proposal for the fiscal year 1985 would have cut spending for such New Deal programs as social security and unemployment insurance by 11 percent (compared with prior policy levels), but it would have cut medicaid, food stamps, rent supplements, and other Great Society low-income assistance programs by more than 25 percent (compared with the same pre-1980 baseline figures). Congress agreed to cut social welfare spending by about half as much as Reagan proposed. As in Roosevelt's case, however, the point was not how far a measure went, but its general direction.

The income tax reduction that the Reagan administration won from Congress in 1981 also represented a reversal of trends established during the Roosevelt years. The measure provided for reductions of 5 percent the first year and an additional 10 percent in each of the succeeding two years. But special interest groups won benefits in the form of accelerated depreciation, lucrative write-offs, and near elimination of the estate tax. As David Stockman, Reagan's budget chief at the time, admitted: "The hogs were really feeding. The greed level, the level of opportunism, just got out of control." The Treasury Department estimated that, over three years, 9 percent of the total tax relief would go to people earning under $15,000, and 36 percent would go to people earning more than $50,000. The 162,000 families with incomes of $200,000 or more saw their taxes cut by $3.6 billion; the 31,700,000 families who earned $15,000 or less realized a savings of $2.9 billion. From 1980 to 1984, the real disposable income of the poorest fifth of American families declined by nearly 8 percent, while the real disposable income of the wealthiest fifth jumped by almost 9 percent. The Reagan administration has presided over a major redistribution of income away from the poor and toward the rich.

Reagan seems to have been as successful as Roosevelt in institutionalizing his policies. But where Roosevelt introduced programs that offered tangible benefits to large numbers of voters who then had a vested interest in preserving them, Reagan has simply run up a massive federal deficit. By cutting taxes, and by increasing defense spending, Reagan has created enormous pressure on Congress to slash spending for social purposes. When Reagan took office, the national debt was $800 billion; four years later, it had nearly doubled to $1.5 trillion. Nearly as much debt accumulated during Reagan's first term in office as had accumulated in the nation's history prior to his election. About one dollar in every seven spent by the federal government went to pay interest on that debt. As some observers pointed out, such deficits were "a means of advancing the Reagan revolution."

The success of that revolution—or, more properly, counterrevolution—can be gauged not so much by the results of the 1984 election, which saw Reagan capture 59 percent of the popular vote and carry 49 of the 50 states, but rather by the kind of campaign waged by his Democratic opponent. Walter Mondale was properly regarded as a spokesman for a traditional brand of liberalism, but one would not know it from hearing his speech accepting the nomination. Mondale called for a well-managed, not merely well-meaning, government; a president who could say "no" to special interest groups; a strong military posture with no major cuts in defense spending; policies to ensure private rather than public-sector economic growth; and the maintenance of family values. "I will cut the deficit by two-thirds," the liberal Democrat pledged; "we must cut spending and pay as we go." Mondale attacked Reagan for pandering to the rich, but he said little about social welfare or racial justice.

Ronald Reagan established the terms of political debate for the 1980s as surely as Franklin Roosevelt had for the 1930s and 1940s. Whether Reagan's agenda will last for thirty-five years, as Roosevelt's did, remains to be seen.

Chapter Four

Ron, Reaganism, and Revolution: The Rise of the New American Political Economy*

JAMES D. McNIVEN

My aim is to weave a number of suspicions about economic and political trends in America over the past decade into some kind of speculative synthesis. I have chosen the mechanics of revolution as an organizing framework because of the persistent claims that there has been a Reagan revolution.

This paper is not meant to be one in which these speculations and suspicions are proven, but to suggest what the constituents of this revolution are and where it might be going. Only after it reaches the point of orthodoxy will its dimensions be defined and analyzed. However, speculation at this stage is useful since it can help us to predict, however hazily, some political and economic factors in America's future.

THE REAGAN REVOLUTION

The notion that there has been a revolution of sorts during the Reagan administration is a tenacious one. Writers and commentators have sometimes gone to great trouble to show that the phenomenon never

---

* With apologies to the Reverend Samuel Burchard, a James G. Blaine supporter in the election of 1884, whose characterization of the Democrats as the party of "rum, romanism, and rebellion" helped to elect Grover Cleveland president.

occurred or that it was a counterrevolution or that Reagan's actions have only been symbolic and not real.[1] Nevertheless, the feeling persists among too many people that the revolution is real for it to be readily dismissed.

Given its persistent nature, perhaps one should describe some of the features of this revolution and try to show President Reagan's place in it. I will attempt to briefly outline some of the economically related facets of the revolution and suggest how the man who gave his name to it is related to the process.

Eugene Kamenka has provided a useful definition of a revolution. He notes that it is:

> A sharp, sudden change in the social location of power, expressing itself in the radical transformation of the process of government, of the official foundations of sovereignty or legitimacy and of the conception of the social order.[2]

In Kamenka's sense of the word, it is doubtful whether America and the world have experienced a "Reagan revolution"; however, within the established framework of American politics, such may be the case. The 1980 election brought a sharp, sudden change in the location of power, and government processes (in this context) were changed significantly, if only in the resurrection of presidential initiative after a decade of eclipse. The foundations of power that had served to elect presidents for half a century and more were replaced by new ones—both in terms of geographical influence and in terms of symbols and values. Much of this is a throwback to earlier symbols and values, although these ideas (especially rugged individualism) are now interpreted in the context of the 1980s, that is, in relation to urban and suburban life. It is impractical to speak of America moving to the left or the right. Each generation defines anew what is left or right. What was revolutionary in 1933 or 1946 is part of the accepted political framework in 1986.

In most revolutions, a simple model of reality put forth by ideologues is seized upon as a guiding image by people of action. These people of action capitalize on popular discontent to replace the gover-

---

[1] See Herbert Stein, *Presidential Economics* (New York: Simon & Schuster, 1984), p. 314; Robert Dallek, *Ronald Reagan: The Politics of Symbolism* (Cambridge, Mass.: Harvard University Press, 1984), pp. 56–60, 94–104; W. W. Rostow, *The Barbaris Counterrevolution: Cause and Cure* (Austin, TX: University of Texas Press, 1983), pp. 1–2; and Thomas Ferguson and Joel Rogers, "The Myth of America's Turn to the Right," *The Atlantic Monthly*, May 1986, pp. 43–53.

[2] Eugene Kamenka, "The Concept of a Political Revolution," in *Revolution*, ed. Carl Friedrich (New York: Atherton Press, 1966), p. 124.

nors and their structures with ones of their own.[3] In the Reagan revolution, the new ideology centered on a model society characterized by:

1. Smaller government (lower taxes).
2. Less intrusive government.
3. Stronger government with respect to foreign threats.
4. More individual rewards and responsibility.
5. Free markets.

This model was based on an assumption that early American society revolved around these values and that their restoration in the 1980s would restore the country to a greatness it had lost over the previous two decades. At the same time, in many ways these values resemble the values most North American economists assume in their models of our economy. However, they are careful to state that their conclusions are based on these values within a restrictive set of conditions. In the real world, these assumptions ignore political power and processes. One must remember that ideologues are less concerned with the limitations and conditions respected by political scientists than with the moral righteousness of their conclusions. Furthermore, people of action are less concerned with science or morality than with the power that derives from the convictions of the majority. It is normal for ideologues to be exploited and then abandoned by the people of action once their ideas have achieved the goal of bringing activists to power.

Finally, a revolution will reduce an "old order" to ruins. It does not really obliterate it, but it builds a new structure on the old foundation. In this sense, the Reagan revolution has, for example, left the basic welfare state intact, and it has added some new facades and demolished others.

THE REVOLUTIONARY MASSES

There were two major forces that came together in the late 1970s to swing American voters toward a different approach to problems. These forces are different from the traditional or orthodox Republican voter, who is probably older and more established and who was likely to vote Republican with or without a revolution. The first force was the rise of the new consumer. The second force was the new investor. These two powers began to dominate the political agenda of the time, although orthodox Republican and Democratic politicians really did not know how to appeal to them, and in some cases, they were extremely reluctant

---

[3] The mechanics of revolution as discussed here are based on a number of sources and synthesized in Rais A. Khan and James D. McNiven, *An Introduction to Political Science*, 3rd ed. (Chicago: Dorsey Press, 1984), pp. 290–96.

to do so. In the end, these forces helped make a revolution in American politics and because of the residual economic power of the American nation, they have unleashed massive changes all over the world.

The new consumer was just that. One has to return to the so-called baby boom of the 1950s and follow the age cohort born between 1940 and 1960 to see the linked set of pressures and changes that this demographic bulge has caused—first in educational institutions, next in the job market, and finally in the political sphere.[4] In 1980, this age group was 20–40 years old. It is important to note that this is the expanding side of the baby boom; the so-called baby bust that followed 1960 is not important in politics and probably will never be. The powerful baby boom cohort can be split into two parts: people 31–40 years of age in 1980 and people 21–30 years of age in that year. In our age-segregated society, these two groups have different aims but they share certain values.

The older group, as consumers, was entering the age when expensive commitments are made for items such as houses and children. They were concerned about the maintenance of public institutions and services, such as schools and hospitals, but they were also concerned about the amount of disposable income available for mortgages and cars. Employment was not a concern, but advancement was important because career paths in our society tend to leap forward or stop in the late thirties. Political activism in this group was not unknown; baby boomers were associated with the 1960s generation. As the new suburban homeowners in 1980, they added the concerns of a new age to the same political system.[5]

The younger group did not share the concerns of older groups, except in one respect. The younger group was most concerned about employment and saw that the economy of the 1970s was unable to cope with their numbers. They shared with their elders the feeling that the economy and the society had too many people who were either living off the welfare programs of another era or who were incompetent at their jobs and blocking the employment or advancement of these two groups.[6] They saw the solution to these problems in freeing up the economy and in relaxing many rules and constraints that had protected farmers, union members, corporate heads, industries, and government institutions. "Deregulation" would do away with these rigidities and

---

[4] "Baby Boomers Come of Political Age," *The Wall Street Journal*, December 30, 1985.

[5] See Landon Y. Jones, *Great Expectations: America and the Baby-Boom Generation* (New York: Ballantine Books, 1980), especially chapters 17, 18, 20, and 22.

[6] A. F. Ehrbar, "The Upbeat Outlook for Family Incomes," *Fortune* 25 (February 1980), pp. 122–30.

allow these young employees and junior executives to fulfill their dreams.

Allied by necessity to these age groups were the unionized workers of the Northeast, whose jobs were being threatened by migration of capital from their region to other parts of the country and abroad. Generally Democratic by inclination, although increasingly Republican and conservative as their protected status was threatened, union members looked for someone who could produce a revitalization of the manufacturing economy of the Northeast and save their jobs.[7]

To the new consumers and union members, someone had to show a new way to get things moving again, to protect employment, to free up the economy, and to provide new jobs.

The "new investor" is partly a misnomer in that many groups, especially the wealthiest individuals and corporations, were old. However, votes come from people, not corporations, and it was the hundreds of thousands of new small business persons, and the millions who had profited from the growth of commodity industries such as oil and from the migration of manufacturing capital to the Sunbelt, that really counted. These people felt that their success was due in great part to their competitive ability rather than to the fortuitous movement of international price trends and capital flows. They viewed the state and the economy in ways that paralleled those of the baby boomers.

The new investors wanted the government to be less intrusive and smaller, yet tougher internationally.[8] A smaller state meant lower taxes and, therefore, more disposable money to invest. A less intrusive state allowed for more competition and especially allowed the small business person the advantage of speedy reaction to opportunity, often the only advantage over a large corporation. A stronger state, internationally, reflected the pride they had as successful Americans and it also served as a step toward addressing concerns over "unfair" competition from

---

[7] No voting statistics back this up directly; however, middle-income voters in 1980 supported Reagan; no Rust Belt or New England state went to Carter; union members supported Carter 45–46 percent; at least 90 percent of blacks supported him; while a plurality of white union members supported Reagan. Carter's plurality of union voters was the lowest of any Democrat in modern times except for George McGovern. Finally, people who felt they were worse off in 1980 than in 1976 voted three to one for Reagan. Deindustrialization in the Northwest hit union members hardest and made them worse off. See Paul R. Abramson, John Aldrich, and David Rohde, *Change and Continuity in the 1980 Elections* (Washington, D.C.: Congressional Quarterly Press, 1982), pp. 100, 115–16; and Walter Dean Burnham, "The 1980 Earthquake: Realignment, Reaction or What?" in *The Hidden Election*, Thomas Ferguson and Joel Rosen, ed. (New York: Pantheon, 1981), pp. 98–140.

[8] Thomas Moore, "The New Libertarians Make Waves," *Fortune*, August 5, 1985, pp. 74–78. Moore exaggerates when he calls them libertarians.

foreign sources.[9] While a strong defense force was symbolic of this need, which Carter's inability to resolve the Iranian hostage crisis illustrated, a strong dollar was also (paradoxically for exporters) seen as an indication that America's decline had been arrested.

The new investors were helped in their concerns by the emergence of faster and more efficient information technology, which enabled the development of a world capital market that has a more cumulative effect than any of the individual national central banks. The market for manufacturing opportunities opened up as well; it allowed for a greater movement of goods on an international scale—often as part of the product and marketing strategies of multinational corporations. The carefully constructed national protections for groups and industries were being pulled apart by these forces. Only Eastern Europe and the Soviet Union were able to resist the forces, and they did so at a great price. On the other side of the world, Japan, Korea, Singapore, Taiwan, and Hong Kong were taking advantage of these changes to present new challenges to the American economy.

The materials for the revolution were at hand: one could say that the revolution had already begun. It remained for someone to explain the problems and solutions in a simple and concrete manner and for someone else to get in front and lead the revolution.

THE IDEOLOGUES

The economic pressures and changes of the 1970s helped create a coalition that backed the Reagan revolution. There arose a group of ideologues who could explain why the revolution had to happen, and why it was good. The revolutionary supply-side arguments arose in a context of competing ideas about how the American economy ought to be managed.

Capital mobility and employment fears combined to create a range of political pressures acting on the American electorate. Not only was East Asian competition seen as a threat to jobs and corporate survival in the United States, but the very process of American corporate response added to the problem. The questions surrounding the conflict between Sunbelt and Frostbelt, the creation of sunrise industries and protecting sunset industries, picking winners and abandoning losers, and maintaining strategic industrial sectors and even products constituted a new industrial policy debate.[10]

---

[9] Dallek, *Ronald Reagan: The Politics of Symbolism*, pp. 133–34. Dallek notes the connection between domestic pride and a strong international image.

[10] One of the more useful books of the hundreds that have been written on industrial policy is Chalmers Johnson, ed., *The Industrial Policy Debate* (San Francisco: ICS Press, 1984).

In response to these pressures, people in the grass roots movement before 1980 sent two messages: they wanted American business to be able to respond to foreign competition, and they wanted some kind of relief from the instabilities caused by both foreign competition and its domestic response. The general tendency was for the Republicans to listen to the first message and for the Democrats to listen to the second.[11] The economic policy communities in the two parties represent a variety of interests. For a long time after the Depression, these interests were largely the domain of traditional Republicans and New Deal Democrats. Since the shocks of oil prices, inflation, and recession hit in the 1970s, the dominance of these tendencies has been challenged. The Republicans were the first to feel a change as the supply-side economists came to the fore with Reagan's victory in 1980. Before the 1984 election, a similar challenge was launched at the Democrats by the so-called Atari Democrats and the industrial policy economists. This challenge was turned back by the nomination of Walter Mondale, who was seen as the champion of the traditional Democratic coalition.

Traditional Republican economic policy focused on the need to inject fiscal prudence into government. Balanced budgets and careful management of the money supply were its hallmarks. Not surprisingly, this approach was seen by opponents as useful for the rich and threatening to the welfare state. With the exception of the Eisenhower years, it is hard to see where this approach has led to any electoral success.

The challenge of supply-side economics arose as a result of conservative rethinking after the Nixon presidency.[12] Its basic tenet was that economic growth could only be achieved if the tax system was reformed to reward entrepreneurs and producers, thus, allowing them to channel more disposable income into investment. The famous Laffer Curve was added to show that overall tax revenues could rise if tax rates declined. The core political move was the Kemp-Roth tax cut proposal of 1977. This did not win acceptance from the Democrats, but it became a rallying point for the new, conservative supply-side ideologues. The promise of supply-side economics lay in the notion that government revenues to support the welfare state and defense expenditures could be maintained in the face of a massive tax cut—partly because of the effects of the Laffer Curve and partly due to the increased economic growth that the cut would stimulate. The combination was politically attractive—especially

---

[11] Kevin Phillips, *Staying on Top: The Business Case for a National Industrial Strategy* (New York: Random House, 1984). He notes this on p. 7, but it becomes apparent to anyone who ploughs through the voluminous literature on industrial policy.

[12] Stein, *Presidential Economics*, pp. 256–57, provides a capsule summary of the development of the Reaganite ideology. Paul Craig Roberts, *The Supply-Side Revolution* (Cambridge, Mass.: Harvard University Press, 1984), does it as well.

to voters who had or expected to have high incomes in the future and who felt no need for the welfare state. Essentially this included suburbia, unionized workers, and rural areas. These groups helped to form a voting majority that swept Reagan to power.

A third strand of Republican thinking held little appeal but should be mentioned. This is libertarianism, which is a radical variant of supply-side economics, though libertarianism predates it. Libertarians believe that the state has intruded into people's lives unnecessarily and that a radical trimming of public expenditures, including most programs of the welfare state, would result in a revitalization of the American economy. This extreme position, while it touches on strands of conservative feeling, has virtually no electoral appeal.[13]

The Democrats, by 1983, were also divided into three schools of economic policy. Unlike Republican experience, the mainstream of the Democratic party developed around an approach that was successful at the polls for decades. This centered on a commitment to provide public support for people in need that was justified economically as a means of stimulating and maintaining demand. The traditional Democratic support for this approach came from people whose incomes did not allow for significant savings and investment and who, therefore, needed public support for pensions, unemployment, education, and health. The Democratic coalition fell prey in the 1970s to the very success that had made it electorally popular. Many groups in the coalition were better off and their sons and daughters felt more secure because of education and the changing occupational structure. They began to desert the party in droves.

A second Democratic approach was not so concerned with the maintenance of the old coalition as with competing for the allegiance of people who had been attracted to supply-side Republicanism. To them, the central concern was not protecting the welfare state in all aspects; instead, they wanted to attack problems caused by economic instability. They agreed with supply-siders that more had to be done to stimulate investment and productivity, and for that they were characterized as right-wing Democrats. They returned to a traditional Democratic mechanism in advocating various methods of planning—government coordination of a national industrial strategy that would allow the country to meet foreign competition.[14] This basic approach was embraced by Gary Hart in the nomination campaign before the 1984 election,[15] but it was

---

[13] Moore, "The New Libertarians . . . ," p. 74.

[14] Portraits of the Democrats' industrial policy thinkers are presented in Sidney Blumenthal, "Drafting a Democratic Industrial Plan," *New York Times Magazine*, August 28, 1983, pp. 31ff.

[15] Gary A. Hart, *A New Democracy* (New York: William Morrow, 1983).

implicitly rejected by the party when it nominated Mondale, who represented the traditional Democratic approach.

The Democrats also had their radical wing. This group dates from the 1960s and may be called the community developers. In the 1960s, one of the approaches tried in Johnson's War on Poverty was encouraging inner city organizations to set up local economic development groups to provide productive employment. By the 1980s, with the shock of recessions in 1974–75, 1980, and 1982 having provided a large degree of job uncertainty, the call for more effort to provide employment in areas of high and chronic unemployment through publicly owned or cooperative organizations had a certain appeal.[16] The Reverend Jesse Jackson was able to enlist many supporters of these ideas in his Rainbow Coalition.

The post-1984 election scene has been confusing. The defeat of Walter Mondale rebuffed the wing of the Democratic party that is still dominant in the Democratic congressional delegation. There is no guarantee that an Atari Democrat could overcome the opposition in his own party, let alone win the next election. At the same time, the long period of prosperity since 1983 has made the traditional Democratic coalition look even more outdated to the majority of voters. Any hope for a Democratic victory depends on a severe recession in 1988.

The Republicans also face uncertain prospects with the approaching end of Reagan's term. He won the last election handily, but he did not have long coattails and there is speculation that a less personable successor might not catch the eyes and votes of a nation with five years of prosperity behind it. Also, the voting coalition that made the Reagan revolution may not be there to support a successor.

REAGAN'S ROLE IN THE REVOLUTION

Normally, a revolution is captured by its leadership, if that is the proper term, once it is underway. This was true of the Reagan revolution as it was of others. The ideologues and the discontent in the Republican party and across the country were both at work in 1980 when Ronald Reagan allied himself with the supply-side economists. He was able to promise smaller government, stronger defense, lower taxes, and growth to people who wanted all of this strongly, and he backed it up with claims from vocal segments of the business and economic communities.

Reagan did not invent the ideology of the Reagan revolution. In-

---

[16] See Gar Alperovitz and Jeff Faux, *Rebuilding America* (New York: Pantheon, 1984); Robert Lekachman, *Greed Is Not Enough: Reaganomics* (New York: Pantheon, 1982); and Samuel Bowles et al., *Beyond the Wasteland* (Garden City, N.Y.: Anchor Press, 1983).

stead, he adopted it as a means to differentiate himself from mainstream Republicans and orthodox Democrats, and in so doing he won two presidential elections. The old order crumbled and new power bases began to emerge.

Winning these elections was, in part, due to the personality of the man, but it was also due to his ability to capture the feelings of people who were experiencing new trends and forces and who were looking for solutions. In revolutions, however, the people of action do not bring the revolution to a culmination; they hasten it. This is what Ronald Reagan has done.

It mattered little that the revolution hardly met the expectations of its thinkers and activists.[17] What was more important was that it satisfied the hopes of people who voted for it. There were tax cuts promising that profits gained by people who were ready to risk and to try would be respected. The recession of 1982, ironically, took some of the heat off expectations of opportunities for all by virtually denying them to everyone for the subsequent two to three years. At least everyone was sharing the same privations. The protests of the Russians over the American missile buildup in Europe, the invasion of Grenada, and the SDI proposals indicated to many people that America was strong once again; so did the rising dollar, even though it brought a number of trade difficulties. Fiscal deficits were not nearly as important as the fall of OPEC— regardless of the noise coming from betrayed ideologues. At the same time, and ironically, the welfare state was safe, even while it was being attacked by its political saviours.

Reagan captured the revolution and brought it partway along its path. He also protected, willingly or not, the vast majority of the institutions and programs of the old order, while he gave a voice to their critics. In effect, he took them off the American political agenda and made them a part of the historical scenery. The revolution has had its Robespierre, and it awaits, in some future election, its Napoleon—the leader who establishes the revolutionary tenets as the new orthodoxy.

CONCLUSION

My aim has been to provide some speculation about the nature of the Reagan revolution, especially emphasizing the points of industrial policy and economic expectations. There is also an attempt to identify the major actors in this revolution, the revolutionary masses, the ideologues, the people of action, and the old order. Since we are in the middle of the revolution, it is not possible to be completely definitive.

---

[17]Among others, Paul Craig Roberts and David Stockman have publicly decried the divorce between their "truth" and the pragmatic politics of Reagan and the people closest to him.

Still, it is possible to make some conjectures about the future of American politics within this revolutionary scenario. As the population bulge ages, we can expect a breakdown of common interests between the two groups of younger people who played a key role in 1980. The collapse of OPEC has brought a collapse in almost all commodity prices, a phenomenon exactly the reverse of what happened in 1973–74. This has somewhat restored the *status quo ante*, when the Rust Belt manufacturing economy was still dominant in America, while it has taken some of the self-congratulation out of the Sunbelt business community, possibly pushing it out of the 1980 coalition. The resurrection of the Rust Belt has also taken away much of the pressure for an active industrial policy from the political groups based in this area, and it has helped to split union members from the 1980 coalition. The forces behind the Reagan revolution are still strong, but they are changing, and the next group of politicians will have to adapt their positions to these new realities and perceptions in order to be elected. The Napoleon of the revolution is not in sight, but one must remember that he was an unknown only two years before he emerged as the dominant political force in France.

Chapter Five

Cultural Sources of the Reagan Revolution: The Antimodern Legacy

ALAN WOLFE

The Reagan Revolution needs to be understood on its own terms. Reagan's abilities to soothe American anxieties, conservative abilities to arouse grass-roots support, and the agility of Reagan's advisers, especially—if not exclusively—in his first term, were all contributing factors to the Reagan revolution. Since aspects of this revolution are discussed so well in other chapters, I will take a different approach. The success of the Right is due, in part, to the failure of the Left. From the New Deal until 1980, the American Left was a factor in American politics. Its agenda from the 1930s set the stage for issues debated at the national level. But now the Left is in crisis, and Reaganism is the result.

THE FETISHISM OF MODERNITY

All explanations of the failure of the American Left seem to begin with Werner Sombart, an otherwise discredited sociologist from imperial Germany.[1] Sombart had few illusions about either America or capitalism. "The worker in the United States," Sombart concluded, "is more exploited by capitalism than in any other country in the world, and . . . in no other country is he so lacerated in the harness of capitalism or has

---

[1] For fascinating background on Sombart, see Arthur Mitzman, *Sociology and Estrangement* (New York: Alfred A. Knopf, 1973).

to work himself so quickly to death as in America."[2] Why, then, does the American working class find socialism repugnant? Ironically, capitalism's greatest success meant socialism's greatest failure. It was because America developed according to Marxist principles of economic accumulation, Sombart argued, that socialism was doomed to fail. A society that could satisfy material expectations aroused little ideological discontent. Using a metaphor proposed by Lord Bryce, Sombart suggested that if one sinks a shaft deep into the American mind, one will only pass through laissez-faire principles and never touch a deep vein of socialist sentiment.[3]

For American sociologists, particularly from the immediate post–World War II period, Sombart's reflections offered a fascinating interpretation of the uniqueness of American politics. The writings of Marx, Max Weber, and Emile Durkheim, when interpreted a certain way, all point to material success as an end product of a process of economic complexity and a differentiated division of labor. By contrasting American experience with the developing world, and by implication with the less economically advanced parts of Europe as well, one could posit the existence of a continuum of political modernization with America standing securely at one end and all other societies arrayed below. As I have argued elsewhere, the two dominant postulates of postwar political sociology were that modernization was good and that America was the most modern society in the world.[4] It followed, from this Parsonian myopia, that the failure of the American Left was a reflection of its inability to be modern. Socialism was a strain, a nineteenth century anachronism in a twentieth century universe. It was only a matter of time before the crass ideological politics and romantic utopianism of the Marxist vision gave way to a secure foothold for the working class in a technologically dynamic but politically placid society.

The most ambitious attempt to explain the failure of the American Left as a by-product of modernization was offered by Daniel Bell. Citing Lord Acton, Bell suggested that there is an irreconcilable tension between ethics—the *ought* of distribution, and politics—the *mode* of distribution. Older forms of society, especially before the advent of liberal democracy, often combined them, but—argues Bell—"a distinguishing feature of modern society is the separation of the two."[5] Modernity, therefore, consists of the recognition that "the redivision of the rewards

---

[2] Werner Sombart, *Why Is There No Socialism in the United States?* (White Plains, N.Y.: M.E. Sharpe, 1976), p. 112.

[3] Ibid., p. 13.

[4] Alan Wolfe, "Is America Modern?," in *Socialist Perspectives*, ed. Phyllis and Julius Jacobson (New York: Karz-Cohl, 1983), pp. 185–99.

[5] Daniel Bell, *Marxian Socialism in the United States* (Princeton, N.J.: Princeton University Press, 1967), p. 6.

and privileges of society can only be accomplished in the political arena."[6] Modern political actors are capable of separating their ethics from their politics—demanding pragmatic compromise and political brokerage. American socialism failed, Bell concluded, because it was unable to participate in the transition to modernity—hunkered down as it was by ethical baggage:

> The socialist movement, by its very statement of goal and its rejection of the capitalist order as a whole, could not relate itself to the specific problems of social action in the here-and-now, give-and-take political world. It was trapped by the unhappy problem of living "*in* but not *of* the world," so it could only act, and then inadequately, as the moral, but not political, man in immoral society. It could never resolve but only straddle the basic issue of either accepting capitalist society, and seeking to transform it from within as the labor movement did, or becoming the sworn enemy of that society, like the communists. A religious movement can split its allegiances and live *in* but not *of* the world (like Lutheranism); a political movement cannot.[7]

There is some validity to Bell's argument. America's most famous socialist, Eugene V. Debs, as a recently published biography points out, was periodically moved by a vision of small city Indiana life destroyed since his boyhood, and a substantial part of his appeal lay in his ability to conjure up visions of a better past in the face of the rapacious consequences of modernity.[8] Yet, while Debs may have led a protest against modernity, other American socialists—one thinks of the technological harmony enshrined by Edward Bellamy[9]—were ruthless in their distemper toward a less efficient and mechanistic past. Bell's reading of the

---

[6] Ibid., p. 6.

[7] Ibid., p. 5.

[8] Nick Salvatore, *Eugene V. Debs: Citizen and Socialist* (Urbana: University of Illinois Press, 1982). Debs, however, like most Americans since Emerson, had an ambivalent relationship with modern technology and its implications. As Salvatore concludes, "In his ability to fuse the personal and the political, Debs personified a more holistic vision that affirmed the older moral values, while accepting, even welcoming, technological innovation and economic progress." Salvatore, p. 343.

[9] Bell, *Marxian Socialism*, p. 17. According to John L. Thomas, not only Bellamy, but Henry George and Henry Demearest Lloyd also became socialists out of a rejection of the irrationalities of capitalism—hence their later attraction to city planners like Patrick Geddes and Lewis Mumford. While a good part of their aim can be seen as the restoration of a balanced life lost in the rush toward modernity, they also anticipated modern society with their emphasis on efficiency and responsibility. Thomas' discussion of the relationship between *Looking Backward* and Taylorism is contained in John L. Thomas, *Alternative America* (Cambridge, Mass.: Harvard University Press, 1983), pp. 251–52. The influence of these men on city and regional planning is discussed on pp. 354–66. If it is

American socialist experience, as John H. M. Lassett has pointed out, puts the emphasis entirely on the movement—not on the society.[10] Thus, Bell cannot explain how European socialist movements, many of which were *more* ideologically driven than the American movement, could nonetheless flourish in an alternative situation of modernity. The failure of American socialism, in short, may have more to do with America than with socialism.

Daniel Bell is not the only sociologist to rely on the modernity of American life as an explanation for the failure of the socialist project. Seymour Martin Lipset, in his book *The First New Nation*, explicitly used modernization theory to explain American exceptionalism. One of the most potent indications of the modernization process, Lipset suggested, is the degree to which "achievement orientation" permeated society. Nowhere in the world is such a commitment to the modern principle of achievement more securely established than in the United States. From this principle, Lipset derives two conclusions: the American labor movement is both more hostile to class interpretations of politics and more aggressive and militant in its union tactics than other labor movements shaped less by premature modernity.[11] When combined with explanations that emphasize other aspects of modernity such as social mobility,[12] a fairly complete picture emerges: the American Left, fighting a hopeless battle against the dynamic rationalizing features of capitalist and industrial life, needs to be understood as a Luddite dream of the past—not a coherent, articulate, and compelling vision of the future.

My complaint with this literature is not so much with its conclusion—I agree with Bell and Lipset that American socialism has been a failure—but with its attribution of cause. Indeed, postwar American sociology posed the problem backwards. The problem was not that American capitalism was modern and the Left reactionary; it was the other way around. American life is characterized by a legacy of pre-

---

true that America's most popular socialist thinkers were as much prophets of modernity as critics of it, it follows that the attraction to their ideas came as much from middle class reformers as from working class activists. In this context, R. Jeffrey Lustig is surely correct to stress that Henry George "succeeded . . . in identifying the class content of a wide range of what are normally seen as 'middle class' issues." R. Jeffrey Lustig, *Corporate Liberalism* (Berkeley: University of California Press, 1982), p. 65.

[10] John H. M. Laslett, "Comment," in *Failure of a Dream*, ed. John H. M. Laslett and Seymour Martin Lipset (Garden City, N.Y.: Anchor Books, 1974), p. 112.

[11] Seymour Martin Lipset, *The First New Nation* (Garden City, N.Y.: Anchor Books, 1967), pp. 202–33. Lipset relies on the term *achievement* from David McClelland, *The Achieving Society* (New York: Free Press, 1967).

[12] Stephan Therstrom, "Socialism and Social Mobility," in Laslett and Lipset, *Failure of a Dream*, pp. 509–27.

modernism far more striking than other advanced capitalist societies in Europe. American exceptionalism lies not in the degree to which the United States is *ahead* of the rest of the world, but in the degree to which it lags *behind*. The problem facing the Left, from this perspective, is not that it resists modernization but that it is called upon to speak for modern principles—rationality, efficiency, equality, and fairness—in a culture still attracted to irrationality and romantic ideologies of an arcadian past. American socialism has not been utopian but prosaic. It offers reason when the culture demands romance. Especially in the 1980s, when a drive toward a new wave of capitalist growth is accompanied by a right-wing ideology that worships fantasy,[13] the American Left stands out like an old-fashioned bore in a fast crowd—perversely insisting on restating experience that few wish to hear.

THE LEGACY OF PREMODERNITY

Whether modernity was viewed as an iron cage entrapping its inhabitants or a harmonious utopia of planning and consensus, most writers in the sociological tradition can agree on their definition of its essential features. Urbanization, industrialization, bureaucratization, the division of labor, technology, and the drive toward equality are accompanied by certain changes in social life; the sum can be considered the essence of modernity. Foremost among these features are the following: a strengthening of the state as an alternative to the market, whether under advanced capitalism or some form of socialism; greater stress on problem solving and pragmatism against ideological modes of thought; secularization and the decline of superstition; the substitution of merit for favoritism; enhanced material satisfaction and choice; reliance on science as a world view; greater democratization, understood as the necessity to provide mass benefits to majorities through the political process; the spread of Enlightenment modes of thought, almost, in the opinion of some, to the point of tyranny; increasing cosmopolitanism and the decline of parochialism and localism, growing out of facilitated communication and transportation; and an emphasis on planning and predictability, undermining a resigned belief in fate. Modern man is Faustian and given ever greater access to wisdom even if at the cost of a certain loss of innocence.[14]

Along many of the key dimensions of modernity, America was in

---

[13] For a spirited defense of the proposition that at this point in history capitalist growth requires the cultivation of unreason, see George Gilder, *Wealth and Poverty* (New York: Basic Books, 1981).

[14] The costs and benefits of modernity have been sympathetically analyzed in Marshall Berman, *All That Is Solid Melts into Air* (New York: Simon & Schuster, 1982).

the lead. It perfected not only industrialization, but the techniques of organizing industrialization as well. Its democracy seemed far in advance of others; it extended universal (white, male) suffrage (and the political techniques based upon it) far earlier than European societies. It pioneered the development of scientific and technological innovations that left the old world both angry and fascinated, imbuing the term *Americanism* with both positive and negative connotations. Yet, for all the dazzling surface of American life in the late nineteenth century and early twentieth century, underneath, had one plumbed deep enough, one could discover the persistence of habits of thought and details of social life that retained an eighteenth century character. The United States imposed a dynamic and extremely modern economy and society upon an antique and outmoded political system and set of beliefs. The result was an important legacy of premodernity that lasted long beyond the drive to create an ever more dynamic technological system.

One can point to any number of examples of the legacy of premodernity in American life: the absolute insistence on not using the metric system; the survival of creationism—in some places accorded equal time in schools with evolutionary theory; the refusal to ratify the Equal Rights Amendment to the Constitution—the last of the major nineteenth century correctives to legal inequality; the distrust of urbanism and praise for small-town virtues that persists in a society that has farms but precious few farmers; the astonishing persistence of a rumor attributing diabolic motives to Procter & Gamble despite all the best efforts of the corporation to dispel it; and the remarkable popularity of romantic fiction sold right next to computerized cash registers that automatically record the price of supermarket goods. But since my purpose in this essay is to understand the problems facing the American Left at the present time, I wish to emphasize just four aspects of the legacy of premodernity that have left their mark on contemporary politics: the importance of religion; the persistence of ideology; the relative weakness of the state; and the anticosmopolitan approach to global politics that characterizes mass public sentiment.

The relationship between modernization and secularization has been carefully studied by Walter Dean Burnham. Based on a 1976 Gallup survey taken in fourteen countries, Burnham found that when societies were contrasted along a strong belief dimension compared to a level of socioeconomic development, an almost perfect correlation was discovered—so long as Canada and the United States were excluded from the analysis. When Canada was added, the significance of the correlation dropped a bit. When both Canada and the United States were added, the correlation plummeted. The consequences of this religious legacy are immediately obvious to any observer of American political behavior. On the one hand, U.S. politicians are careful to make widely known their religiosity—even as the society formally recognizes a separation between church and state. Also, secularization, as Burnham notes, "has been an essential precondition for the emergence of leftist parties, and therefore for the entire matrix of developed alternatives in the electoral market."[15] The persistence of religion and the late arrival of socialism, in other words, are two sides of the same process in American political life.

One influential attempt to account for the persistence of religion in American life has been offered by Robert N. Bellah, who has called attention to the side-by-side existence in American culture of a fairly methodical utilitarianism accompanied by a tradition of Protestant evangelicalism. Bellah has stressed the existence of America's "civil religion," a complex of attitudes and beliefs suggesting a kind of secularized or modern religion emphasizing the importance of having faith— not the details of an individual's faith.[16] One wonders, however, why Bellah feels the need to add the adjective *civil*, for the civil religion of America is surely religion pure and simple. A long-standing commitment to theological doctrine, despite America's technological and worldly success, has, as Bellah has brilliantly argued, made socialist millenarianism a taboo subject. "Socialism," Bellah has written, far from constituting itself as an alternative to capitalism in American political culture, "has often seemed merely to compound the evil that is contained in capitalism. . . . The American aversion to socialism," he continues, "goes deeper than rational argument."[17] It is the unspoken premise of a society that not only still believes in God but to this day views itself as the instrument of God's will on this earth.

Faith in God coexists in the United States along with faith in the efficacy of a moral and ideological stance toward important issues of public policy. Despite reams of agreement in the sociological literature that ideology was incompatible with modernity—and that America, as the most modern society in the world, was destined to be the least ideological—American political culture retains an ideological flavoring that both European Social Democrats and technocratic capitalists find bizarre and inexplicable. The United States is supposed to be the natural home of pragmatism yet, as Paul Starr discovered in his effort to explain why the United States did not develop a public health insurance system —surely a symptom of modernity—when Europe did, the answer has a great deal to do with the persistence of ideological discourse as a way of life in American politics:

---

[15] Walter Dean Burnham, "Social Stress and Political Response: Religion and the 1980 Election," *The Hidden Election,* ed. Thomas Ferguson and Joel Rogers (New York: Pantheon, 1981), pp. 132–40.

[16] Robert N. Bellah, "Civil Religion in America," *Daedalus,* Winter 1967.

[17] Robert N. Bellah, *The Broken Covenant* (New York: Seabury, 1975), pp. 121–22.

America is frequently described as a less ideological society than Europe, more given to interest-group than ideological politics. The AMA's battle against health insurance is often cited as a premier case of interest-group political influence. But throughout the debate over health insurance in the United States, the conflict was intensely ideological, much more so than in Europe. The interest groups opposed to health insurance repeatedly found it useful to cast the issue in ideological terms. By accusing the supporters of health insurance of being the agents first of German statism and then of Soviet communism, they meant to inject a meaning into health insurance that the reformers deeply resented. The reformers' efforts to detoxify the conflict were to no avail. And their attempt to present national health insurance as a technical matter of the 'health needs' of the society had its ideological bias, too.[18]

On only one point does Starr's extremely insightful analysis need correction, in my opinion. The point is not that proponents of national health insurance—indeed, the American Left in general—resorted to ideological language when they talked about health needs. The point is that the Left's position in the debate over health insurance used a language of technical need and social service, which, in its excessive pragmatism, had little to offer against the romantic, moralistic, and heavily ideological presentation of the AMA and its allies. In American political life, it is often the dominant interest groups who use the language of utopia, while the Left remains committed to utilitarian principles.

As health insurance went, so went many of the other reforms that in Europe would be considered the essence of social democracy. In the modernization process, social democrats have played a major role, for Marx was more enthusiastic in the welcome he offered modernity than, for example, Max Weber. The relative weakness of social democracy in the United States, in other words, deprived American politics not of a tradition of ideological vision, but it stripped the United States of that powerful movement toward rationalization, predictability, scientific public policy, and moderate progress which Fabianism and Social Democracy came to embody. The excessive ideological language of groups like the AMA in its heyday—or the similar moralistic discourse utilized by both the fundamentalist religious Right and the anticommunist supporters of cold war military spending—persists in the gap left by the absence of a clinical and dispassionate tradition of statist reform. Socialism in America failed not because *it* was ideological but because *America* was ideological; the kind of political culture that enables a purely ideological administration like Ronald Reagan's to flourish is the exact political culture that makes it impossible to make a compelling case for a

---

[18] Paul Starr, *The Social Transformation of American Medicine* (New York: Basic Books, 1982), pp. 286–87.

political and social reform based on its efficiency and rationality. (One would be hard pressed to find a system of paying medical costs that is more inefficient and irrational than the one used in the United States.)

The quite remarkable inability of the United States to establish a state-directed system of medical insurance—a feature that makes American public policy distinct from that of all other advanced capitalist democracies—is symptomatic of a third legacy of premodernity: the relative weakness of the state in American political life. In the literature on modernization (sometimes called development), the state was called upon to play a major role. For example, Cyril Black defined modernization as "the process by which historically evolved institutions are adopted to the rapidly changing functions that reflect the unprecedented increase in man's knowledge, permitting control over his environment, that accompanied the scientific revolution."[19] To bring these changes about, certain transformations in the sociopolitical environment became necessary, including a "transfer of power from traditional to modernizing leaders in the course of a normally bitter revolutionary struggle often lasting several generations."[20] Such a transformation could only take place successfully where states accumulated sufficient power to break down pockets of power based on premodern or feudal obligations. Without a strong state, modernization becomes impossible.

The necessity of a strong state, in the sociological literature, begins from the premise that modernizing elites will always face resistance from entrenched interests. Even the creation of a liberal economic order rooted in a distrust of state action, as diverse writers such as Polanyi, MacPherson, and Tilly have all pointed out, required the consolidation of political power in the state before it could be turned into reality.[21] From this perspective, the American experience remains uniquely fascinating because, as Samuel P. Huntington has argued, America retained many of the features of a Tudor political system even though it earlier adopted the fullest commitment to capitalist development.[22] The legacy of Tudor policy continues to haunt the process of political change in the United States. It has significantly affected the political behavior of both dominant elites and opposition movements.

---

[19] Cyril Black, *The Dynamics of Modernization* (New York: Harper & Row, 1966), p. 7.

[20] Ibid., p. 67.

[21] Karl Polanyi, *The Great Transformation* (Boston: Beacon, 1957); C. B. MacPherson, *The Political Theory of Possessive Individualism* (Oxford: Claredon Press, 1962); and Charles Tilly, "Reflections on the History of European State Making," in *The Formation of Nation States in Western Europe*, ed. Charles Tilly, (Princeton, N.J.: Princeton University Press, 1975), p. 73.

[22] Samuel P. Huntington, *Political Order in Changing Societies* (New Haven, Conn.: Yale University Press, 1968).

"What does the ruling class do when it rules?" one sociologist recently asked.[23] Without engaging all the details of the resulting answers, a fundamental political task of a dominant class is to overcome resistance to modernization. All economic systems, especially capitalism, go through periodic changes of such a magnitude that political coalitions that seek to organize and transform change to their liking are often left behind. The paradox of capitalist growth lies in the fact that, as Mancur Olson has stressed, those who benefit from a privileged position in the previous wave of change must yield their privileges to make the next wave of change possible.[24] Even in the United States, which did not possess Europe's feudal legacy, there were sufficient entrenched elites, especially among Southern planters and New England Federalists, to make one wonder how an emerging capitalist ruling class would assemble sufficient power to build a new form of state.

Without a tradition of political absolutism, America developed its own solution to the problem of political modernization. The Hamiltonian project of leading a transition to a modern political economy in the face of local resistance could not be accomplished without a significant ally, and that ally was found in an alliance between modernizing elites from above and a democratic movement stimulated from below.[25] Rationalizing reformers attached their political fortunes to an expansion of the electorate as a method of circumventing the entrenched power of local elites. The result was an ambiguous tradition of progressive reform in the United States; the Left was a combination of corporate rationalizations and popular democratic pressures simultaneously—two tendencies that might, in another political context, be in opposition to each other. Yet, the weakness of the American state left no choice; a highly decentralized political system, emphasizing the division of authority between Washington and the state capitals and divided into separate sovereignties of power in both places, made the ʰ ·· of implementing modernization solely from above nearly imposs.

The implications of this pattern of political deveⅬopment for American socialism were enormous. Where centralized political authority existed—ironically, given the literature on modernization, in states where an absolutist tradition persisted—socialist movements (for example, in Germany, Austria, and Scandinavia) could develop entire opposition cultures as if they were creating an alternative state due to take over when the existing one ran its course. But in the United States,

---

[23] Goran Therborn, *What Does the Ruling Class Do When It Rules?* (London: New Left Books, 1978).

[24] Mancur Olson, *The Rise and Decline of Nations* (New Haven, Conn.: Yale University Press, 1982).

[25] Alan Wolfe, "Presidential Power and the Crisis of Modernization," *Democracy* 1 (April 1981), pp. 10–32.

where political authority was weak, modernizing elites needed to coopt the energy and mobilizing potential of left-wing movements in order to win passage of their programs. The Left, small as it was, was constantly tempted by the opportunity to participate in such political transformations; socialist rhetoric, and some socialist activists, played a role in both the Progressive Movement and the New Deal. The legacy of premodern political authority in the United States compelled the American socialist movement to play a role as a modernizing force—substituting itself for the partial weakness of the ruling elites. In periods when entrenched local elites were in the ascendency—the conservative phase of the political cycle—the Left was tempted to moderate its oppositional urges in order to bring a more favorable political atmosphere into being. This point will be discussed in detail in the next section of the chapter, where I consider the contemporary Left's response to such a conservative period—the present one—but for the moment, it is sufficient to stress that if a strong central authority is an essential criteria of political modernization, then America's political system to date has sufficient premodern legacies to make one question how much can be explained by references to America's modernity.

One final legacy of premodernity that is relevant to understanding the plight of American socialism lies in the special relationship that the United States has developed with the world. Cosmopolitanism—an appreciation of and respect for the world at large—is, according to the sociological tradition, an important aspect of the modernizing experience. For postwar sociologists, intoxicated by the Parsonian emphasis on universality, the assumption by the United States of a global role in world affairs seems to prove the maturation of the American polity. Parochialism and isolationism, so characteristic of U.S. foreign policy in the nineteenth century, had no place in a social system that values moderation, rationality, balance, and tolerance. Postwar sociology became a part of the cold war—offering a theory of why the projection of American power beyond its borders was essential not only to political modernity in the United States but to the replication of the experience for other societies as well. Communism was a false God, a revolution *manqué*; the real revolution, if only the world would hear, was the inevitable drive to create modern men and women living roughly in the way people in the United States lived.

To be sure, America did assume an imperial role in the postwar period, but to describe the consequences as a growing cosmopolitanism misses how it did so. The isolationist strain in American culture was not so much vanquished as transformed; the United States became that rarest of creatures, an isolationist empire—just as intent on ruling the world as it was on closing its mind to learning about the world. (The British engaged in a much greater give and take with their imperial subjects than did the Americans, although the U.S. empire has lasted for a far shorter time.) From the first outburst of imperial ambitions in the last decade of the nineteenth century straight through to the Reagan administration, America's attempt to project its power abroad, as one historian has written, "was more the product of troubles at home than of opportunities abroad." It represents "a succession of modern episodes in which foreign affairs had greater symbolic than substantive importance in the nation's life."[26] America retained a political culture emphasizing its parochialism and uniqueness just as much during its imperial years as during its isolationist ones; the domestic political culture did not essentially change even if the outward form of American foreign policy changed radically.

British globalism, as Bernard Semmel has described it, was a combination of imperialism and social reform.[27] Active British socialists, most especially the Fabian Society, were far from hostile to the assumption of an imperial role; if the Webbs were any example, socialist reformers were second to none in their enthusiasm for empire. In America, as well, one can discover in the Progressive tradition the same combination of warfare and welfare; there is an extensive commitment to action, national purpose, reform, and moral regeneration.[28] There is a kind of modernizing socialism that flourishes when a society assumes a role as a global power. (When the underlying rationale for global hegemony is anticommunism, the political culture of Social Democracy is especially compatible, given the historic hostility between socialism and communism.) To engage for a moment in counterfactual speculation, had America become an ideal-type imperial power, rooted in a strong welfare state at home and seeking the creation of a stable world order under its global leadership, such a movement could easily have supported and, in turn, have been essential to the aims of a reformist tradition of socialist interventionism. (French society, at the moment, contains an example of a modernizing socialist party committed to increasing French power in the world arena.)

But what did not happen in the United States is precisely this link between mature imperialism and progressive social reform. The pro-

---

[26] Robert Dallek, *The American Style of Foreign Policy* (New York: Alfred A. Knopf, 1983), pp. 4–5.

[27] Bernard Semmel, *Imperialism and Social Reform* (Cambridge, Mass.: Harvard University Press, 1960).

[28] For a fascinating interpretation of the culture of Progressivism, see Robert M. Crunden, *Ministers of Reform* (New York: Basic Books, 1982). Crunden emphasizes that the religiosity and moral rectitude of Progressive reformers like George Herron and Richard Ely created a vocabulary that formed the basis of Woodrow Wilson's "Presbyterian foreign policy"—one that "asserted the virtue of American motives and the superiority of American ideals and insisted on the right to export those ideals to any unstable area in the world." Crunden, p. 226.

cess, which began under Theodore Roosevelt, ran out of steam under Lyndon Johnson. Instead of the empire serving the cause of domestic reform and regeneration—opposed for precisely those reasons by the conservative Right—the imperial urge became the first priority of the American Right in the 1980s. As it did so, a legacy of premodern ideological values—including faith in America's unique mission combined with a somewhat primitive nationalism and disdain for other cultures—became the basis for imperial resurgence. Particularism was retained even as American foreign policy sought a universal mission.

This combination of modern imperialism with premodern ideology has contributed to the isolation of the American Left from public discourse. Again, in comparison with the British case, Fabianism and social reform, while contributing to the assumption of an imperial role, also legitimized a tradition of state intervention and equality—one must have better education and public health if one is to rule the world. But in America, where primitive, premodern imperialism became the rule, there was no need for leftist or progressive rhetoric to rationalize the empire. Moreover, and this reason may be more important, the reassertion of American needs onto the world scene provided a set of symbols for mass consumption that constituted a viable alternative to socialist symbols. It was not so much, as Leon Samson first argued, that Americanism was a form of surrogate socialism.[29] I have in mind the important argument made by Trent Schroyer that American political culture, far from being purely Lockean, contains in its republicanism and religiosity a critique of materialism which, however removed from practice, constitutes an ethical alternative to a socialism that often seems too materialistic and secular.[30] Parochial Americanism, the belief in a premodern Eden with its own virtues and distinctive moral code, is such an effective accompaniment for the empire that there is no need to rely on social reform to solidify the imperial consensus. Ironically, the American Left might have had a greater role in political life if America's assumption of empire had been based more thoroughly on the British model.

Religion, ideology, a weak state, and an eighteenth century projection of moral virtue abroad all constitute a healthy legacy of premodern symbols and practices that belie the often-made claim that America stands at the end of a modernization continuum to which all other nations aspire. There is enough strength left in eighteenth century concepts to make one wonder how fully the American polity has joined the twentieth century. But there is one exception to the rule—one example

---

[29] Leon Samson, *Toward a United Front* (New York: Farrar and Rinehart, 1935), excerpted in *Failure of a Dream*, pp. 426–42.

[30] Trent Schroyer, "Cultural Surplus in America," *New German Critique* 26 (Spring–Summer 1982), pp. 81–117.

of a portion of American culture that has aspired to modernity: the Left itself. To understand the failure of American socialism, one cannot focus exclusively on the premodern legacy of American political and social patterns; one must also examine the ambivalent relationship of left-wing dissent to the dynamics of the modernization process.

AN AMBIVALENT PROJECT

The American Left, Gerry Watts has suggested, has been afraid to face the consequences of modernity.[31] Rooted in romantic and utopian longings, he has concluded, the Left will never be a force until it proves itself willing to accept the fundamental premises of a modern political culture. I disagree; the Left has been seriously divided over its approach to modernity; part of it has assumed an ultramodern stance in the face of the refusal of dominant elites to assert their own modernizing project, while another portion of the Left has retained an Emersonian transcendentalism and longing for nineteenth century life. Weak, in any case, the American Left has been further paralyzed by its internal differences toward the whole question of how modern it should be.

The emergence of a New Left in the 1960s seemed to indicate that an indigenous radical movement had developed in the United States that rejected the hierarchical, working-class oriented, and popular-front style of traditional left organizations in the United States. Yet, the rapid fall from grace of the New Left, almost as spectacular as its rise, has led some people to conclude that the differences between old and new have been exaggerated; James Weinstein, for example, writes that "in style, as well in their social situations and their age, the new leftists were different from the old. But even so, many of their underlying assumptions about social change were shared with the old left."[32] I disagree. The New Left stood for a critique of urban-industrial society—a reaction against the major tendencies of modernity, while the Old Left viewed its project as the completion of urban-industrial society, the extension of its benefits to all. My aim is not to take sides, but to point out that the American Left has been working at cross purposes; one constituency aims to negate the gains that the other constituency seeks to effect.

For the Old Left, which significantly called itself progressive, the problem facing American society was its lack of progress. Implicit in its world view was the notion that society was moving inevitably toward greater equality, fairness, and political participation—but without the intervention of a body of activists speaking in the name of the underclass, such a motion would be stopped. Therefore, the task of the Left

---

[31] Gerry Watts, "The Socialist as Ostrich: The Unwillingness of the Left to Confront Modernity," *Social Research*, 50, no. 1 (Spring 1983), pp. 3–56.

[32] James Weinstein, *Ambiguous Legacy: The Left in American Politics* (New York: New Viewpoints, 1975), p. 115.

was to bring to the working class, minorities, and other deprived groups the gains in government access that the middle class had already won. Accompanying this project was rhetoric about a future socialist society, but the short-term objectives, the ones that current political activity could tangibly produce, goaded the conscience of liberal politicians to take a position just beyond what was acceptable at any given time and, as a result, they pushed the bounds of the possible toward the left. At its best, for example, during the New Deal, the presence of an organized left in American politics served as a partial counterweight to the permanent influence of big business—opening up the political system both in terms of the constituencies served and in terms of a broadening of electoral groupings making legitimate demands.

Even this relatively moderate project, however, seemed impossible, so unaccustomed was the United States to the notion of a well-functioning welfare state. American liberalism, even at the height of New Deal popularity, faced sufficient conservative obstructionism to force a moderation of its objectives. A rightward bias in American politics had a domino effect that shifted each constituency along the continuum one or two steps rightward to legitimize itself under the reigning ideology. Since corporate liberal tendencies were weak among American businessmen, who retained an attraction to pure laissez-faire ideology even as many of their colleagues in Europe were abandoning it, liberal social reformers shifted to the Right and spoke for the long-term interests of capital. As that took place, the resulting vacuum in liberalism was filled by people whom Europeans would call Social Democrats. As the Social Democratic territory was vacated, whatever pressure that existed for a more activist socialism was invariably tempted to move into the open slot. Socialist tendencies, in other words, were sublimated into a drive to complete the modernization process that the bourgeoisie had essentially abandoned.

If modernization means the tendency to replace a resigned belief in fate with the principles of planning, predictability, human intervention, and protection against uncertainty, then reliance on the market—which Max Weber had viewed as the primary cause of calculability and rationality—at some point turns on itself and destroys the drive toward modernity it once helped create. The drive made by capital to organize into a predictable world that can be managed, a drive that leads to the replacement of competitive capitalism by its organized and monopolistic counterpart, spills over into demands from all other groups in society to obtain the same access to the regulation of fate. Yet, as each group in the society seeks protection against the ravages of the market, the logic of capitalism and profit making is questioned. Capital seeks modernity for itself and passive resignation for everyone else—an intolerable position for everyone else if they have the political power to avoid it. A singular task of the Left is to complete the modernizing process that capitalism began but is afraid or unable to bring to fruition.

In the United States, the modernizing tendencies in the Left were strong for necessity because similar modernizing tendencies on the part of business and other dominant groups were so weak. The incompleteness of American political modernization affected the tasks of the Left in two significant ways. First, the relative strength of capitalism, combined with its commitment to an excessively ideological understanding of its class interests, created a vacuum in which relatively few corporate leaders could speak for the long-term interest of capital as a whole. It fell by default upon the Left to fill that gap and, as a consequence, a pattern was established whereby reform from below became the precondition for reorganization from above. If, following Habermas and others, we understand advanced capitalism as a system of state planning designed to organize and make more predictable the process of capitalist accumulation,[33] then significant credit must be given to the tradition of progressive and socialist reform for creating the conditions that made advanced capitalism possible in the face of the unwillingness of business to recognize what was in its best interest.

Secondly, political modernization in the United States was as incomplete as the state-led organization of the accumulation process. The logic of citizenship in liberal democracy is a logic of inclusion—the extension of the rights gained by the first group to be accorded political recognition to all other groups that seek it. As a class becomes integrated into society politically, it becomes, to use a term associated with John Goldthorpe, "nature."[34] Its demands, instead of being visionary and militant, become interests to be bargained among all other classes or groups that have gained entry into the system. From this perspective, a modern polity is one that extends the principle of inclusion to as many deserving constituents as possible—meaning that a class had demonstrated some claim to legitimacy under which its exclusion would be seen as so basic a violation of the norms of a mature liberal democracy that no such exclusion can be countenanced. Interest-group bargaining among legitimately contending groups, in a modern polity, replaces overt class struggle and extraparliamentary militance as a means of reconciling issues of distribution; the findings of political scientists like Douglas Hibbs—that polities according political rights to the working class are less likely to have strikes—reflect these trends.[35]

---

[33] Jurgen Habermas, *Legitimation Crisis* (Boston: Beacon Press, 1975); James O'Connor, *The Fiscal Crisis of the State* (New York: St. Martin's, 1973).

[34] John Goldthorpe, "The Current Inflation: Towards a Sociological Account," in *The Political Economy of Inflation*, eds. Fred Hirsch and John Goldthorpe (London: Martin Robertson, 1978), pp. 186–214.

[35] Douglas Hibbs, "Trade Union Power, Labor Militancy, and Wage Inflation: A Comparative Analysis" (Cambridge, Mass.: M.I.T. Center for International Studies, 1977).

By this criteria of political inclusion, the United States is significantly more premodern than similar societies in Western Europe. As late as the 1980s—more than a century after the struggle to incorporate legitimate access to political power began—constituencies in the United States are still struggling to win basic nineteenth century rights of legal access to the state. The defeat of the Equal Rights Amendment—in its wording and in its strategy of the bourgeois revolutions of past times—is one indication of the relative immaturity of the American polity. Another sign is the inability of minorities—who also won legal rights extraordinarily late in the political development of the United States—to transform those gains into concrete political victories. The effect of these political delays on the Left is obvious. Instead of taking for granted basic rights and building upon them for a transition to a future society, the Left must assume the burden of attempting and often failing to secure the victories of a previous generation. A political movement that in theory is supposed to be concerned with the future finds itself operating in the political language and rhetoric of the past.

If the inability of the Left to respond to the premodern aspects of American culture helps explain its weakness, it also helps explain the Reagan Revolution. The American Right has had no trouble responding to premodern themes. It emphasizes religion, for example, even though the sources of its wealth—franchised hamburgers, plastic dinnerware, and other such goods—are ruthlessly secular. It is unabashedly ideological—speaking a language of hopes and dreams and blithely unconcerned with practical realities as President Reagan's position on SDI illustrates. It is against the state even though, like all modernizing tendencies, it uses the state for its own purposes. Also, its foreign policy is moralistic and idealistic—having more in common with Wilsonian visionary notions than hard-headed European efforts at *realpolitik*.

Yet, if this rejection of modernity is the source of Reagan's emotional appeal, it may also be the cause of his increasing political weakness in the real world. For all the premodernity of its culture, America is capitalistic, bureaucratic, and a global power—all of them as modern as can be. Americans may want to pretend differently, and they may resound enthusiastically to a president who tells them what they like to hear, but the real world does have a nasty habit of making itself felt every now and then. The troubles currently facing the Reagan administration seem to indicate that the real world has done it again.

Part IV

THE "REAGAN REVOLUTION" IN ECONOMICS

He had promised, as it were, to alter the laws of arithmetic.
DAVID STOCKMAN

Not many years ago, economist Walter Heller delivered the Godkin Lectures at Harvard University. He surveyed the accomplishments of his discipline and found it was good. The economists had understood how the economy works; it was now only a matter of fine-tuning the instruments.[1] This, of course, was before the discovery of supply-side economics, the arrival of Ronald Reagan in the White House, and the emergence of the "magic asterisk" as a new tool of economic management.

It is easy to dismiss scornfully the claims of "the Hellers": we did learn a lot about how our economy works and it is when we disregard what we have learned that troubles come. That is one of the points implied in the following essay by James Tobin, a Nobel Prize winner in economics. Although economic science can be both dismal and abstruse, the central issues of political economy can be stated with relative clarity and ease.

One issue concerns answers to the question: "Who should pay for our government and its policies?" The answer deals with taxation and deficits; it also concerns our notions of justice; our answers depend on how we view questions of wealth, income (and how they are created), and benefits bestowed by the government.

The question of benefits also inevitably implies questions about who

---

[1] Walter W. Heller, *New Dimensions of Political Economy* (Cambridge, Mass.: Harvard University Press, 1966).

should pay for them and the wisdom of these policies. There is far less clarity and agreement in this area. William Niskanen, president of the Cato Institute and former chairman of the Council of Economic Advisors to President Reagan, focuses on the ambiguous experiences of the Reagan economic policies. His claim, far more modest than the claims of Heller, is that "we need to rebuild our understanding of macroeconomic phenomena."

Perhaps the difficulties economists experience with political economy is that they do not really agree on how the economy works—and even less on how it *should* work. Adherents of various schools—supply side, monetarists, Keynesian, and so forth—offer various interpretations of our economy and various policy suggestions. Superimposed on these differences are the different visions of a better society that they hold: What should be the right balance between the results brought about by the invisible hand of the free markets and our conscious attempts to ameliorate the same results through governmental actions?

There is also another danger that economists engaged in public policy debate face: The elegance and clarity of what Tobin calls "the central paradigm of economic theory" is easily subverted and vulgarized not only by ignoring the *ceteris paribus* caveats but by filling in the "remaining things" with ideological assumptions and slogans. It is the ideological assumptions of the Reagan administration that often go unexamined; they are explored, together with their consequences in macroeconomic management, in Tobin's paper.

These consequences are not always clear. Niskanen suggests that no existing school of economics "has yet offered a coherent explanation of the most unusual and unanticipated economic conditions" of the Reagan administration. The Reagan magic, it seems, works wonders even for economists.

SUGGESTIONS FOR FURTHER READING

Aaron, Henry J., Harvey Galper, Joseph A. Pechman, George L. Perry, Alice M. Rivlin, and Charles L. Schultze. *Economic Choices 1987.* Washington, D.C.: The Brookings Institution, 1986.

Eisner, Robert. *How Real Is the Federal Deficit?* New York: The Free Press, 1986.

Hulten, Charles R., and Isabel V. Sawhill, eds. *The Legacy of Reaganomics: Prospects for Long-Term Growth.* Washington, D.C.: Urban Institute Press, 1984.

Roberts, Paul Craig. *The Supply-Side Revolution.* Cambridge, Mass.: Harvard University Press, 1984.

Stone, Charles F., and Isabel V. Sawhill. *Economic Policy in the Reagan Years.* Washington, D.C.: Urban Institute Press, 1984.

---

[1]Walter W. Heller, *New Dimensions of Political Economy* (Cambridge, Mass.: Harvard University Press, 1966).

Chapter Six

Reaganomics In Retrospect

JAMES TOBIN

Rarely in a democracy does a new government take office determined to change course radically and endowed with the electoral mandate that enables it to do so. Franklin Roosevelt in 1933 and Lyndon Johnson in 1965 were the only United States presidents in my lifetime who had and used this opportunity, until Ronald Reagan was inaugurated in 1981. Most administrations veer only moderately from the established compromise consensus they inherit. Their minor course adjustments reflect the difference from their predecessors and opponents in the balance of interests in the coalition that elected them. Leaders like FDR, LBJ, and Reagan—and across the sea, Margaret Thatcher—manage to shift boldly the whole path of policy. After them, the centrist consensus from which successors will deviate is forever different.

Ronald Reagan came to Washington with a strong and distinctive social and economic ideology. Roosevelt and Johnson, both pragmatists, were definitely not ideologues. They responded decisively and imaginatively to the situations they confronted; the New Deal and the Great Society were not preordained by any long-held doctrinal beliefs of their builders. Liberalism, in its twentieth century meaning, is a loose set of attitudes and values rather than a coherent ideology. But there is a ready-made right-wing ideology, and Reagan came to Washington in 1981 with a programmatic agenda conceived in its image.

THE ECONOMIC IDEOLOGY OF THE REAGAN ADMINISTRATION

What was the economic ideology President Reagan brought to Washington? Basically, it was the ancient theme of nineteenth century liberalism—celebrating the miracle of Adam Smith's Invisible Hand, the virtues of free markets, free enterprise, and laissez faire. It has long been espoused by the Right in the United States. After World War II, conservative intellectuals, business leaders, and politicians rallied to this flag even when it was outside the general consensus. Barry Goldwater was their hero in 1964, but Johnson clobbered him. Ronald Reagan became a public figure and a potential political leader by his talent for communicating the ideology on radio, television, and in person under the sponsorship of General Electric.

The Invisible Hand

Free-market ideology is an extravagant version of the central paradigm of economic theory. The modern theory of general competitive equilibrium and its theorem that such an equilibrium is, in some sense, a situation of optimal social welfare make rigorous the intuitive conjectures of Adam Smith and subsequent classical and neoclassical economists. Economists know the restrictive conditions of these proofs; they can list the standard caveats and qualifications. They are lost in the arena of politics and public opinion, and they are increasingly glossed over by economists. At the same time, and for the same reasons that conservative ideology was gaining public favor, its counterpart in economic theory was being taken more and more uncritically throughout the economics profession.

Every ideological movement has its own version of history. As Reagan tells it, the U.S. economy was a shambles when he came to its rescue in 1981. He lay all the blame on federal economic policies under previous administrations since World War II: chronic deficits, overtaxation, large and growing government, loose monetary policy, macroeconomic fine tuning, intrusive regulation, bureaucratic waste, misguided welfare handouts, and so on. In this story, there is no credit for the remarkable performance of the economy in the 1950s and 1960s, and there is no acknowledgment of the roles of OPEC, the Iranian revolution, and other external shocks in the 1970s.

Government as Leviathan

In renascent conservative doctrine, government "is the problem, not the solution." In the 1970s, this message found receptive ears in a populace disillusioned by Vietnam, Watergate, and the economic disappointments of the decade. Government regulations and taxes, according to candidate and President Reagan, shackle the energies and initiatives of the citizens. Government, especially central government, has become a Leviathan, devouring the resources of the nation. Government has expanded far beyond its proper functions of national defense, internal order, protection of property rights, and enforcement of contracts. Government has no business redistributing income and wealth beyond minimal safety nets for the truly poor and disadvantaged. Even these needs should be met primarily by private charity supplemented by local governments.

The highest priority for the Reagan administration has been from the beginning to reduce the size of the federal government and budget relative to the economy. This implied severe cuts in federal civilian spending; Reagan was also committed to a sharp increase in military expenditures. The nondefense budget had been growing faster than the GNP. This growth was almost entirely in social security benefits: for old age and disability, medicare, and health insurance for the aged, introduced by Lyndon Johnson in 1966. These are universal entitlements, not needs-tested, and the growth of spending for them had been closely matched by earmarked payroll taxes. Social security growth reflected a combination of demographic trends, economic developments, fiscal miscalculations, and political generosities—notably by the Nixon and Ford administrations and their Democratically controlled Congresses. The experts in the Reagan team knew these facts, but the president preferred to ignore them and talk about the excessive size of the budget as a whole.

The Strategy of Cutting Taxes First

The idea that the federal budget must stop growing faster than the GNP was not new; both Presidents Ford and Carter were committed to this objective. Reagan, however, was ready to slaughter cows that previous administrations and Congresses regarded as politically sacred. He was also ready to follow a strategy that his predecessors eschewed as unsound. That was to cut taxes first, accept the resulting deficits, and use the abhorrence of deficit spending among politicians, financiers, and the general public, as a bludgeon to force Congress to cut civilian spending. Cutting the budget—both civilian spending and taxes—was and is the prime goal.

Only a conservative Republican president could have adopted this strategy without provoking an outraged response from the financial community and negative reactions in financial markets. Such responses forced Jimmy Carter to modify several of his proposed budgets. For example, when his budget for fiscal 1979 was proposed in January 1978, it showed a deficit of $60 billion. The outcry forced Carter to submit a revised budget with a much lower expected deficit and to abandon some expenditure initiatives and scale down some tax cuts. While Reagan and his spokesmen routinely have given lip service to the old conservative orthodoxy of budget balance, it has always been a distinctly subordinate objective. The president has often explained the strategy of lowering taxes first by saying that the way for parents to keep kids from overspending is to cut their allowances.

The strategy did not work quite the way President Reagan had hoped. Although Congress acquiesced in drastic cuts for civilian spending, other than for social security entitlements, these cuts were insufficient to bring the federal deficit under control. The president succeeded in making it politically impossible for any major restoration of federal tax revenues. His landslide victory in 1984 over Walter Mondale, who courageously but recklessly told the electorate that taxes would have to rise, closed that road to fiscal sanity for the foreseeable future. The president eventually lost to Congressional opponents about half of his ambitious buildup of defense spending. Even so, the "unacceptably large" deficits continued. The Gramm-Rudman law of 1985 acknowledged the impasse. Its purpose was to force the president and Congress to agree on how to eliminate the deficit over the five fiscal years 1987–91 or else face mindlessly automatic cuts in both defense and civilian spending—cuts that neither side would like.

Supply-Side Economics and the Budget

Supply-side economics gave Reagan another argument for reducing taxes faster than he could hope to lower expenditures. This argument is not wholly consistent with the strategy just discussed, but ideology and political economics do not have to be consistent. The argument was that cutting tax rates would actually raise tax revenues—a claim that made famous the economist who made it famous. Arthur Laffer drew his curve on a cocktail napkin for the instruction of Congressman Jack Kemp. The curve dramatized the incontrovertible truth that beyond some point a rise in tax rates will discourage taxable activities so much that revenues actually decline. Laffer and Kemp jumped to the unsupported conclusion that U.S. rates were already there. This assertion was naturally an instant sensation in conservative political and business circles, lending apparent scientific authority to something they very much wanted to believe. Ronald Reagan believed it, and he still does. Raising taxes, he continues to say, will devastate the economy. Economic growth propelled by tax cuts, he continues to say, will balance the budget. Members of his administration who thought otherwise and had the courage to speak up—like Martin Feldstein, who never bought the Laffer line, and David Stockman, who once agreed but learned better— are now in private life.

Supply-side fiscal economics as espoused by Laffer, Kemp, and Reagan is reminiscent of extravagant claims advanced by some Keynesian enthusiasts that tax cuts would pay for themselves in revenues generated by the expansion of economic activity. The expansion they had in mind was demand-side. The scenario was that in an economy with excess unemployment and redundant industrial capacity, the spending of tax cuts would prime the pump. Sober Keynesians believed that tax cuts—or additional government expenditure—would stimulate activity in a slack economy—but not by enough to avoid an increase in the deficit.

The label *supply side*, which had a great deal to do with the attention the doctrine rapidly received, was coined satirically by Herbert Stein to distinguish what he called supply-side fiscalism from the old Keynesian demand-side brand. There are several differences in logic. From a demand-side viewpoint, additional government spending is at least as expansionary as private spending—mostly on consumption, induced by tax reductions. The supply-siders, however, contend that both cutting tax rates and *reducing* public spending are stimulating. The supply-side recipe is supposed to work by giving private individuals greater after-tax incentives to work, save, invest, innovate, and take risks—not to consume. These responses are supposed to augment productivity and raise the economy's capacity to produce from a given employed labor force, while demand-side fiscal stimuli are intended to raise the economy's production from given capacity by employing more of the available labor force. Laffer's theory, if valid, should work even if unemployment were at and remained at its full employment minimum, while a Keynesian fiscal prescription is intended only as therapy for recession or as a tonic for an uncompleted recovery.

These differences did not prevent the supply-side protagonists from claiming the 1964 Kennedy-Johnson tax cut as a precedent, even though its motivation and success were demand-side and even though there is no credible evidence that it alone led to a net reduction of the deficit. Also, logic has not prevented them from staking claim to the 1983–85 U.S. recovery, even though that fits a standard Keynesian scenario.

There is a less flamboyant, less novel, and more professional supply-side economics—namely good, straight microeconomics. Economists of all shades of opinion recognize that taxes and transfers have incentive and disincentive effects. This has been recognized in policy, too—for example, the Investment Tax Credit introduced in the Kennedy administration and the sliding scales relating welfare benefits and food stamps to recipients' own resources introduced under Johnson and Nixon. Martin Feldstein joined the Reagan administration after leading, for a decade, important research on the effects of taxation of capital income on investment and saving. The Reagan ideologues had the directions of effects right; the trouble was, as Charles Schultze observed, that they multiplied reasonable empirical magnitudes tenfold.

Monetarism

Monetarism was another ingredient in the triumphant conservative ideology of 1981. Strict control of money supply growth was accepted as necessary and sufficient for disinflation; the Federal Reserve should stick to noninflationary "M" targets and hit them. Supply-siders were somewhat uncomfortable; they feared that the Fed would not accommodate the expansion that their policies would generate. The administration feebly tried to argue that monetary stringency would take care of prices while supply-side stimuli raised output. Inflation is, after all, "too much money chasing too few goods," and their policies would shrink the money and multiply the goods!

Later, the supply-siders became downright hostile with the Fed. They blamed Paul Volcker, the chairman of the Federal Reserve, whom Reagan inherited from Jimmy Carter and reappointed, for the incomplete success of their program. They joined voices with some Keynesians in urging more accommodative monetary policy and lower interest rates. Unlike the Keynesians, they also attacked the present international monetary regime, floating exchange rates, and called for a return to the gold standard, the Bretton Woods fixed-parity system, or some variant. This always had been a plank in the platform of the original supply-side guru, Robert Mundell, and his popularizer, Jude Wanniski, who were important influences on Kemp, Stockman, and Laffer. The president has flirted publicly with this idea, but the pragmatists of his administration have kept it from becoming serious policy. The ambivalence of Reaganomics intellectuals towards monetarism and floating exchange rates sets some distance between them and the world's leading conservative economist, Milton Friedman.

Supply-side thinking also differentiates Reaganomics from the more orthodox conservatism guiding the policies of other governments such as Japan, West Germany, which sets the tone for Europe, and the United Kingdom. Those governments share Reagan's faith in laissez-faire, but they also subscribe to traditional budgetary prudence and firm monetarism. Reaganomics enthusiasts cite the greater recovery of the United States since 1982 as proof of their conservatism's superiority over the conventional variety.

MACROECONOMIC MANAGEMENT 1981–85

In 1981, Congress adopted the president's economic and budgetary programs to an amazing degree. The Democrats retained nominal control in the House and a near majority in the Senate. But, bulldozed by their disastrous defeat in the presidential election, they submitted with docility and me-too-ism. Tax cuts amounting to about 3 percent of the GNP were passed—to be phased in over three years. Simultaneously, a buildup of defense spending, designed to rise from 5.5 percent to 8 percent of the GNP, began. (As the administration points out, defense would still be 2–3 percent lower relative to the GNP than in the 1950s and 1960s.) Civilian budget cuts were passed in almost equal magnitude to defense increases. Entitlements were still growing, however. The administration made some noises about taking them on, but it drew back when the flak made clear that social security was one ancient monument that the opposition could and would defend.

The official 1981 forecasts of the economy and the budget were rosy. In part, they were phony, as Stockman admitted in his unguarded interview with an *Atlantic* writer—for which the president took him to the proverbial woodshed; Stockman reiterated his claim in great detail in a later book. In part, the forecasts reflected unjustified optimism about the economy shared by most private forecasters at the time.

In October 1979, Paul Volcker instituted a strict monetarist regimen designed to rid the economy of the high inflation accompanying the second oil shock. A recession began in the spring of 1980—contributing to the defeat of Jimmy Carter—but there was a slight recovery at the end of the year. Anyone who understood Volcker's policy should have known that this was a temporary blip. Recession resumed with a vengeance only months after the inauguration—too late to be taken into account in the budget and economic prospectuses of the new administration.

Later in 1981, people began to recognize realities: Deficits of a new magnitude were in prospect. Moreover, they were not just cyclical; they were structural, that is, they would continue even when the economy was operating, and generating government revenues, at normal rates of unemployment and capacity utilization. One big reason was the growth of interest payments on federal debt. High interest rates were, in part, the consequence of the unprecedented fiscal stimulus superimposed on the Fed's monetary policy. High interest payments, in turn, enlarge the deficit—altogether a vicious spiral.

Alarm in the financial community and in Congress about prospective deficits inspired some efforts to contain them. In 1982, Congress passed, and the president reluctantly signed, the Tax Equity and Fiscal Responsibility Act (TEFRA), which enhanced revenues and in particular took back some of the more egregious goodies given to corporations by the Economic Recovery Tax Act of 1981 (ERTA). Furthermore, in one of the finer examples of statesmanlike cooperation between Congress and the chief executive, between parties, and among interest groups, a blue-ribbon commission chaired by Alan Greenspan arrived at compromise recommendations to assure the solvency of social security. The package was enacted in 1983 containing benefit reductions, payroll tax increases, and other provisions projected to put the account in the black for several decades. The Social Security Trust Fund will contribute surpluses up to 2 percent of the GNP to the unified federal budget in the 1990s. In almost every year after 1981, Congress has nibbled at the deficit, making expenditure cuts and enhancing revenues, to use the obligatory euphemism for tax increases. These efforts have added up, and even without Gramm-Rudman, the structural deficit will decline.

The Federal Reserve reversed policy in late summer 1982, and the recession ended a few months later. There were several reasons for the reversal: The downturn, which took unemployment close to 11 percent, three and a half points higher than on inauguration day in January 1981, was deeper and faster than the Fed had expected. An unexpected slowdown in the velocity of money had made the Fed's monetary growth targets even more restrictive than intended. Third-world debtor countries and banks in the United States and other advanced countries who had lent to them were on the brink of a financial crisis. Congress, by passing TEFRA, showed some appreciation of the federal budgetary problem and withdrew some of the fiscal stimulus that the Fed regarded as excessive.

In 1983 and 1984, after Volcker had turned the economy around, the 1981 tax cuts and defense programs came into force and delivered a massive fiscal stimulus to aggregate demand. This was a well-timed Keynesian recovery policy of unprecedented magnitude. It was quite serendipitous. The administration had not expected a recession in the first place, and it had, on principle, repudiated countercyclical demand management. Fortunately for business activity, taxpayers appeared not to realize that the cuts they were enjoying were supply-side measures designed to be saved rather than spent. Also, defense procurement and contracts percolated through the economy. The fiscal stimulus to demand led to such a rapid recovery at some times that the Fed felt it was necessary to apply the monetary brakes. As a result, real interest rates, that is, market rates corrected for inflation, remained high—certainly much higher than if the same recovery had been driven by monetary policy combined with pre-1981 budget policies.

The United States drifted into a bizarre and extreme mix of tight monetary and easy fiscal policies with several unpleasant consequences: The federal debt grew faster than the GNP as far as the eye could see, because interest on the debt alone increased the debt faster than the sustainable growth rate of the economy, while expenditures other than debt interest exceeded revenues even when the recovery was complete. High interest rates induced a net capital inflow and appreciated the dollar enough to yield an equivalent current account deficit. As a result, the recovery was unbalanced; manufacturing industries and agriculture suffered formidable international competitive disadvantage while services and other nontrade sectors flourished. Pressures for protection of jobs and markets in the disadvantaged sectors threatened the political consensus that had long supported a liberal U.S. commercial policy.

Let no one underestimate the drastic extent of the change in fiscal policy in 1981. While the federal government seldom ran surpluses in the last forty years, before 1981 its deficits were modest, virtually always less than 2 percent of the GNP—compared to the 4–5 percent deficits of the Reagan years. Before 1981, cyclical recoveries brought deficits down close to zero, and the structural high-employment budget was often in surplus. Now we have *structural* deficits of 3–4 percent of the GNP. Before 1981, the debt/GNP ratio had declined from more than 100 per cent at the end of World War II to 25 percent in the 1970s. Five years of Reaganomics raised it to almost 40 percent. That figure is not a catastrophe, but the prospect that it will rise and accelerate endlessly portended future disaster.

Proponents of the political business cycle hypothesis will cite the first Reagan administration as a stunning confirmation. Nearly two years of painful disinflationary recession were followed by recovery through election day 1984. Poor Jimmy Carter first had recovery, then a new surge of inflation, and then recession throughout his campaign for reelection. Reagan's success, however, was another example of his incredible luck. As argued above, the decisive demand management policies were Volcker's—not those of either president. Reagan's fiscal contributions to recovery were unintentional. In 1984, Reagan ran on his restoration of prosperity, as if 1981–82 had occurred on some predecessor's watch. Actually, the unemployment rate was the same in October 1984, just before the election, as it had been in December 1980, just before Reagan's inauguration.

WHERE DO WE STAND TODAY?

The Unfinished Recovery

The economy is still not recovered fully. The United States has done better than the six other economic summit nations. But, through 1986 unemployment remained nearly a point higher than at the peak of Jimmy Carter's recovery in 1978–79, two points higher than at Nixon's peak in 1973, and the same as at the peak of the short-lived recovery in 1981. Utilization of industrial capacity stayed around 80 percent—compared to 85–87 percent in previous prosperities.

The decline in the inflation rate is the great victory—it is 4 percent or even lower now—compared to 9 or 10 percent after the two oil shocks of the 1970s (year-to-year changes of the GNP deflator). Recall that inflation rates of 4–5 percent were considered intolerable before 1973 and were the occasion for counterinflationary recessionary policies. But few have quarreled with Paul Volcker's decision to declare victory in the war on inflation when it fell below 5 percent. Moreover, inflation is stable or even declining; it has been well-behaved throughout the recovery. The appreciation of the dollar may be credited with as much as one-third of the disinflation of the years 1981 to 1985. This assistance—the one redeeming feature of our high interest-rate policy—was borrowed from our trading partners, and it will be repaid in extra U.S. inflation as the dollar depreciates. On the other hand, declining oil prices—another striking proof of Reagan's "luck of the Irish"—have moved U.S. price indexes in a benign direction. We could have hoped to enjoy the reverse of a stagflationary shock, a boost to domestic consumption demand and a fall in prices. However, the sharp decline in domestic oil drilling and exploration in 1985–86 was a stronger adverse blow to aggregate demand. It seemed, not for the first time, that oil news is bad news whether it heralds abundance or shortage.

The major question before macroeconomic policymakers—in practice, the Federal Reserve today—is whether or not to allow or engineer a demand expansion to bring the unemployment rate down to 6 percent or lower. The Fed seems comfortable with about 7 percent unemployment—where the economy has been stuck since May 1984. Yet, there is little reason to regard 7 percent as the lowest inflation-safe unemployment rate. No significant bottlenecks, shortages, or signs of domestic wage and price inflation loom on the horizon.

The Fed lowered its discount rate in seven half-point steps from 9 percent in November 1984 to 5½ percent in August 1986. Other short-term rates fell in concert. Long-term rates also fell dramatically, but they still carry a premium over short rates—fluctuating around 200 basis points as market expectations about deficits and inflation swing between optimism and pessimism. *Ex post* real rates have declined much less because of the continuing fall in inflation; they remain high compared to previous cyclical upswings. The interest rate declines have not sufficed to shake the economy out of its doldrums.

The stubborn U.S. trade deficit, 3½ percent of the GNP in 1986, has been an immense drag on aggregate demand. Federal Reserve interest-rate policy was instrumental in bringing the dollar down from the heights to which its previous tight policy had raised it. But U.S. exports and imports have been painfully slow to respond. The Fed is afraid of further depreciation—especially a free fall of the dollar if foreign investors should be turned off—largely because higher dollar prices for foreign foods would show up in U.S. price indexes. However, the high exchange rates of 1981–85 may have done such durable damage to the competitive strengths of numerous American industries that the trade account cannot be corrected without further depreciation. U.S. authorities urge Europe and Japan to fire up their sluggish "locomotive" economies by expanding domestic demands. But those governments seem unwilling to do enough to make a noticeable difference in trade imbalances. They, in turn, complain that the dollar's fall is hurting their exporters and their economies. The United States is stalled by a domestic political impasse on the budget deficit and by an international political impasse on the trade deficit.

Prospects of Budget Deficit Reduction

The fiscal-monetary policy mix is still bad, but some correction is gradually occurring. The Gramm-Rudman drama still has to be played out.

In the summer of 1986, the Supreme Court upheld a lower court decision declaring unconstitutional the provisions of the law that were meant to force automatic spending cuts if Congress and the president had not agreed on a budget consistent with the prescribed schedule of deficit reduction by the beginning of the fiscal year. Although both branches of the federal government profess allegiance to the Gramm-Rudman targets, they seem resigned to miss them. Congress and the president are far apart regarding the roles of defense spending, civilian spending, and tax revenues in deficit reductions.

Nevertheless, given the mood in Washington in which Gramm-Rudman was a symptom, the structural deficit is likely to decline in the next several years. One big help is the decline in interest rates, which removes one source of explosive deficit growth. Another help is the success of Congress in freezing the real size of defense spending.

The Federal Reserve may face the pleasant task of offsetting some withdrawal of fiscal demand stimulus, and we must hope that residual monetarism will not stand in the way. If recession or growth recession should occur in the remaining years of the decade, the Fed will have to act with uncharacteristic boldness, because in the present Washington mood even cyclical deficits are interpreted as reasons for austerity.

The Failure of Supply-Side Nostrums

Supply-side effects have been disappointing. Budget outcomes show that we were not on the wrong slope of the Laffer Curve. That is scarcely a surprise. A more credible objective of Reagan policy in 1981 was to shift the composition of the GNP from private and public consumption to private investment—particularly business investment in plants and equipment. But comparing real final sales (GNP less inventory investment) in 1985 with 1978, the last pre-Reagan normal year, more than 95 percent of the increase went into personal consumption and government purchases. In 1981 and 1982, critics of Reaganomics said that the tax cuts would result in more government dissaving than additional private saving; their warnings were correct. Personal saving in percent of disposable personal income actually declined from about 7 percent in the late 1970s to 5 percent in 1985 and 4 percent in 1986. Personal consumption in percent of pretax personal income rose by nearly two points between 1978 and 1986, and consumer interest payments rose by another point.

Business-fixed investment did well in the 1983–84 recovery, but, considering that it started from rock bottom, it was not any better than in other cyclical upswings. The strongest gains occurred in equipment, computers, and motor vehicles, for which the incentives added by ERTA were negligible. The investment boom slacked off in the next two years. Growth of private domestic investment during the Reagan years was virtually equaled by the rise in the country's international current account deficit. The decrease in net claims of the United States against the rest of the world, now negative, is as bad for future generations as low domestic capital formation. Private research and development expenditures have slowed despite new tax incentives. Public expenditures on basic science and civilian research and development have been victims of federal budgetary stringency.

There is no sign that Reaganomic measures have increased the supply of labor—corrected for normal cyclical effects. The secular downward trend in average hours of work has continued without a break. The labor-force participation by men has actually declined; the long upward drift in female labor-force participation has continued—but at a somewhat slower pace.

For supply-side economics, the bottom line is productivity growth. Its mysterious decline and disappearance in the 1970s was the most fateful disappointment of that decade. Alas, there is no sign that it has come back to the 2½–3 percent per year characteristic of the economy before 1973. Recession and recovery in the 1980s have had their usual cyclical effects on measured labor productivity; after they are allowed for, the trend growth rate is only 1 percent or less. The ten million jobs added since the trough of the recession have been good news, although there are 2 million fewer jobs than the administration foresaw in 1981. The bad news is that the added employment has not produced as much of a gain in the GNP as it should have.

Greater Poverty and Inequality

During the Reagan years, poverty and inequality have increased in the United States. The president's promise that supply-side incentives would create a "rising tide" that "lifts all boats" has not been fulfilled. Even in 1985, after three years of recovery, 14 percent of all United States citizens were living in households below the official absolute poverty line—the same rate as in 1981, up from 11.4 in 1978 and 12.1 back in 1969. Inequality has increased in the 1980s—reversing modest trends in the other direction since 1960. In the two previous decades, families in the lowest quintile consistently received 5.2 to 5.5 percent of aggregate family money income; together, the lowest two quintiles received 16.8 to 17.6 percent; and the top quintile received between 40.9 and 41.6 percent. In 1984, the share of the lowest fifth was less than 5 percent, the share of the lowest two fifths was below 16 percent, and the share of the highest fifth was 43 percent. These figures are for pretax cash incomes. Tax changes in 1981 added to the absolute and relative gains of the higher income groups. The 1986 tax reform of personal income taxes will do the same, although it will also remove households in poverty from the tax rolls.

Cynics, like me, are bound to notice that the emphasis of supply-side tax reduction and reform has been to cut top-bracket income tax rates. The emphasis on marginal incentives is reversed in the administration's policies toward transfer programs for the poor, where needs tests have been made more stringent and implicit tax rates (benefit losses consequent to additional earnings) have increased significantly. In the welfare area, the Laffer Curve has been matched by Murray's Law—that cutting welfare spending will reduce poverty. Thanks to his book, *Losing Ground*, Charles Murray has become a popular favorite of the conservative convention speaker circuit, and the president appears to have embraced Murray's philosophy in his proposals for welfare reform.

Income Tax Reform

Faced with mounting federal and international debts but unable to agree on how to deal with them, President Reagan and Congress spent 1986 reforming personal and corporate income taxes. To most objective observers, the urgent need was to increase federal revenues. But the president insisted that the outcome of tax reform must be revenue-neutral, and Congress acquiesced. Future economic historians will shake their heads in disbelief at this distortion of priorities.

The history of this legislation is confusing and ironic. Before 1984, two tax reform proposals were before the Congress; one was a Republican bill sponsored by Congressman Jack F. Kemp (R-N.Y.) and Senator Robert W. Kasten (R-Wis.), and one was a Democratic initiative by Senator Bill Bradley (D-N.J.) and Congressman Richard A. Gephardt (D-Mo.). They were similar in lowering tax rates, broadening tax bases, attacking loopholes, and purporting to be revenue-neutral. To gain some initiative on this issue in a campaign year, the president asked the Treasury to come up with a proposal, a task that took almost all of 1984 and put the matter on the political back burner until after the election. The proposal, known as Treasury I, was remarkably apolitical. It was prepared by dedicated experts who were committed to making the system economically neutral—not just revenue-neutral. The distortions they sought to correct were mostly ERTA provisions enacted at the behest of the same administration only three years before. The anguished howls from businesses that had benefited from the provisions, and from other interested parties, led, in 1985, to Treasury II, a political compromise that sacrificed the purity and incentive neutrality of Treasury I, and it led to the passage of a different political compromise, closer to Treasury I, in the House of Representatives.

The Senate took up the matter in 1986. The proposals on the table were variations on a common strategy. A principal objective was to lower marginal tax rates and to reduce the number of brackets. A game rule that the president adamantly insisted on was the reduction of the top marginal rate of personal income tax from 50 percent to 35 percent or less. Before 1981, it had been 70 percent for unearned income, and before 1971, top tax rates of 70 percent or higher had applied to all income. Revenue lost by rate cuts was to be regained by broadening the tax base and eliminating or limiting some deductions, exemptions, tax credits, and shelters. The same strategy applied to the corporate income tax. The rates were to be reduced, but the taxable base was to be broadened by phasing out the investment tax credit (ITC), accelerated depreciation and expensing of capital outlays, and other incentives for investment. The ITC dated from the Kennedy administration, but most of the other loopholes were part of the ERTA in 1981, when the Reagan administration and Congress seriously promoted investment. Another common feature was shifting the tax burden from the personal to the corporate tax. This politically feasible base-broadening in the personal tax was insufficient to render its reform revenue-neutral, and individuals were unlikely to discern the indirect burden of higher corporate taxation on them.

Even so, it appeared that protests from lobbyists representing taxpayers with vested interests in the provisions slated to be sacrificed to rate reduction would prevent the Senate from agreeing on a bill that both the House and the president would accept. But Senator Bob Packwood (Ore.), Republican chairman of the Finance Committee, with help from the Democratic Senator Bradley, pulled off a political miracle. The secret was to reduce personal tax rates so much—the top marginal rate to 32 percent and the top average rate to 28 percent—that the bait would disarm opposition about the rates from defenders of all but the most invulnerable immunities. Even so, the sponsors had to buy the votes of many members of Congress by agreeing to an unprecedented number of particular transitional exceptions, which totaled $14 billion in lost revenue, one of the most distasteful episodes in the unsavory history of tax legislation. The president and congressional leaders in both parties held an orgy of self-congratulation once the act was passed and signed.

The tax reform act of 1986 improves the personal and corporate income tax codes in horizontal equity and in economic neutrality and efficiency. It shuts down outrageous shelters that allowed wealthy operators to avoid taxes that ordinary wage-earners could not escape— for example, claiming paper losses on highly leveraged real estate investments by deductions of fast depreciation and interest charges and then selling the property but paying low-rate capital gains taxes. While eliminating concessionary investment incentives in the corporate tax law, the new act makes effective profits tax rates much more uniform among industries and among different types and durabilities of capital assets. The regressive cuts in tax rates are a high political price for these improvements. There is no evidence that low top rates will stimulate enterprise, innovation, and effort. Our economy and many foreign economies have flourished with progressive rate schedules. Viewing the whole tax reform history since 1980, I observe that the 1981 reduction of high-bracket rates was obtained without any compensatory sacrifice of loopholes—with the enactment of provisions further eroding the tax base. Starting from this new status quo, in 1986, the wealthy successfully extracted further reductions in top rates as the price for closing loopholes that never were justified.

THE LEGACY OF REAGANOMICS

The Crippled Public Sector

Ronald Reagan will bequeath a crippled federal government to his successor. He tried to squeeze ambitious growth for defense spending into a budget he was simultaneously depriving of tax revenues. Legislators of both parties, most of whom knew better, deserve a share of the blame for their supine surrender to the president's program.

President Johnson lost the place in history his domestic social policies could have earned him by the tragic error of embroiling the United States in the Vietnam war. His by-product error in fiscal policy, his insistence on "guns *and* butter," and his delay in asking for taxes to pay for the war all fatefully destroyed the economic stability achieved prior to 1966. The lesson of the Vietnam war may be saving President Reagan and the country from pushing his obsessions with communist threats in Central America to the point of U.S. military intervention. Yet, he is also likely to be seen in history as repeating the "guns and butter" mistake.

President Reagan is right that the country can afford the arms buildup he has asked for. Whether it is needed and whether it is good national policy are questions where an economist has no special expertise. Assuming the buildup is needed, it should neither be the victim of budget deficit control nor should its burden be placed narrowly on other government programs and their beneficiaries. A rich country can afford the defense it needs, and it can also afford the Library of Congress, public broadcasting, good statistics, environmental protection, and humane treatment of the poor and disadvantaged. Reagan's "butter" is different from Johnson's; it consists in the tax reductions he is determined to protect—largely to the benefit of the wealthier citizens of the country. The policy has had the adverse macroeconomic consequences discussed above—notably including the trade deficit. The policy has also brought federal budget making to the political impasse that ended in the colossal irrationality of Gramm-Rudman.

Income taxes have long been the major source of federal revenue. They yielded revenues equal to 11.3 percent of the GNP in 1959, 13.3

percent of the GNP in 1969, and 11.6 percent of the GNP in 1979. They will yield only 10.7 percent of the GNP in 1989. It is true that payroll tax revenues have risen from 2.4 percent of the GNP in 1959 to an estimated 6.8 percent for 1989. They are, however, earmarked for social insurance benefits—mostly for Old Age and Survivors Insurance. Social security stands on its own feet; it will run surpluses over the next twenty years—building a trust fund that will be needed later in the next century. These accounts are now officially off budget once more. Regular on-budget governmental activities depend on income taxes—or on deficits. In 1979, defense and debt interest took 6.4 percent of the GNP, and income tax revenues amounting to 4.1 percent were available for other activities. In 1989, defense and interest will take 8.7 percent of the GNP—leaving income taxes of only 2.0 percent for other activities.

The social costs and dangers of the resulting austerities in the civilian budget are already evident. Here are some examples:

- The federal government is abandoning revenue-sharing—federal support of state and local government expenditures on infrastructure investments, education, and social programs. Those governments have responded partly by curtailing those expenditures, as the administration intended, and partly by raising their own taxes—generally more regressive than the federal income tax.

- Secretary of State Shultz is right in complaining that Congress does not provide enough funds for foreign aid, for effective diplomatic representation around the world, and for meeting U.S. obligations to international organizations. He should address his complaint to the White House, too.

- President Reagan promised action on acid rain to Canadian Prime Minister Mulroney, but the funds are missing from the president's budget. President and Mrs. Reagan made headlines when they solemnly proclaimed an all-out war on drug abuse, but his next budget cut the funds. American airports and skies are increasingly congested, but there are no funds for expanding facilities, air control personnel, and safety enforcement. National highways deteriorate, but gasoline taxes supposedly earmarked for their maintenance and improvement remain unspent to hold down the deficit. The federal government relies on tax-deductible private donations for more and more purposes: for example, advancing the cause of democracy throughout the world, and enabling the White House and State Department to receive foreign dignitaries in facilities worthy of a great and rich republic. Cutbacks in federal statistical programs hamper academic researchers, businesses, and others who rely upon them. Our national parks deteriorate. Federal support of education and science is shortchanged. Federal service is underpaid relative to the private sector, and at the same time reviled by its chief as a parasitic, power-hungry bureaucracy. (As I told an undergraduate class recently, Paul Volcker, the most important economic official in the world, is paid less than Green Business School graduates hired to guess what Volcker will do next week.)

There never was any reason to believe the Reagan thesis that the trouble with the U.S. economy was that the public sector was too big, either in its real economic activities or in its welfare-state transfers. On both counts, the United States had smaller public sectors relative to the size of the economy than any advanced capitalist democracy except Japan and Australia. The administration's view that only the formation of physical capital by private business provides for the future of the nation is a vulgar error that has sacrificed public investment in human capital (education, health, natural resources, and the public infrastructure) to the construction of shopping malls and luxury casino hotels.

The current conservative fad is privatization. The administration's budget makers have hit upon sales of federal assets as a cute technical way to appear to comply with Gramm-Rudman. No business accountant would regard asset sales as deficit-reducing for current revenue. But privatization is welcomed by free-market ideologues anyway. Although some privatization may be desirable and cost-effective, current proposals reflect budget cosmetics and doctrinaire principle rather than case-by-case examinations of long-run costs and benefits.

Certainly some federal programs cut or eliminated over the past six years deserved Stockman's ax, and that is also true of some parts of the president's proposed budget for fiscal 1988. These expenditures would not have been vulnerable under the business-as-usual budget politics of previous administrations and Congresses. Yet, other cows that deserved slaying under free market principles have remained sacred. The most expensive example is federal agricultural policy; this administration has spent record amounts for farm price supports and related subsidies. Another example, of interest to Canadians, is our maritime policy. In both these cases, costly budgetary subventions are accompanied by regulations restricting competition.

As for deregulation, the major initiatives in energy, air and surface transportation, and finance were begun under President Carter. They have been continued and extended. The Reagan administration's own initiatives have concentrated less on dismantling anticompetitive regulations than on relaxing the regulations designed for environmental and social purposes. As Canadians know, it has been hard to get the president excited about acid rain. As blacks know, the administration is against affirmative action.

The administration deserves credit for defending liberal trade policies against the pressures of protectionism—all too tempting to Democratic politicians. But it was the administration's macroeconomic policies that, by appreciating the dollar, made American producers uncompetitive in world trade and invited protectionist demands from desperate industries and displaced workers. Moreover, the administration's rhetoric has been more liberal than its actions. Like his predecessors, the president has arranged import quotas and special duties for particularly hard-hit industries.

Missing Agenda

Two major economic problems have not been on the Reagan agenda at all. The first problem is macroeconomic; it has to do with unemployment and inflation. The greatest basic obstacle to full prosperity is the fear of policymakers at the central bank and throughout the government, and of the influential public, that a return to the low unemployment rates we reached in the prosperities of the 1970s would set off another inflationary spiral. This fear may be obsolete and unjustified, but it is a reality. If it is justified, then the inflation-safe unemployment rate is too high at 6 percent or more, and we should actively seek structural reforms that would lower it. These reforms could include pro-competitive labor market policies, changes in trade union legislation, incentives for employers and workers to adopt profit-sharing or revenue-sharing contracts, and the use of wage-price guideposts with tax-based inducements for compliance. This is not the occasion to discuss specific proposals; yet, this administration has no concern about this crucial matter.

The second problem conspicuously missing from the Reagan agenda is the pathology of urban ghettos inhabited by blacks and other minorities. These neighborhoods, the people who live in them, and the cities where they are located have been "losing ground," to use the title of Murray's book. The war on poverty and the Great Society did not prevent or arrest the vicious downward spirals in these areas and populations. Subsequent neglect and a decline in the real public resources channeled to them also hurt. The only current administration response is to cut welfare spending further in the belief that this will cut both welfare dependency and poverty. Meanwhile, the lower Bronx and Harlem, Roxbury in Boston, Woodlawn and the West Side of Chicago— and in similar areas of many other small and large cities—are a disgraceful and dangerous contrast to the affluent styles of life displayed in the centers of the same cities and flaunted on national television. President Reagan is fond of likening America to "a shining city on a hill." There is a Hill district here in my own New Haven, and it does not shine.

At the outset, I placed Ronald Reagan in the select class of government leaders who substantially and durably shift the course of policy and the center of political debate. Yet, I have some doubts about the permanence of the rightward Reagan counterrevolution. Prior to the Iran-contra scandals, opinion polls showed Ronald Reagan's high approval rating to be without precedent for a president in his sixth year; he still is remarkably popular as a person—even among citizens critical of his role in the adventures recently revealed. On few specific issues, however, have polls shown majorities favoring Reagan's side. In the nature of the case, an antigovernment president leaves few public monuments. This president will leave none comparable to Roosevelt's social security or Johnson's civil rights and health insurance.

The awful truth is that Reaganomics was a fraud from the beginning. The moral of its failures and of its legacies is that a nation pays a heavy price when it entrusts its government and economy to simplistic ideologues—however smooth their performances on television.

Chapter Seven

Reflections on Reaganomics
WILLIAM A. NISKANEN

Reaganomics represents the most serious attempt to change the course of U.S. economic policy of any administration since the New Deal. A common belief, in the president's words, that "only by reducing the growth of the government can we increase the growth of the economy" guided this program. The common direction was to reduce the role of government in the U.S. economy by reducing the growth of government spending, tax rates, regulation, and the growth of the money supply.

It is too early to write the history of Reaganomics. The second-term agenda is not fully revealed. There is usually some time lag between changes in economic policies and conditions. Ideas cast an even longer shadow. It is not too early, however, to reflect on the major lessons of at least the first five years of this ambitious program. The following remarks summarize my reflections on some of these lessons.

The growth of real government spending proved to be very difficult to reduce—despite the most conservative president since the 1920s, a Republican Senate, and a remarkable budget director. From fiscal 1981 through fiscal 1986, real federal spending increased at a 3.4 percent annual rate—lower than the 5 percent annual increase during the Carter administration but higher than the growth of the economy. Moreover, the growth of real federal spending would have been somewhat higher if Congress had approved the full defense budget requests. Some calculations that I made in 1985 suggest that the pattern of total federal spending during the Reagan administration was not significantly different from the pattern of prior postwar years.

The continued high growth of real federal spending was the major failure of the Reagan economic program. Moreover, the deficits that were caused primarily by continued growth in real spending threaten to undermine the major accomplishments of this program—specifically the reduction in tax rates and inflation. There is plenty of blame to go around.

First, the initial Reagan budget plan severely constrained the potential for budget restraint. A substantial increase was proposed for the defense budget—equal to 25 percent of total outlays in fiscal 1981. The initial budget also promised to preserve and maintain the "core social safety net" programs, for which the budget was 35 percent of total outlays in fiscal 1981. Interest payments on the outstanding debt were another 10 percent of fiscal 1981 outlays. To reduce the growth of total outlays, the budget plan required a substantial reduction in spending for the many domestic programs that constituted the other 30 percent of the fiscal 1981 budget.

Part of the problem is that contemporary campaign politics undermines the potential to govern. At no time during the 1980 and 1984 campaigns, for example, did Reagan acknowledge that a substantial reduction in domestic programs was necessary to permit both a defense buildup and a tax cut without an increase in the deficit. The 1980 solution to this budget problem was to reduce "waste, fraud, extravagance, and abuse." The 1984 solution was to increase economic growth. Both of these solutions to the budget problem were illusory. There is plenty of waste in the federal budget, but most of this waste is there for the same reason that the programs are there—because someone wants it. Cutting waste proved to be no easier than cutting programs. An increase in economic growth proved difficult to achieve. In the absence of any campaign commitment to reduce domestic programs, substantial election victories did not provide a sufficient mandate to reduce these programs.

Another part of the problem is that Reagan's agenda included a number of controversial proposals that required congressional approval. The total budget cost of proposals such as the sale of weapons to Saudi Arabia, the MX missile, additional funding for the IMF, and aid to the contras, was often much higher than the direct budget cost.

A major problem is that the phased tax-rate reductions approved in 1981 were not made contingent on subsequent budget restraint. The initial budget proposals were not sufficient to offset the revenue loss of the tax cuts, and not all the initial proposals were approved. Once the tax cuts were approved, the only case for budget restraint were the vague general benefits of lower deficits—benefits that became increasingly implausible after inflation and interest rates declined and the economy recovered. The political problem of reducing the deficit was due to a developing recognition that the deficit did not lead to substantial economic problems in the short term.

The most important problem, as David Stockman has documented, is that there are few consistent advocates of spending restraints in the administration or in either party in Congress. Almost every self-styled fiscal conservative strongly supports some part of "the social pork barrel." Stockman may be wrong that the public also supports these programs, but there is no doubt that the contemporary welfare state is broadly supported in Congress.

A related lesson of this period involves the relation between spending and taxes. For many years, economist Milton Friedman has argued that an increase in taxes would increase spending, a view shared by President Reagan. Economist James Buchanan maintains the contrary view that an increase in taxes, by increasing the perceived current price of government services, would reduce spending, a view apparently shared by British Prime Minister Thatcher, West German Chancellor Kohl, and, more recently, Canadian Prime Minister Mulroney. The developing evidence is that neither view is correct. A recent study concludes that changes in taxes do not appear to have any effect on changes in spending. Spending restraint, apparently, must be addressed head-on without much effect from whatever is happening to taxes. These findings may be small comfort to people who share the traditional view that major tax cuts must be earned by spending restraint.

The growth of real domestic output proved to be very difficult to increase. Real GNP increased at a 2.4 percent annual rate during the Reagan first term, compared to a 2.9 percent annual rate during the Carter administration. The slower growth of real GNP, however, was entirely attributable to a slower growth of the adult population. On a per adult basis, the growth of real GNP and other measures of domestic output were the same or slightly higher than during the Carter administration. The growth rates did not change much despite policies that most economists regarded as stimulatory. For the Keynesians, the record peacetime deficits should have increased demand. For the monetarists, the record rate of money growth since mid-1982 also should have increased demand. For the supply-siders, the reduction of tax rates and some deregulation should have increased output. As it turned out, economic growth does not appear to have been affected by the combination of these policies. There was reason to expect that the growth rate might increase after inflation was stabilized, but the growth rate during the second term, to date, is about the same as during the first term.

The most interesting effect of the Reagan policies is that the growth rate of each major component of real purchases—consumption, domestic investment, and government purchases—was higher than during the Carter administration, despite a somewhat slower growth of real GNP. How can this be? The answer is that U.S. imports grew very rapidly—allowing the United States, for a limited period, to use more goods and services than the United States produced. The magnitude of the current account deficit, now over $100 billion, is not sustainable. As this deficit is reduced, we may experience the opposite pattern—an increase in the growth of real GNP and a lower growth of each major component of real purchases.

The reduction in inflation was much less difficult than expected. The last *Economic Report* of the Carter administration estimated that each percentage point reduction in inflation would cost about $100 billion (1980 dollars) in lost output. In fact, the inflation rate was reduced about 6 percentage points without any change in the growth of real GNP per adult. The temporary loss of output relative to this trend was less than half that implied by the prior estimates. The substantial and continuing decline in inflation is the one economic condition that is superior to the initial Reagan forecasts.

It is much less clear *why* the inflation rate declined so much. The most obvious reason was the reduction in money growth from late 1979 through mid-1982. The rest of the story is much less clear. Since mid-1982, M1 has increased at the highest sustained peacetime rate without reigniting inflation due to a corresponding reduction in the velocity of money, a condition that was not anticipated and is not yet well understood. The most probable reasons for the reduction in the velocity are that the reduction in market interest rates and bank deregulation reduced the cost of holding assets as bank deposits. A third condition was the sharp increase in the real foreign exchange value of the dollar through early 1985, a condition that was primarily the result of the reduction of the effective tax rate on business investment approved in 1981. A fourth condition was the growing excess supply of oil, in part, the result of the stronger dollar. The earlier reduction in money growth contributed only to the initial reduction in inflation—an important contribution but not the dominant contribution for which Paul Volcker is credited.

On issues such as regulation and trade, a good defense is not enough. All too often, those of us responsible for reviewing regulation and trade issues faced a no-win situation. On numerous occasions, often with considerable effort, we managed to defeat or defer some new regulation of trade restraint. On other occasions, we lost. The net result of this process is that we ended up with more regulations and more trade restraints than at the beginning of the administration. The reason for this is that most regulations and many trade restraints do not automatically expire, and most of the new proposals are for more restraints.

An aggressive strategy of deregulation is the only way to avoid a net increase in regulation. The total amount of regulation increased during both the Carter and Reagan administrations—but for different reasons. Under Carter, there was a substantial reduction of the regulation of prices and entry in the airline, trucking, railroad, and financial industries, and there was a substantial increase in the regulation of health, safety, the environment, and the uses of energy. Under Reagan, there was little deregulation and less new regulation; the only deregulatory legislation approved so far involves banks and intercity buses.

Similarly, an aggressive strategy of reducing existing trade barriers is now necessary to avoid a net increase in protection. Average U.S. tariffs are now about 5 percent, and the automatic reductions in these tariffs are correspondingly smaller. There is no automatic mechanism, however, to relax most of the nontariff barriers. For the first time in many decades, the new trade restraints exceed the automatic reductions. For several years, the administration had proposed a new trade round, but the prospects for the new Uruguay round are not promising.

For the most part, the president's convictions on these issues are admirable. My disappointment is that the administration did not have the political commitment and energy to follow through on these convictions.

The experience of the early 1980s has been, or should have been, chastening to economists of all persuasions. Only an econometrician could love this period because it produced such a high variance of the key policy variables. Keynesians, for example, may wish to reflect why record peacetime deficits did not apparently increase total demand, inflation, or interest rates, and did not reduce domestic investment. Monetarists need to explain why the record sustained peacetime rate of money growth since mid-1982 has not (yet) increased inflation. Supply-siders, not to be left out, should consider why the reduction in tax rates has not (yet) increased economic growth.

None of these schools has yet offered a coherent explanation of the most unusual and unanticipated economic conditions of this period:

- The combination of strong domestic investment and high real interest rates through 1984.

- The strong increase and recent decline in the exchange value of the dollar.

- The rapid increase in the trade deficit.

- The rapid reduction in the velocity of money.

For economists, one of the more important lessons of this period may be that we need to rebuild our understanding of macroeconomic phenomena. A little more humility would also be appropriate.

The major lesson of Reaganomics is that those of us who share the Jeffersonian vision of limited constitutional government have not yet changed much of the wondrous ways of Washington.

Part V

THE REAGAN
REVOLUTION IN POLITICS

Government is not the solution to our problem. Government is the problem.
RONALD REAGAN

That voters change their preferences between political parties is unre-markable. After all, that is how democracies change governments. When, however, there are long and fairly regular periods when one party dominates, it is only natural that we should ask about the nature of the phenomenon. Unless one ascribes these approximately thirty-year cycles to the influence of sun spots, we must ask questions not only about their irregularity, but about the reasons for shifts in voter preferences.

There are inevitably arguments about the periodic realignment of voters. Even if an agreement can be reached on the magnitude and timing of the fundamental shifts—by no means an easy matter—questions about the reasons for and significance of their occurrence are debated. Are these shifts comparable? That is, are their causes due to the same *kind* of social change? This comparison of events across time assumes that changes in electoral behavior are caused by similar influences. If it can be done, then the only sensible way is to account for the broader changes that society and government have experienced. Elections do not take place in a vacuum. For example, one of the reasons for electoral victories may be demographic changes or changes in the character of the voting population—as demonstrated in the shifts from Democrats to Republicans in the South. The experience of the South demonstrates another facet of realignment: party loyalties are difficult to change. Moreover, assuming that a typical voter abandons his or her old party, will the voter then forge an allegiance to the new party? Or, will there be an increase in the number of both independent voters, who shift votes from election to election, and voters who do not vote at all? Is there evidence that the American electorate is experiencing not realignment but dealignment?

Changes in electoral behavior often also assume changes both in the ruling party and in policies followed by the new governing party. It can be argued that a realignment occurs only when the changes in voter preferences result in changes in policies and, more importantly, that these changes will be reflected in the institutionalization of new policies. Judging from the rhetoric of the Reagan campaign, this is certainly what was expected.

The record can be read in a number of ways. It can be argued that the Reagan administration, mostly because it was able to institutionalize its policies—through the budget deficit and either cuts or a slowing in the growth of social programs—has marked a realignment of American politics. The following essay discusses the issues of realignment, dealignment and institutionalization.

SUGGESTIONS FOR FURTHER READING

Burnham, Walter Dean. *The Current Crisis in American Politics.* New York: Oxford University Press, 1982.

Ferguson, Thomas, and Joel Rogers. *Right Turn: The Decline of the Democrats and the Future of America.* New York: Hill and Wang, 1986.

Rockman, Bert A. *The Leadership Question: The Presidency and the American System.* New York: Praeger Publishers, 1984.

Salamon, Lester M., and Michael S. Lund, eds. *The Reagan Presidency and the Governing of America.* Washington, D.C.: Urban Institute Press, 1985.

Sundquist, James L. *Dynamics of the Party System: Alignment and Realignment of Political Parties in the United States.* rev. ed. Washington, D.C.: The Brookings Institution, 1983.

Chapter Eight

Realignment, Institutionalization, and the 1986 Elections

JOHN E. CHUBB

How significant have the Reagan years been for American politics?[1] Will scholars look back at them as a historic turning point—a political realignment? Or, will the days of Ronald Reagan's presidency be viewed as more ordinary than special? It is generally agreed that at five junctures in American history one party seized control of the national government, reoriented its politics, and remained in command for a generation to come. Historically, this happened with great regularity, roughly once every thirty years. But a major realignment has not occurred for some fifty years since Franklin Roosevelt and the New Deal—giving rise, along with other developments, to skepticism about realignments occurring again at all. The most common view today is that the Reagan years represent a brief interruption of a secular trend of dealignment—or a popular movement away from parties altogether.

Nevertheless, there is renewed interest in the issue of realignment, kindled by the Reagan presidency, and a real debate about whether something like a historical realignment may be occurring. On the one side, an unabashed conservative, Ronald Reagan, won smashing electoral victories in 1980 and 1984; as of 1988, the Republicans will have controlled the presidency for sixteen of the last twenty years; and the Republicans have controlled the Senate for the last six

---

[1] Part of this presentation is adapted from John E. Chubb and Paul E. Peterson, "Realignment and Institutionalization," in *The New Direction in American Politics*, Chubb and Peterson, eds. (Washington, D.C.: The Brookings Institution, 1985), Ch. 1.

years—the longest uninterrupted period of Republican control since the 1920s. There are also important Republican gains in partisanship, for example, in the South. On the other side, Democrats control the House of Representatives (realignments have never had the opposing party in control of the House) and the overwhelming majority of state governments. Public opinion, on most issues, has not become more conservative. It is possible that were it not for a fortuitous turn of the business cycle, Ronald Reagan would not have become a political success at all. Just as Jimmy Carter was perhaps done in by rising oil prices and economic decline, Ronald Reagan may simply have been a beneficiary of good luck, falling oil prices, and the economic surge that resulted.

But however pertinent these points are to a debate about realignment, are they the terms in which the realignment issue should now be discussed? In my view and in the view of my collaborator Paul Peterson, they are not. Arguments such as these miss the point. To appreciate the significance of the Reagan years, just as to appreciate the significance of previous realignments, we have to change the terms in which we debate the question. There are two basic flaws in the way the realignment issue has been discussed heretofore. The first flaw is that the discussion has been exceedingly narrow—focusing almost exclusively on voters and elections. The second problem, and this is more fundamental, is that assessments of realignment have been based on criteria that essentially require history to repeat itself—demanding that realignments follow a single pattern. This is a naive view of how political systems evolve. Realignments must be assessed with criteria that accommodate the changes that political systems experience as they mature.

Let me begin by developing these two arguments. Once they are understood, the evidence of change—in policy, institutions, partisanship, and elections—can be more clearly interpreted. That evidence indicates that if our arguments are sound, the Reagan years are a period of historic significance, a contemporary version of a political realignment.

A NEW VIEW OF REALIGNMENT

Our first argument is that the significance of the Reagan years, and of general historical realignments, cannot be appreciated unless their analysis is broadened to include more than elections and voters. Specifically, it must look at institutions and policy. It is change in policy and institutions that really gives realignments their historical significance. Were it not for such change, if realignments were only transformations of public attitudes and loyalties, they would not be nearly as significant.

American government, as its founders so thoroughly ensured, is not designed to deal with problems in the most efficient manner. It is designed to do the opposite. Because of checks and balances, the separation of powers, federalism, and the like, the characteristic response of American government to public problems is sluggish. Difficult problems, therefore, tend to fester. In the 1970s, for example, the United States experienced two energy crises without ever coming to grips with the problem. Today, the national government is locked in a protracted struggle to reduce its budget deficit. Realignments, however, have provided the American government with an occasional vehicle for overcoming this characteristic sort of inertia. During a realignment, the government is able to break deadlocks, take strong policy actions, put crises behind it, and move on to new things—usually items that will occupy politicians for a generation to come. Perhaps the main reason, then, that realignments are historically significant is that they have helped the U.S. government to overcome its inherent constitutional limitations, to put serious problems behind it, and to get on a new path of progress.

For example, in the 1860 realignment, the important development was not so much that the Republicans became the dominant party, but that through the realignment process, not to mention the Civil War, the government resolved the slavery issue and began an agenda of new issues crucial to national economic development. In 1896, the realignment enabled the government to dispatch the persistent issues of cheap money and agrarian subsidies and chart a new course of industrial development. In the 1930s, the realignment allowed the government to come to grips with the demands of a modern economy, and to push forward with economic management, social insurance, and the establishment of the welfare state. These periods deserve historical prominence as turning points in party politics. Their general importance for American government is great: As a result of the institutional and policy changes that accompany electoral realignments, the government can manage some of the most intractable problems of the times and take up a new agenda better-suited to the future. Unless this is recognized, the significance of realignments may be seriously underestimated.

Another reason why attention should be paid to policy and institutions is that it is hard to fathom how a realignment could be consolidated without changes in these areas. There are many examples of landslide victories in national politics in the United States—1964, for example, for the Democrats. But these landslide victories and massive voter protests are seldom turned into enduring political change. Durable political or electoral change seems to require that the party benefiting from the landslide take measures to give the voters a reason to convert their protest into new loyalties. Without some kind of strong, positive, and ultimately successful government response, landslides can be temporary phenomena. Realignments, in contrast, are more enduring because they are reinforced with changes in policy and institutional practice. Our first argument is that realignments involve equal measures of electoral change and governing change, both of which must be examined if the process of historical realignment is to be understood.

Our second argument is that the relationship between these two elements, electoral and governing change, has evolved in a predictable and regular way. In particular, institutionalization—or the transformation of governing institutions into large, complex organizations characterized by specialization and stability—has insulated government from elections or at least from major changes in their outcomes. This has happened steadily, and unless it is appreciated, expectations about realignment in the late twentieth century are apt to be anachronistic.

Institutionalization means, among other things, that as political offices become more attractive and their occupants take more steps to hold on to them, mass voter protests are less likely to sweep the membership of an institution clean. We have seen this, for example, in the House of Representatives since the turn of the century. Institutionalization also means that as political systems mature, leadership succession becomes increasingly routinized: When a new political party takes over, no matter how dramatic its victory, the leadership of the government may not change in a dramatic fashion. For example, when the leadership of the Senate Finance Committee passes from Russell Long to Robert Dole to Robert Packwood there are notable changes, but there is also real continuity—a result of years of expectations associated with the position. A hundred years ago, a change in a chairmanship, particularly in the absence of seniority rule, could lead to genuine upheaval in committee operations. But that is much less likely today. Finally, institutionalization means that public policy and the bureaucracy that implements it become more extensive, interdependent, complex, and deeply entrenched. This makes it more difficult for the government to change its course because actions that promise to do so will be resisted by increasing numbers of officials and clients whose interests are threatened.

Institutionalization largely has been ignored in the writing on realignments—historical and contemporary. Most discussions of historical realignments give the impression that this country's five major realignments were more or less identical. True, there is theoretical value in such generalizations. But the differences between those realignments have not been entirely idiosyncratic—and at least one of the differences is quite systematic. In each successive realignment, institutionalization dampened the process of change. In the early realignments, such as in 1800 and 1828, electoral change destroyed or transformed basic institutions—suffrage, public administration, the presidential nominating process, and the national banks. In 1860, the realignment process threatened the union. But, by the end of the nineteenth century, electoral upheavals did not pose a serious threat to political institutions.

One striking piece of evidence of institutionalization is the decreasing sensitivity of institutions to electoral shocks—a process that sharply distinguishes the realignments of 1896 and 1932. In 1932, there was three times as much permanent change in the party loyalties of American voters as there was in 1896. But, in 1896, electoral change was converted more effectively into institutional change. Despite the greater electoral upheaval of the 1930s, Franklin Roosevelt benefited from only two-thirds as much turnover in the House of Representatives, one-third as much turnover in state government, and considerably less party cohesion in Congress. The Republicans and William McKinley enjoyed more institutional benefits, even though the electoral protest that swept them into office was much weaker. Notwithstanding the major initiatives that Franklin Roosevelt was able to launch, electoral protest was not converted into institutional change as effectively in the 1930s as it had been three decades earlier.

Since the New Deal, this pattern has continued. Institutionalization has diminished the response of national institutions and national policy to electoral change. One implication of this steady trend is that current realignments cannot be assessed by asking whether history has repeated itself. History has never repeated itself; each realignment has reflected the increasing force of moderation imposed by institutionalization. The significance of political changes must be evaluated against the constraints that impede them. Standards of evaluation must make historical sense. The ongoing argument about realignment during the Reagan years lacks this kind of historical sensitivity. When the definition of realignment is broadened to include institutions and policy, and when the complication of institutionalization is introduced, a new direction in American politics is evident.

VOTERS AND ELECTIONS

Consider partisanship and political behavior as traditional indicators of realignment. There are a number of signs pointing to a period of intense two-party competition—rather than Democratic dominance —for the first time in more than thirty years. Partisanship has changed in important ways. During most of the years after the New Deal, the Democratic party enjoyed the loyalty of 45–50 percent of the American public. Republicans were often stuck in the mid-twenties, and in the wake of Watergate, they fell to the low twenties. In other words, the ratio of Democratic to Republican support was at least two to one. This began to change in 1978; it changed more substantially after the Reagan victory of 1980; it slipped during the recession of 1982; it jumped dramatically in the Republican's favor in 1984; and it has mostly sustained that gain since then. In contrast to the Democratic lead that once left the Republicans in the small minority, most polls now show the Democrats enjoying the support of somewhat more than 35 percent of the American public and Republicans somewhat less than 35 percent. There has been a decided convergence of the levels of party support.

In addition, the movement toward voter independence—the unwillingness to identify with either major party—peaked in aggregate terms in the early 1970s, and it has declined somewhat since then. Even more significant, it appears that the voter independence movement was driven by the so-called 60s generation, and it affected other generations much less substantially. Voters who came of age in the late 60s and early 70s were extraordinarily high in their level of partisan independence, and they have remained near that level. The generation that succeeded them, however, has not followed the same path toward independence. They have shown a much greater tendency to identify—and to identify with the Republicans. A prime reason why the Republican gain in partisanship may signal a realignment is that young people, shedding their independence and aligning with the Republican Party, will increasingly dominate the electorate. If the Republicans can hold on to young people, among whom they now enjoy a 10 percent edge over Democrats, they may become the dominant party—rather than just a competitive party—in the near future. Clearly, there are questions about the ability of the Republicans to maintain this support—for example, will young people tolerate the conservative social agenda of the party's right wing?—but the questions about the Democrats are as numerous.

One final note about partisanship: No one disputes that the South has undergone a secular process of realignment toward the Republicans for some time. The Republicans now enjoy a partisanship plurality among white southern voters, and they are competitive in the southern electorate as a whole. If the Democrats are to control the national government in the future, they will need to find a basis other than tradition to make their appeals in the South.

Turning to the parties themselves, the Republicans have not only gained supporters; they have changed the image they convey. This signals the kind of shift in the political cleavage of the party system that may also be integral to realignment. The Democrats are no longer thought to stand for pragmatism, moderation, effectiveness, and prosperity, as they did during the 1930s and the decades thereafter. The Republicans are no longer derided as the party of Wall Street and big business. On a host of major issues, the Republican party is now regarded as more effective. Symbols such as opportunity, prosperity, and national pride are now associated with the Republican party rather than the Democratic party. The Democrats are no longer viewed as the party of the middle class; they are viewed more as the party of special interests. Their image has become decidedly negative. These are big changes with real significance for the respective abilities of the parties to recruit new members.

It is worthwhile to note that the Democrats did nothing to disabuse the American public of these shifting images when they ran Walter Mondale for the presidency in 1984. Despite his considerable merits, Mondale's image was that of the liberal Democratic party and of the Carter presidency—both of which voters had arguably repudiated in 1980. His earnest pleas to the country to face its fiscal problems and to accept higher taxes only reinforced the negative image of his struggling party.

One additional aspect of party change also suggests realignment. Party organizations used to be exceedingly decentralized operations that played relatively small roles in directing realignments. Now, the national committees of the parties play major roles in financing and training candidates for national and state offices. The partisan significance of this is that the Republicans have built stronger organizations. They have five or six times the financial resources of the Democratic party and a parallel advantage in formal organization. The Republican committees contribute more money to congressional campaigns than all political action committees put together. The overall partisan distribution of money in national elections continues to be fairly even because the Democrats have more incumbents, and incumbents receive more money by virtue of interest group's concern with government access. The Republicans, nonetheless, derive an advantage from campaign finance because they can contribute substantially to races where there is a chance to unseat a Democrat—open seats previously held by Democrats, and seats that are held by weak Democratic incumbents.

So, let us consider elections. The Senate followed realignment form in 1980 with Republicans gaining an astonishing twelve seats and taking control of the chamber. In 1982, during the most adverse economic conditions imaginable, the Republicans gained a seat (at least nominally), and in 1984, despite defending twenty out of thirty-four seats, they lost only two. After six years, the Republicans remained in control of the Senate fifty-three seats to forty-seven. The question remains whether they can maintain control in 1986. But, if they can, control of the Senate may stay securely Republican for some time.

House and state elections, however, have not followed realignment form—or at least not the conventional definition of that form. But, it is here that the role of institutionalization must be recognized. As mentioned before, the House of Representatives was relatively unresponsive to the electorate during the New Deal—that is, relative to its responsiveness during previous realignments. What the 1930s illustrated is a development that the next fifty years served mostly to confirm, namely, the insulation of House incumbents from electoral shocks and surges. The swing ratio, which measures the responsiveness of seat shares to vote shares, declined after the New Deal, and it left members of the House well-protected against electoral tides from the mid-1950s to the present. This insulation is a major reason that Democrats continue to control the House of Representatives.

Some observers argue that today we have a split-level realignment: People like Ronald Reagan are in the White House, but voters want Democrats in the House of Representatives to check his power. In other words, voters have made an affirmative choice for divided government. They want Republicans in the presidency and Democrats in Congress. Or, because both parties field candidates who are more extreme than voters who are middle-of-the-road, the people can only satisfy their preferences by choosing one extreme for the presidency and the other extreme for Congress; on the average they are satisfied. There is only weak support, however, for this interpretation. It also has the perverse implication that a Democratic victory in the 1988 presidential elections should increase the prospects of a Republican takeover of the Congress: Won't the people want a conservative Congress to counterbalance a liberal president? In any case, the evidence is strong that voting for Congress is driven substantially by loyalty to incumbents. So powerful is voter loyalty to incumbents that most incumbents even succeed in discouraging bona fide challengers. Under these conditions, it is likely that the failure of the Republicans to capture the House of Representatives has less to do with the popularity of Democrats and more to do with the extraordinary security of incumbents.

At the state level, the lagging performance of Republicans has much to do with incumbency. But there may be another factor of general importance. State elections have become increasingly insulated from presidential tides because most gubernatorial elections have been moved from presidential election years—when an ascendant party would do best to run—to off years, when popular presidents like Reagan are of little electoral value and may even cause harm. State elections tend to go decisively against presidents in the off years. In short, the rules are stacked against concomitant Republican gains in the states.

INSTITUTIONS AND POLICY

While the changes in partisanship, parties, and elections indicate a substantial political movement in the Republican direction, they do not point unambiguously to a historic realignment. This indication is provided mostly by changes in policies and institutions that look much like the changes that characterized past realignments.

When Ronald Reagan took office in 1981, like his strongest predecessors, he seized control of the national policy agenda. Reagan knew precisely what he wanted: Above all else, he aimed to reduce the size of government—and he kept political and popular attention focused on that issue alone. His strategy for accomplishing the goal was quite simple; spread the burden of government cutbacks as wide as possible—but spare defense—and increase the pressure for cooperation by proposing a popular tax cut that, if enacted, would necessitate spending restraint. The strategy was helped by the desperate public mood; after ten years of stagflation, the country was ready for radical measures. The country was not in a depression, as in earlier realignments, but there was a popular perception of economic crisis; inflation raged at 18 percent in 1980; recessions had been recurrent; and the nation had been rocked by two energy crises. There was a sense that something dramatic needed to be done, and the new president capitalized on that.

To implement his plan, Reagan had unusual help from the institutions of national government. More than any of his predecessors, Reagan took firm hold of the executive branch. He centralized executive and budgetary decision making in the White House to an unprecedented degree with the able assistance of James Baker and David Stockman. In addition, he politicized the bureaucracy with loyal appointees. He did this to prevent end-runs by bureaucrats—around the White House and to the Congress—that may have undermined his budget-slashing objectives. Finally, Reagan stimulated an extraordinary level of cohesion in Congress—unanimous support among Senate Republicans, virtually unanimous support among House Republicans, and a conservative majority in Congress. Republicans greatly strengthened their position by picking up thirty-three seats in the 1980 House elections and by gaining tenuous control of the Senate. But the support that Reagan enjoyed in 1981 owed a great deal to his ability to convince conservative Democrats and even establishment Republicans that his agenda was really the public's agenda. The result of this is that in 1981, although not since then, President Reagan controlled the national government almost as assuredly as any party ever had controlled it.

In his first year, when his goals, strategies, and support were in sync, Reagan engineered policy changes that have been with us ever since and that will likely be with us for a long time. They include: massive cuts in domestic discretionary spending that reversed a process of centralization in the federal system that had occurred since the country's founding; dramatic increases in the responsibilities of state governments; a complete reversal in spending priorities with defense undergoing the largest peacetime buildup in history, switching places with domestic policy—or at least the directly controllable categories thereof; and a 25 percent reduction in taxes. The effect of these changes on Reagan's major goal—reducing the size of government— can be debated. But if Reagan's accomplishments are evaluated against a proper counterfactual consideration—that is, the growth that would have occurred in the absence of Reagan—chances are that he accomplished his original aim; federal spending is probably lower than it would otherwise have been.

These policy changes were associated with, although they may not have caused, a vast improvement in economic conditions. Inflation, which had been a persistent problem for a decade, went away. Economic growth did not reach unprecedented heights, but it was steady and prolonged. The public feeling, as a result of this improvement, was that Reagan's policies had worked. In addition, because of Reagan's commitment to defense, the public feeling about the nation's international standing also improved. Through a mixture of popular policy and good fortune, President Reagan and the Republican party rode a crest of public support that rose as the "bad" times of the 1970s (and Reagan's second year, too) gave way to the "good" times of the 1980s.

Most of this, moreover, is unlikely to change soon. In particular, Reagan's budgetary priorities and stingy spending levels are likely to persist. The main reason is another product of the Reagan revolution; a federal budget deficit unlike any in American history. As long as the deficit remains large, the government in Washington will be forced to address a very different agenda than the one it had addressed from the days of the New Deal through the late 1970s. This simple fact, perhaps more than any other, is what distinguishes the Reagan years from other periods of substantial political upheaval. The New Deal policy agenda, by and large a positive one—of federal programs aimed at all of society's ills—has been replaced by an agenda of retrenchment—of proposals to eliminate or reduce federal programs and to make programs that remain more efficient or affordable. New agendas are a large part of what realignments are all about. The establishment of one in the United States is a clear signal that American politics is moving in a new direction.

THE 1986 ELECTIONS

The transformation of the nation's policy agenda should not be permitted to obscure, however, the real changes that have occurred and that seem likely to continue to occur in the nation's elections. There is reason to believe that further evidence of realignment will be provided by the 1986 elections. According to most observers, the main contest in 1986 is for control of the Senate. Today, the Republicans have a precarious fifty-three—forty-seven edge in the Senate. The Republican's electoral problem is that they must defend twenty-two of the thirty-four seats that are up for election; to retain control, they must win at least nineteen of the thirty-four contests—or 56 percent of them. That is a tough task in a midterm election when your party controls the White House, and an even more difficult task when some of your incumbents were swept into office by a presidential landslide, which happened to several Republican freshmen in 1980. Should the Republicans lose the Senate, the last two years of the Reagan administration will be years of stalemate in which the Reagan agenda will make little progress. But the Reagan agenda is unlikely to be reversed; whichever party gains the competitive edge in 1986 and thereafter will have to work within the severe constraints that the Reagan administration created. As a result, the importance of controlling the Senate after 1986 may be exaggerated.

Indeed, it may be that the most important elections in 1986 are not in the Senate but in the states. With the next census fast approaching, redistricting is a major concern of both parties. Redistricting is controlled by state governments, and they have traditionally used that process to strengthen the electoral position of the party in control of the state. It is estimated, for example, that in the 1982 House elections, when the Republicans lost twenty-six seats, ten or eleven of those losses were caused by gerrymandering. Because redistricting has electoral potential, the Republicans would like to be in a position in 1991 to do to the Democrats what they did to Republicans in 1981. Consequently, there are very vigorous efforts being made by the Republicans and Democrats to win state elections and to gain control of state legislatures after 1990. However that battle goes, the 1986 elections are also important because they will indicate whether the Republicans have made any progress in pushing their popular strength down to the state level, where they have been very weak.

History suggests that the 1986 elections will be dreadful for the Republicans and for the president at all levels. 1986 is a second midterm for President Reagan, and presidents have historically done very badly at such junctures—though often because of special circumstances such as Vietnam in 1966 and Watergate in 1974. But even if 1986 is like any other midterm election, the news for Reagan still promises to be bad. The last time the president's party picked up any seats in a midterm House election was 1934—and the Great Depression had a lot to do with that. The Senate pattern is less regular, but it is not encouraging for presidents. Less often recognized, presidents have suffered similar problems in the states. The president's party has not picked up a net state house, a net state senate, or a net governorship since 1934. History is clear: 1986 figures to be a bad year for the president and a good year for the Democrats.

But history does not have to repeat itself. It all depends on the causes of the patterns that history records. In House elections, these causes are well understood. In Senate elections, and especially in state elections, they are not well understood. In research that is still exploratory, I have investigated some determinants of election outcomes in those arenas. With considerable trepidation, I will use the results of that work—dynamic models of state and U.S. Senate election outcomes—to venture some predictions about 1986.

The current partisan lineup in the states finds the Democrats in control of two-thirds of the state legislatures—sixty-four out of ninety-nine, to be exact. What accounts for this? The partisan composition of these bodies hinges on several of the same factors that influence the control of the U.S. Congress: the popularity of the standing president, changes during the previous year in national economic conditions, and swings in voter turnout. In fact, a model employing these factors explains most of the variation in state election outcomes. Because at midterm presidents are usually less popular, economic conditions are ordinarily worse, and the president's supporters are less likely to turn out, the president's party typically loses control of a number of state legislatures in off-year elections.

Considering, however, that Reagan has been and remains a popular president, that economic conditions this year are likely to be better than last year, and that through recruitment efforts the turnout may not decline as much as in previous midterm elections, there is a good chance that the Republicans will not lose state legislatures. Given the current party divisions in state legislatures, the model indicates that if today's political and economic conditions hold up, the Republicans will reverse the historical trend and pick up four state chambers.

As for governorships, not too much is known about the causes of systematic variation in gubernatorial election outcomes. In addition, gubernatorial elections are influenced by personalities and are somewhat difficult to predict. Currently, the Democrats dominate governorships holding thirty-four out of fifty. In 1986, there are thirty-six governorships up for election—twenty-seven of which are Democratic. Some pundits have suggested that because of this vulnerability, the Democrats will not be able to maintain the historical trend against the president's party; the Democrats, having to defend twenty-seven out of thirty-six offices, may not prevent a Republican gain. But the facts do not support that supposition. The statistical relationship between office vulnerability in gubernatorial elections and the outcomes of those elections at midterm indicates that the midterm punishment of the president's party is so severe that with thirty-six offices up for election, the out-party must defend at least thirty offices before it fails to pick up a governorship. Even with twenty-seven governorships at stake, the Democrats are not in a no-win position. If this were an ordinary midterm election, they would nonetheless come out of it with twenty-eight or twenty-nine. But this is not an ordinary midterm election. The factors that appear to decide elections are not going against the president; hence, the Democrats are likely to lose.

Gubernatorial elections, like state legislative elections, can be modeled successfully as a function of presidential popularity, national economic conditions, and turnout. Unlike the legislative election models, however, the prediction errors are somewhat large—and the electoral conditions suggest close races in any case. What the model predicts for 1986 is not a single unambiguous change in the control of a governorship, but seventeen races that are too close to call statistically. Unfortunately for the Democrats, they control thirteen of the closely contested governorships. If we assume that the parties split the seventeen close races fifty-fifty, the result will be a shift toward the Republican Party of four governorships. If this unprecedented presidential gain should occur, it might signal real improvement in the long-term competitive position of the Republican Party.

Finally, in the Senate, the popular argument is that with twenty-two of the thirty-four seats at stake in the election being Republican, the Republicans will almost certainly lose control of the Senate. Aggregate modeling of Senate seat swings, although limited, supports this argument and, given current conditions, it predicts a narrow Senate victory for the Democrats in 1986. My efforts at modeling Senate elections have focused on individual outcomes—predicting the results of Senate races state by state. Using the same type of model and the same pooled cross section/time series data set employed in the state election analysis, I estimated the influence of various forces on Senate election outcomes. The results indicate that Senate races depend on presidential popularity, the condition of the national economy, and incumbency. Fortunately for the Republicans, all of those factors are in their favor in 1986. The seldom-mentioned corollary of

Republican vulnerability in 1986 is that incumbents will run in many of the twenty-two seats that Republicans must defend. Historically, incumbency has been worth about 5 percent of the vote. Overall, the model predicts that there are no clear-cut switches to one party or the other in the upcoming Senate elections. But, again, there are a number of races that are too close to call, eleven to be exact. Seven of those are now Republican seats, and only four are Democratic. Assuming a fifty-fifty split in tight races, the net outcome in November will be a Republican loss of a seat and a half. Since the Republicans need to lose four seats to lose control of the chamber, the Senate may remain Republican. As the personalities of the candidates and the idiosyncracies of state issues come into play, this prediction could be upset easily. But the important point is that the regular forces of Senate elections do not add up to inevitable losses by the president and his party in 1986.

If these predictions hold, 1986 will be a special year in American electoral history: it will mark the most successful performance by a president's party in a midterm election in the twentieth century. Such an outcome would also lend support to our thesis about the competitive edge in American politics.

EPILOGUE

Since this presentation was given, several notable political developments have raised questions about the "new direction in American politics." First, the 1986 elections saw the Republicans lose eight seats in the U.S. Senate and badly fall out of control of the chamber. This will almost inevitably make President Reagan's final two years in office a struggle. More importantly, it will put the Democrats in a better position to capture the public's attention with a policy agenda and philosophy that may help them win the 1988 presidential election. This, of course, is important for the competitive balance of the parties, but it does not negate the central accomplishment of the Reagan presidency: establishing a new agenda—of limited government and budget deficits—that the Democrats, even if they are on the ascendance, will have to work with.

Additionally, the elections were not a complete Democratic triumph. The Democrat's Senate victory owed much to the weaknesses of Republican incumbents and to the pockets of economic hardship in an otherwise sound economy (the main reasons the model failed so badly), and it provided little evidence of a repudiation of the president. Outside of the Senate, the Democrats picked up only five U.S. House seats—a poor midterm performance—and only three state legislatures, a mere one-fourth of the usual out-party gain in those races. Most significantly, the Republicans gained eight governorships

—the first midterm pickup since the 1920s—and they drew nearly even (twenty-four to twenty-six) with the Democrats in the vital contest for control over redistricting. Idiosyncrasy helped the Republicans in the states as much as it helped the Democrats in the Senate. But as the models suggested, the conditions were ripe for the Republicans to have a good year in the states—and they did. The fact that Republican successes were greatest in the South and the Midwest suggests that in those states party politics may finally achieve the competitiveness that was achieved earlier in national elections. That is part of the new direction in which the country is heading.

The other provocative development is the Iran-contra arms scandal. It has cost President Reagan roughly one-fourth of his popular approval and left him, at this writing, looking very much like other lame-duck presidents in American history. The short-term significance of this is that it undermines an already weak presidential position in relations with Congress. But the long-term significance, as yet uncertain, could be much greater. If the scandal and its investigation drags on—and that is likely given the troubling findings of the Tower Commission and the control of further inquiries by the Democratic Congress—the Republican Party could suffer permanent political damage. The chances of a Republican presidential victory in 1988, especially by Vice President Bush, are reduced, and that undermines the image of the party—as the Iran affair by itself also does—as the Republicans try to recruit and retain partisans. Current polls indicate that the Republicans have already lost some of the ground that they gained in partisanship in the 1980s. Because so many Republican converts are young and weakly committed, that loss could be durable. If the Reagan administration fails to put the scandal into the past and recapture the public's attention, party politics could turn back in a Democratic direction. Party politics would still be more competitive than during the 1970s, and the policy agenda and lines of party conflict would be stamped with the changes of the Reagan years, but the nation would be charting a different course than the one that it has been on since Ronald Reagan's first election.

Part VI

THE REAGAN REVOLUTION AND SOCIAL POLICY

. . . wee must entertaine each other in brotherly Affeccion, wee must be willing to abridge our selves of our superfluities, for the supply of others necessities . . . wee must delight in each other, make others Condicions our owne . . . for wee must Consider that wee shall be as a City upon a Hill . . . .
JOHN WINTHROP

The two essays in this section examine in some detail the impact of the Reagan administration on welfare policy and on the disadvantaged. "The 'Reagan Revolution' required a frontal assault on the American welfare state," according to David Stockman, and the repudiation of the welfare state's growth was central to the ideology with which President Reagan began his administration. Both Peter Gottschalk and Kent Weaver agree, however, that there has been no rollback of welfare programs. There has been no *expansion* of programs, but commitment of federal funds to various social programs remains larger in the late 1980s than in 1966. Even the retrenchment undertaken by Reagan can be seen less as a new initiative than a continuation of a trend begun in the 1970s under Presidents Ford and Carter. There has been an increase in poverty during the Reagan years, but Gottschalk argues that this was due as much to a rise in unemployment as to cutbacks in social programs.

Why has so much presidential determination and rhetoric produced so little substantial change in this area? Kent Weaver suggests that the major social programs are all hedged with various forms of protection—

procedural, political or ethical—which makes it extremely difficult to cut them out or even cut back to any substantial degree. The high point of retrenchment was in 1981 at the beginning of the new administration; by 1984, additions and the liberalizing of eligibility requirements indicated a substantial easing of ideological assault on the welfare state. Public opinion polls also demonstrate that while the public does not like welfare chiseling, it is unwilling to countenance really deep cuts in support payments to the less fortunate. Peter Gottschalk suggests paradoxically that the Reagan administration may mark both the end of retrenchment in programs for low-income people, and a culmination of the trend that began in the 1970s, as well as the beginning of a modest upturn.

It may be that some form of state welfare is a necessary and inevitable part of a functioning mature capitalist system—a fact recognized by Congress when it exempted social security and Aid to Families with Dependent Children from the automatic provisions of Gramm-Rudman. Thus, revolution in welfare policy is hardly possible although reform may be possible. What is emerging in the late 1980s is a bipartisan consensus—not on slaying the "welfare monster" but a hardnosed, unsentimental approach designed to cut costs and streamline welfare rolls by tying welfare to work in nineteenth-century style. This new consensus on welfare policy indicates what may be the essence of the Reagan Revolution: On the continuum from Left to Right, the Reagan administration has succeeded in shifting the debate and the limits of what is desirable and possible toward the Right, and the Democrats have acquiesced in this redefinition of the boundaries of political terrain. This does not mean that the basic welfare achievements of the New Deal and its successors will be overturned; it means, however, as Gottschalk comments, that certain items, like a comprehensive health care plan, are off the political agenda for the foreseeable future.

SUGGESTIONS FOR FURTHER READING

Bawden, Lee. *Social Contract Revisited*. Washington, D.C.: The Urban Institute, 1984.

Danziger, Sheldon, and Daniel Wineberg. *Fighting Poverty*. Cambridge, Mass.: Harvard University Press, 1986.

Harrington, Michael. *The New American Poverty*. New York: Holt, Rinehart & Winston, 1984.

Kaplan, Marshall, and Peggy L. Cuciti, eds. *The Great Society and Its Legacy*. Durham, N.C.: Duke University Press, 1986.

Murray, Charles. *Losing Ground: American Social Policy 1950–1980*. New York: Basic Books, 1984.

Palmer, John, and Isabelle Sawhill. *The Reagan Record.* Cambridge, Mass.: Ballinger, 1984.

Rogers, Joe, Tom Rogers, and Cheryl Rogers. *By the Few for the Few: The Reagan Welfare Legacy.*Lexington, Mass.: D. C. Heath, 1985.

Sowell, Thomas. *The Economics and Politics of Race.* New York: Morrow, 1983.

Weicher, John. *Maintaining the Safety Net.* Washington, D.C.: American Enterprise Institute, 1984.

Chapter Nine

Retrenchment in Antipoverty Programs in the United States: Lessons for the Future

PETER GOTTSCHALK

*The Reagan Revolution required a frontal assault on the American welfare state. . .
It required an immediate end to welfare for the able-bodied poor.*

We had a tumultuous national referendum on everything in our half-trillion dollar welfare state budget. . . . I am as qualified as any to discern the verdict. The failure of the Reagan Revolution. . . . represents the triumph of politics over a particular doctrine of economic governance.

DAVID STOCKMAN, *The Triumph of Politics*

President Reagan's first year in office was heralded as offering a sharp break with the past. At the heart of the Reagan Revolution was the Omnibus Reconciliation Act of 1981 (OBRA), which reduced expenditures and restructured major social welfare programs.

These changes were met by a variety of responses. Detractors of the administration predicted that the cuts in programs for the poor would lead to sharp increases in poverty. Reagan supporters argued that the safety net had not been cut. Since only people above the poverty line were to be eliminated from the rolls, little hardship would result. The detractors seemed to be vindicated when poverty rates rose steadily from 13.0 to 15.3 percent between 1980 and 1983. However, the decline in poverty rates to 14.4 percent in 1984 was used to bolster the claim that the economic recovery resulting from the Reagan Revolution was starting to reduce poverty.

The reality is considerably more complex than either of these explanations of recent history. In specific terms:

1. Benefits were cut during the early years of the Reagan administration, but this completed a long-term decline in real benefits for low-income people.

2. The safety net was weakened but not destroyed for people at the bottom of the distribution. The working poor suffered disproportionately from budget cuts.

3. While growth in total spending on human resource programs slowed, these programs remained substantially larger in 1985 than in 1966—the Reagan Revolution was a skirmish when viewed in its historical context.

4. Taxes on low-income people increased, but the trend toward higher taxes had started five years earlier.

5. Poverty rates increased substantially during the Reagan years, but budget cuts account for only about half of the increase. Higher unemployment and increased inequality of income were about as important as the budget cuts.

6. There are signs that retrenchment peaked during the Reagan years. The American public may want programs to be redesigned, but they show little enthusiasm for cutting programs below 1970s funding levels.

7. A redesigned income support system should take account of underlying American values reflected in the recent changes. Work opportunities and decreased taxes are preferred to transfers for the able-bodied poor.

SCOPE OF BUDGET CUTS

President Reagan and Speaker of the House O'Neill seem to agree that the Reagan administration reversed a decade of growth in social welfare spending. Reagan lauds this accomplishment while O'Neill bemoans the retrenchment. Unfortunately, the factual premise of the argument is wrong. The growth rate of human resource programs was cut during the Reagan administration. However, this retrenchment continued a trend that predates the Reagan administration, and the resulting cuts still left programs substantially larger than in the mid-1960s.

The top panel of Table 1 shows the commonly cited figures that are used as evidence to show that a revolution in government spending did occur during the Reagan years. Average annual rates of

TABLE 1   Annual rates of change, percent of federal outlays and percent of the GNP for selected federal programs aggregates

	(1)	(2)	(3)	(4) Human resource	(5)
	Total	All	Work-related entitlement	Low-income health and income assistance	Education, training, and social services
Average annual rate of change in real outlays					
1967–73	1.9	9.9	10.1	13.5	9.6
1973–79	3.7	5.6	5.7	5.3	8.7
1979–85	4.2	3.2	4.4	3.1	−4.8
Proposed					
1985–91	−.3	.4	2.4	−.5	−7.0
Percent of federal outlays					
1966	—	32.2	21.2	4.3	1.0
1985	—	49.9	34.4	6.8	1.8
1991	—	52.4	40.6	6.8	1.2
Highest year	—	1976	1991	1976	1979
(percent in highest year)		(54.8)	(40.6)	(7.9)	(3.0)
Percent of GNP					
1966	18.2	5.8	3.9	.8	.17
1985	24.0	12.0	8.3	1.6	.44
1993	18.9	9.9	7.6	1.3	.23
Highest year	1983	1983	1983	1983	1980
(percent in highest year)	(23.3)	(12.8)	(9.2)	(1.7)	(.65)

SOURCE: Gene Falk, "1987 Budget Perspectives: Federal Spending for Human Resource Programs," Report no. 86–46 EPW, (Washington, D.C.: Congressional Research Service, 1987).

change in real outlays are shown for all federal programs, all human resource programs, and human resource programs offering health and income assistance to low-income people. Data are shown for the three six-year periods between 1967 and 1985. Proposed outlays in the Reagan budget are shown for the following six years.

Column 2 shows the rate of growth in outlays for all human resource programs. While these programs grew at a 9.9 annual percentage rate between 1967 and 1973, the rate declined to 3.2 percent in the 1979 to 1985 period, and the projected rate over the next six years in the Reagan budget is only .4 percent.

The next three columns of Table 1 disaggregate human resource programs into three broad groups: work-related entitlements (including social security), low-income health and income assistance programs (including medicaid, Aid to Families with Dependent Children, and Supplemental Security Income) and programs that offer education, training, and social services. The disaggregate data show that retrenchment was particularly sharp in programs that provide education, training, and social services (column 5). These programs, which grew at a rate of 9.6 percent between 1967 and 1973, started declining in real terms between 1979 and 1985. If the proposed Reagan budget was passed without alterations, these programs would decline even faster in the following six years. The next most severely affected programs provide health and income assistance to low-income people (column 4).

Note, however, that the growth rates in all but the training and education programs are roughly comparable to the growth rate in total outlays on all federal programs—shown in column 1. Between 1979 and 1985, human resource programs grew roughly three-quarters as fast as total outlays. In the following six years, human resource programs are proposed to grow modestly while total outlays are proposed to fall slightly as a result of cuts in other nondefense programs. The past decline in growth rates of human resource programs would, therefore, reflect as much the retrenchment in the overall size of government as a reorientation of priorities within the budget. Given the recent history of cutting human resource programs in Congress by less than what was requested by the Reagan administration, no future reorientation seems likely.

The bottom two panels of Table 1 show that the Reagan administration could rightfully claim in 1985 that, while programs would grow more slowly in the future, and in some cases might be scaled back, human resource programs would still be larger in 1991 than they were in the mid-1960s—even if the Reagan budget were fully adopted. Human resource programs grew from 32.2 percent of federal outlays in 1966 to 49.9 percent of federal outlays in 1985. Largely as a result of continued increases in social security outlays, human resource programs will continue to grow to 52.4 percent of all federal outlays by 1991. Even programs for health and income assistance for low-income people (column 4) and education, training, and social services (column 5) will make up a larger proportion of federal outlays in 1991 than in 1966 (6.8 percent versus 4.3 percent for assistance programs and 1.2 percent versus 1.0 percent for training and service programs).

While human resource programs may not shrink in relationship to total outlays, they could shrink in relationship to the GNP if government outlays grow slowly. The bottom panel of Table 1 shows that even when measured in relationship to the GNP, human resource programs still will not return to their 1966 levels. While these programs will be smaller in 1991 than they were at their peak in 1983 (9.9 versus 12.8 percent of the GNP), they will still be considerably larger than they were in 1966 (5.8 percent of the GNP). Even the training and social service programs, which have taken the largest cuts, will take up a larger percent of the GNP in 1991 than in 1966 (.23 percent versus .17 percent).

While these figures show that the retrenchment in broad categories was not large enough to offset prior growth, some programs within these broad aggregates were reduced below their 1966 share of the GNP. Particularly hard hit were the cash income assistance programs, which shrank from .37 percent of the GNP in 1966 to .22 percent in 1985 and are slated to decline to .16 percent in 1991. Likewise, compensatory education grants have been reduced from .7 percent of the GNP in 1966 to .4 percent in 1985. Thus, one should not conclude from the data in Table 1 that specific programs were not cut, but that broad aggregates of programs for low-income people were not cut sufficiently to turn the clock back to 1966.

We have shown gross changes in outlays by viewing changes in six-year periods. The exact timing of these changes is, however, masked by the aggregation across time. To get a better picture of the timing of the changes, Table 2 shows the yearly data on total federal outlays (column 2), all human resource programs (column 3), and two narrowly defined human resource programs (columns 4 and 5)—all measured as a percent of the GNP.

Several conclusions stand out. First, total federal expenditures, and human resource expenditures in particular, started declining as a percent of the GNP after 1983. However, declines after cyclical increases are not unprecedented, as illustrated by the declines after the 1975 recession, and expenditures were still larger in 1985 than when Reagan entered office. Second, if one focuses on the narrowly defined programs (columns 4 and 5), which were chosen because of their sharp decline as a percent of the GNP, one finds that the decline predates the Reagan administration. Cash income assistance programs (column 4) started declining in 1973 and compensatory education grants (column 6) reached a peak in 1971.

Thus, many of the cuts in the programs for low-income people experienced since 1980 are a continuation of trends that started during the Ford and Carter administrations—retrenchment did not start with the current administration. In fact, it is hard to see large Reagan effects in these data except in the area of compensatory grants. This is not to deny that benefits were cut or that they would not have been cut even more if the Reagan program had been fully implemented. However, the enacted cuts were not so large that they couldn't be offset by recession-induced expenses in spending.

The data on total expenditures include the impact of changes in

TABLE 2   Real federal outlays as a percent of the GNP

(1) Fiscal year	(2) Total federal outlays	(3) Human resource programs	(4) Cash assistance payments	(5) Compensatory education grants
1966	18.17%	5.84%	0.37%	.7%
1967	19.84	6.55	0.34	.9
1968	20.90	3.93	0.37	.8
1969	19.76	7.08	0.39	.8
1970	19.75	7.61	0.42	.8
1971	19.88	8.69	0.52	.9
1972	20.04	9.31	0.57	.8
1973	19.11	9.30	0.46	.7
1974	19.01	9.58	0.38	.6
1975	21.81	11.37	0.34	.7
1976	21.87	11.98	0.34	.6
1977	21.14	11.46	0.32	.7
1978	21.11	11.15	0.29	.5
1979	20.53	10.91	0.26	.6
1980	22.15	11.75	0.26	.6
1981	22.71	12.12	0.26	.6
1982	23.74	12.37	0.24	.5
1983	23.34	12.83	0.24	.4
1984	23.05	11.69	0.23	.4
1985	24.04	11.99	0.22	.4
1986*	23.38	11.44	0.22	.3
1987*	21.90	10.79	0.18	.4
1988*	20.94	10.51	0.18	.4
1989*	20.19	10.25	0.18	.3
1990*	19.45	10.07	0.17	.3
1991*	18.85	9.88	0.16	.3

*Proposed budget.

SOURCE: Gene Falk, "1987 Budget Perspectives: Federal Spending for Human Resource Programs," Report no. 86–46 EPW, (Washington, D.C.: Congressional Research Service,1987).

the number of recipients as well as changes in benefits per recipient. It is possible that benefits per recipient would show a sharp break in trend during the Reagan years. To address this thesis, Table 3 shows the maximum AFDC and food stamp benefits for a family of four with no other sources of income with the median benefits in each year between 1968 and 1984. Column 1 shows a steady drop in AFDC benefits from $570 in 1968 to $376 in 1984. It is true that benefits dropped from $440 to $376 during the Reagan years, but this is also a continuation of past trends—not a sharp reversal.

Focus on AFDC benefits may be inappropriate since states, not the federal government, set benefit levels in this program. Furthermore, food stamp guarantees are adjusted automatically for inflation while AFDC adjustments are discretionary.

TABLE 3   Maximum AFDC and food stamp
benefits for a family of four in
the median state, 1968–84 (constant
1983 dollars)

Year	(1) Maximum AFDC benefit	(2) Maximum AFDC benefit plus food stamps	(3) Percent of poverty threshold
1968	$570	—	—
1969	566	—	—
1970	601	—	—
1971	581	$737	86.9
1972	584	730	86.1
1973	568	716	84.5
1974	577	769	90.6
1975	507	716	84.5
1976	536	720	84.8
1977	536	705	73.1
1978	525	700	82.6
1979	484	659	77.7
1980	440	599	70.6
1981	409	579	68.3
1982	393	550	64.9
1983	383	558	65.8
1984	376	542	63.9

SOURCE: Congressional Budget Office, *Children in Poverty*
(Washington, D.C.: Government Printing Office, 1985),
p. 644.

However, Column 2 shows that the combined maximum AFDC
and food stamp benefits also declined. The resulting decline in the
percent of the poverty threshold covered by these programs docu-
ments the steady erosion of income protection. While the benefits under these two programs were large enough to cover 86.9 percent of
the poverty budget in 1971, the percent had declined to 77.7 by the
eve of the Reagan administration. The decline continued through
1984, when a family of four receiving the maximum AFDC and food
stamp benefits could buy only 63.9 percent of the poverty budget in
the median state. When viewed in this context, the Reagan era again
marks not so much an abrupt change but rather an acceleration of
past trends.

CHANGE IN PROGRAM RULES

The Reagan administration's unique contribution to dismantling the
U.S. version of the welfare state lies not so much in its ability to reduce the size of the budget but in the method used to cut programs.

This was the first administration in recent years to propose nominal decreases in some programs. Previously, benefits had been eroded because they were not raised enough to keep up with inflation. During the Reagan administration, it became acceptable to advocate explicit cuts for some recipients.

Benefits were cut primarily by changing eligibility standards. Rule changes made many of the working poor, who had previously received both assistance and earning income, ineligible for assistance. AFDC rules were changed in 1981 to limit benefits to people at the bottom of the income distribution. After working four months on a job, benefits would be reduced by a dollar for every dollar earned by the working recipient. The result was that large numbers of working poor became ineligible for AFDC benefits.

This was a sharp break with the recent past. The so-called thirty-and-a-third rule, which allowed a recipient to keep the first $30 and one-third of any additional savings, had been instituted in the mid-1960s to provide equity and work incentives—recipients who worked were allowed to keep some of their earnings so that they would have a higher income than nonworking recipients. The principle that benefit reduction rates should be kept below 100 percent was well-accepted prior to the 1981 OBRA changes.

Likewise, large "notches" were introduced into the AFDC and food stamp programs in 1981. Under the new rules, AFDC benefits would drop to zero if earnings exceeded 150 percent of the poverty line (130 percent for food stamps). Placing these gross income ceilings limited payment to the poorest of the poor at the cost of creating strong incentives to stay just below these ceilings to maintain eligibility.

By abandoning the principle that notches should be avoided and tax rates should be low enough to encourage work, the Reagan administration shifted away from the stress on work incentives. In place of work incentives, the Reagan administration introduced new work requirements by instituting Community Work Experience Programs, better known as workfare. Under these state-run programs, recipients with children over six would be required to work for their AFDC grants. Failure to accept a workfare job resulted in ineligibility for benefits.

TAXES AND THE POOR

Did the Reagan era mark a sharp break with the past in tax policy toward the poor? Table 4, which shows the amount of federal income tax and social security tax that a family of four at the poverty line paid in selected years, suggests that the break with the past was not sharp. Taxes on low-income people increased dramatically during the 1980s. However, this was again an acceleration of earlier trends.

TABLE 4   Federal direct tax bill for a family of four with poverty-line earnings, 1965–84*

	(1) Poverty line earnings	(2) Personal income tax[†]	(3) Social security tax (employee's share)	(4) Total federal tax	(5) Effective tax rate[‡]
1965	$ 3,223	$ 31.22	$116.83	$ 148.05	4.4%
1969	3,743	104.02	179.66	283.68	7.6
1971	4,137	54.18	215.12	269.30	6.5
1973	4,540	33.60	265.59	299.19	6.6
1974[§]	5,038	3.32	294.72	298.04	5.9
1975	5,500	−250.00	321.75	71.75	1.3
1977	6,191	−180.90	362.17	181.27	2.9
1978	6,662	−133.80	403.05	269.25	4.0
1980	8,414	−54.00	515.78	461.78	5.5
1982	9,860	285.00	660.62	945.62	9.6
1984	10,609	366.00	710.80	1,076.80	10.1

*Assumes a married couple with two children not living on a farm; only one earner per family; all income is from earnings.

[†]From 1975 to the present, it includes the earned income tax credit. A negative entry represents a refund to the family.

[‡]Defined as total federal tax as a percentage of family income.

[§]The Tax Reduction Act of 1975 rebated $100 of 1974 personal income taxes to a family at this income level.

Prior to 1975, the standard deduction and personal exemption had been adjusted periodically to reflect the effects of inflation and higher social security tax rates on the poor. Column 3 shows that even though social security taxes increased steadily between 1965 and 1974, these taxes were offset by reductions in federal income taxes. The result was a decline in effective tax rates (shown in column 5) from 7.6 percent in 1969 to 5.9 percent in 1974.

Taxes on low-income people were further lowered in 1975 by the introduction of the earned income tax credit (EITC). This refundable tax credit for families with children equaled 10 percent of earned income up to $5,000. Families with incomes between $5,000 and $10,000 received a reduced credit. As a result of the EITC, a family of four with earnings at the poverty line had a federal income tax liability of −$250 in 1975 (column 2). This offsets a greater part of the social security tax—leading to a $71 total tax liability and the lowest effective tax rate (1.3 percent) in recent history.

After 1975, the personal exemption, standard deduction, and earned income tax credit were not adjusted for inflation. The result was that total tax liabilities (column 4) rose to $461 or 5.5 percent of income by 1980. The continued increase in social security taxes and the failure to reduce personal income taxes in the Economic Recovery Tax Act of 1981 led to a continued increase in tax liabilities for low-income people. By 1984, a poverty-line family paid $366 in personal income tax and $711 in social security taxes or 10.1 percent of income.

The more than doubling of the tax burden for low-income households in the four years between 1980 and 1984 is unprecedented in recent history. In this sense, the Reagan era was revolutionary. The fact that the trend toward higher taxes started in 1975 indicates that the Reagan changes were akin to a large battle in an ongoing war.

IMPACT ON POVERTY

One premise of the Reagan revolution was that only the "truly needy" should be helped by the government. This was to be accomplished by concentrating budget cuts on the working poor. While this policy was defended on the ground that it redistributed funds from the near poor to the more destitute, it consequently increased the total number of families in poverty.

Table 5 shows the growth in poverty between 1979 and 1984 under two definitions of income. The first definition includes the value of in-kind and cash transfers; the second definition counts only cash income. Neither measure includes the impact of increased taxes.

By either measure, poverty rose substantially between 1979 and 1984—the last year for which we have data. The number of poor per-

TABLE 5 Number and percent of persons in poverty and unemployment rates, 1979–84

	Number of persons in poverty		Percent of persons in poverty		Unemployment rate
	Cash plus in-kind benefits	Cash benefits	Cash plus in-kind benefits	Cash benefits	
1979	20,478	26,072	9.2	11.7	5.8
1980	23,895	29,272	10.6	13.0	7.0
1981	26,784	31,822	11.8	14.0	7.6
1982	29,407	34,398	12.8	15.0	9.7
1983	30,720	35,515	13.3	15.3	9.6
1984	28,917	33,700	12.4	14.4	7.5
Percentage change 1979–84	41.2	29.3	34.8	23.1	29.3

SOURCES: Cash plus in-kind definition from "Estimation of Poverty Including the Value of Noncash Benefits," U.S. Bureau of the Census, Technical Paper no. 55, p. 6. The in-kind benefits are included at their value to recipients and include food, housing, and medical care for the noninstitutionalized. Cash definition from "Money Income and Poverty Status of Families and Persons in the United States," U.S. Bureau of the Census, Current Population Reports, Series P–60, no. 149.

sons rose by 8.4 million using the in-kind definition and by 7.6 million when only cash is counted. Likewise, the increase in poverty rates is large by either definition—33.8 or 23.1 percent growth over the five-year period depending on the definitions.

These increases in poverty were not solely a result of budgetary retrenchment. Two other factors were as important in raising poverty rates. First, the rapid increase in unemployment between 1979 and 1983 weakened job prospects for the poor. As the last column of Table 5 shows, unemployment rates increased from 5.8 percent in 1979 to 9.6 percent by 1983. The ensuing recovery had only a modest impact on unemployment. By 1984, the unemployment rate had only dropped to 7.5 percent—remaining well above its 1979 level of 5.8 percent.

The second and less well-known factor influencing poverty is the secular increase in inequality that has occurred since the early 1970s. Poverty depends not only on average incomes but also on the distribution of this income. If the poverty-increasing effects of greater inequality more than offset the poverty-reducing effects of higher average income, then poverty can increase even when the average family's income is growing.

Table 6 shows the share of income received by each quintile of families in 1979 and 1984. The increase in inequality is clear from this data—the share of income received by families in the lowest fifth of the income distribution dropped from 5.3 percent to 4.7 percent, while the share for the top quintile increased from 41.6 percent to 42.9 percent between 1979 and 1984.

While it is difficult to separate the impact of retrenchment in programs, unemployment increases, and increases in inequality in terms of poverty, the best estimates are that roughly half of the increase in

TABLE 6   Percentage share of aggregate income received by each fifth of families, 1979 and 1984

	(1)	*(2)*	*(3)* Ratio
	1979	*1984*	*(1) ÷ (2)*
Lowest fifth	5.3	4.7	.887
Second fifth	11.6	11.0	.948
Third fifth	17.5	17.0	.971
Fourth fifth	24.1	24.4	1.012
Highest fifth	41.6	42.9	1.031
	100.0	100.0	

SOURCE: Current Population Reports, Series P–60, no. 129 and no. 149.

poverty between 1980 and 1983 was due to budget cuts. In other words, poverty rates would have gone up from 13 percent in 1980 to 14 percent in 1983 as a result of the budget cuts alone. Instead, they increased to 15.3 percent because of all the other economic and demographic changes that occurred.

FUTURE PROSPECTS

There was a retrenchment in human resource programs in the 1980s, although expenditures were not cut back to the levels of the mid-1960s. Did this retrenchment mark the start of a long-term decline in spending on the poor? Several bits of evidence suggest that this is not the case. While it is too early to predict major changes in the public mood, three actions taken by Congress and the president indicate that we may already have seen the largest cuts in programs for low-income people.

First, several of the changes enacted in the Omnibus Reconciliation Act of 1981 were reversed in later legislation. As described earlier, the eligibility of the working poor for AFDC was limited in two important ways under OBRA legislation—benefits were limited to households with incomes less than 150 percent of the poverty line and the "thirty-and-a-third" disregard was limited to the first four months on the job. Under the Deficit Reduction Act of 1984, the gross income limit was raised to 185 percent of the poverty line and the $30 disregard was extended to the first twelve months of a job. Coverage under medicaid was also extended for a limited period to some persons who lost AFDC coverage. The Food Stamp Act of 1985 also reversed earlier cutbacks in the food stamp program by increasing the gross income limit, liberalizing deductions, and raising the assets limit.

While none of these changes are large, the fact that programs were liberalized rather than cut in the aftermath of OBRA indicates a change in public mood. This is underscored by the decrease in rhetoric that programs for the poor have grown out of control. While the Reagan budget still contains proposed cuts in benefits, these cuts have become increasingly unpopular.

Provisions of the Gramm-Rudman legislation offer the second piece of evidence that retrenchment may have peaked. In brief, this legislation, aimed at reducing the federal deficit, has two parts. The first part sets targets for reducing the deficit to zero by 1991. The second part mandates a set of cuts that will be made if the targets are not met.

While the latter provision requires cuts in both military and domestic spending, some programs are exempt from the mandatory cuts. Exempting social security from mandatory cuts under Gramm-

Rudman is consistent with previous congressional actions that sheltered programs for the elderly from budgetary cuts. Of greater note is the exemption of AFDC and select other low-income transfer programs from mandatory cuts under Gramm-Rudman.

Protecting most income-tested programs has several important implications. First, Gramm-Rudman signals a change in attitude toward programs for low-income people. Not only will these programs not be the first to be cut, they will be protected against any mandatory cuts. Second, while low-income programs are not directly protected from discretionary cuts, they are offered some indirect protection. It will be harder to convince advocates for low-income programs that discretionary cuts in their programs are necessary to meet deficit targets—protectors of these programs will be less likely to make political concessions to avoid triggering the mandatory cuts that they will not have to bear.

The major tax reform proposals offer the third bit of evidence that a backlash may have developed against further cuts in low-income programs. All three major tax reform proposals offered in 1985 would have substantially reduced the federal income tax liabilities of low-income people through a combination of increases in the zero bracket amount, the earned income tax credit and the personal exemptions. Income taxes for a family of four earning a poverty-line income would have been reduced from $400 under 1984 regulations to $85 under the Bradley-Gephardt proposal, zero under the Kemp-Kasten proposal, and −$221 under the Reagan proposal (Bourdette and Weill, 1985).

Again, the links are indirect and the evidence is only suggestive. However, the fact that all the proposals give large tax cuts to low-income people is in sharp contrast to the Economic Recovery Tax Act of 1981, which lowered tax rates for high-income households but failed to protect low-income people.

In summary, the recision of some of the OBRA cuts, the protection of some income-tested programs under Gramm-Rudman and the reduction of tax liabilities for low-income people under all major tax reform proposals suggests that the retrenchment of the early 1980s may not signal a lasting revolution. It is possible that the Reagan administration will mark not the beginning but the end of retrenchment in programs for low-income people.

WHERE DO WE GO FROM HERE?

There is a wide consensus that something must be done to lower the poverty rate from its 1984 level of 14.4 percent back to the 11 to 12 percent range attained in the mid-1970s. While the fact that lowering unemployment rates would have a substantial impact on poverty is not in dispute, the more difficult question is how programs should be restructured. That welfare benefits were reduced during both Democratic and Republican administrations and that there was almost no public outcry when the working poor were effectively cut from the rolls, should tell us something about public support for the form, if not the magnitude, of antipoverty programs that had developed by the mid-1970s.

To return to the income support system of the 1970s would only leave recipients in the same precarious position in which they found themselves in the 1980s. The system needs to be restructured to serve the needs of low-income people without violating widely held values. In keeping with these values, I offer a three-part reform.

First, a national minimum AFDC standard should be enacted. The fact that there has been a public reaction against further major cuts in poverty programs indicates that the American public places a limit on budget cuts in programs that assist persons who are not able to provide for themselves. While there may be little support for across-the-board increases in benefits, there seems to be support for raising benefits in the lowest-payment states. This could be achieved by enacting a minimum AFDC standard that all states must meet.

Second, the earned income tax credit should be expanded. The fact that all 1986 tax reform will sharply cut federal income taxes for low-income people indicates that there is support for helping the working poor through the tax system. While there may be no analytical difference between increases in transfers and decreases in taxes, the American public clearly has indicated a preference for using tax cuts rather than transfers for the able-bodied poor. It would, therefore, be consistent with this basic preference to further help the working poor by expanding the earned income tax credit to all low-income families, whether or not they have children, and to raise the maximum credit.

Finally, programs for the able-bodied should offer work opportunities instead of transfers. Recent evidence indicates that the work ethic is so prevalent that many recipients, as well as taxpayers, prefer work opportunities to welfare for the able-bodied poor. In keeping with this view, President Carter's welfare reform proposal included a public jobs component, and President Reagan has advocated Community Work Experience Programs. While some work programs seek only to reduce the number of recipients, this need not be the case. The issue should not be whether able-bodied recipients must earn their income, but how much income they can earn. Under many workfare programs, recipients can only work until they have earned an amount equal to their welfare benefits. If the programs allowed recipients to work more when they want to, workfare would become a work opportunity program. My third recommendation is, therefore, to eliminate the ceiling on the number of hours a recipient can work under workfare programs.

CONCLUSION

In summary, the Reagan administration did not begin the unraveling of the welfare state in the United States. It continued a process that had started considerably earlier. While it found broad popular support for the shift in program design away from grants to the able-bodied, it found the public unwilling to support continued deep cuts in funding levels.

If low-income people are not to be placed, once again, in the precarious position of heavy reliance on public support, then future changes in the income support system should stress reduced taxes and increased work opportunities as well as restoration of some cuts in welfare programs for persons unable to work.

BIBLIOGRAPHY

Bourdette, Mary, and Jim Weill. "The Impact of Federal Taxes on Poor Families." Washington, D.C.: Children's Defense Fund, 1985.

Danziger, Sheldon, and Peter Gottschalk. "The Impact of Budget Cuts and Economic Conditions on Poverty," *Journal of Policy Analysis and Management* (Summer 1985), pp. 587–92.

Falk, Gene. "1987 Budget Perspectives: Federal Spending for Human Resource Programs." Washington, D.C.: Congressional Budget Office Report, no. 86–46 EPW, 1986.

U.S. Congress Committee on Ways and Means. *Children in Poverty.* Washington, D.C.: Government Printing Office, 1985.

Chapter Ten

Social Policy in the Reagan Era

R. KENT WEAVER

Perhaps no aspect of the Reagan era has been more controversial than the administration's initiatives in social policy—programs that directly affect the welfare and life chances of individuals in American society. Broadly conceived, social policy includes such areas as income transfers (such as social security and food stamps), health care (medicare and medicaid), education and job training, and tax policy (which redistributes income). It can even include policies toward abortion, family planning, and drug abuse. This essay will have a narrower focus on income transfer and health programs.

Even with this restricted focus, social policy comprises a huge portion of the federal government's activities. Approximately one-third of all federal government revenue comes in the form of contributions to social insurance programs—primarily for social security and medicare. Payments to individuals constituted more than forty cents of every dollar of federal expenditure in 1986—compared to less than thirty cents of every federal dollar spent on national defense. More than 37 million Americans—almost one-sixth of the country's population—received payments under the social security system's old age, survivors, and disability insurance programs in 1986. For millions of Americans, federal income and health programs make the difference between near starvation and a poor, but tolerable condition or between poverty and a relatively comfortable existence.

The Reagan administration came into office pledging both continuity and substantial change in social policy. The so-called social safety net of programs for individuals who were not expected to work (such as social security, medicare, and Supplemental Security Income) was to remain relatively intact. But the administration pledged a major effort to get the able-bodied poor off public assistance, and to rid the welfare state of the "waste, fraud, and abuse" of which it was ostensibly full.

The administration's goals were less than revolutionary. Its achievements, especially in public assistance programs, have fallen below the administration's initial hopes and expectations. This essay will outline how and why these developments came about.

The essay is built around three major arguments. First, as suggested above, President Reagan has not brought about a revolution in income maintenance and health care policy, although he has strengthened and reinforced a change in direction from expansion to cutbacks that was already underway. Second, the impact of cutbacks in the Reagan era has not been felt evenly across programs: programs aimed at the poor have been cut more. However, the forces shaping the redirection of politics are more complex than weak clients losing out politically. Clientele strength is important, but it is certainly not the whole story. Third, future changes in social policy are likely to be modest changes from the status quo.

There are three different kinds of measures that can be used to look at social policy change in the Reagan era. A first indicator is changes in *overall spending levels* for specific programs. But this measure can be misleading, especially in examining income transfers, because these programs are affected dramatically by how the economy is doing. In 1982 and 1983, for example, social spending increased substantially because a serious recession made many more people eligible for food stamps, AFDC benefits, and unemployment insurance. This was not, for the most part, the result of policy change, but, it was rather a change in the environment to which the policy was applied. A second measure is the *welfare of individuals*, as covered in the essay by Peter Gottschalk. Again, this measure is heavily influenced by how the economy is doing, even if policy stays the same. A third measure is *changes in program standards*: the criteria for eligibility and the value of the benefits received. This last measure, which most accurately separates the administration's efforts at policy change from other forces, will be the focus of this essay.

REAGAN'S POLICY INHERITANCE

It is helpful at the outset to gain a sense of the policy inheritance that confronted the Reagan administration when it took office. Even before the Reagan era, federal expenditures on income maintenance and health care in the United States were not especially high in comparison to those in other industrialized countries. The reason for this is that many social welfare functions provided through government in other countries—such as health care for citizens under age sixty-five,

income supplements for families with children, and full pensions—
are, in the United States, provided primarily in the private sector with
exceptions only for the poor. Current expenditure patterns are shown
in Table 1. The bulk of federal spending in the United States was and
is for "social insurance" programs—that is, programs where individuals and/or employers make contributions, usually through payroll
taxes (such as social security, medicare hospital insurance, unemployment compensation), and occasionally through premium payments
(medicare supplementary medical insurance). Benefits received in
these programs are linked, often rather loosely, to past contributions.
A much smaller percentage of federal spending on income and health
programs is provided on a means-tested basis—that is, with the requirement that recipients have earnings and assets below specified
levels. Many of the means-tested programs in the United
States—such as Supplemental Security Income (SSI), Aid to Families
with Dependent Children (AFDC) and veterans pensions—are categorical programs. This means that it is not enough just to be poor to
qualify. In addition, recipients must be aged, blind, disabled, have
dependent children, or meet additional eligibility criteria. The major
noncategorical income program is food stamps.

Most federal income maintenance and health programs are enti-

TABLE 1   Federal outlays on major social programs in fiscal
year 1986 (millions of dollars)

Social insurance, retirement, and disability	
Old-age and survivors insurance	179,572
Disability insurance	20,243
Unemployment	
Unemployment compensation	25,137
Means-tested programs	
Supplemental security income	10,345
Aid to families with dependent children	9,877
Low-income home energy assistance	2,046
Veterans pensions	3,874
Earned income tax credit	1,415
Nutrition	
Food stamps	11,619
Child nutrition programs	3,820
Supplemental nutrition for women, infants, and children (WIC)	1,578
Miscellaneous	
Coal miners' disability (black lung)	1,612
Health care	
Medicare hospital insurance	49,685
Medicare supplementary medical insurance	26,217
Grants to states for medicaid	24,995

SOURCE: *Budget of the United States Government*, Fiscal Year 1988.

tlements. That means that anyone who meets the program criteria is automatically eligible for benefits and has a legal right to the benefit specified by statutes. Government cannot simply cut back on spending for the program by not appropriating the money; the statute that defines eligibility and benefits must be changed. Because the American political system provides so many veto points where change can be blocked, lowering spending in these sectors is a politically difficult task.

The major growth in social welfare spending in the United States occurred between 1965 and 1976. This growth had several roots. A first source was demographic change. In social security, more of the elderly who had contributed to the program through most of their working lives became eligible for benefits, and they became eligible for higher benefits based upon their contributions. There were other demographic changes as well. A higher rate of family breakup and illegitimacy increased eligibility for AFDC, for example.

A second source of growth was the creation of new programs—most notably in health care. Medicare and medicaid were created in 1965, and they started in 1966. In the next eight years, they grew to become 6 percent of federal expenditures.

A third factor leading to expansion of social spending was increased benefit levels. In social security, for example, there were a series of ad hoc benefit increases in the late 1960s and the early 1970s that were followed in 1972 by a 20 percent benefit increase across-the-board and then an indexing of social security benefits so that they would remain fixed over time. Unfortunately, a faulty indexing mechanism that overindexed benefits for many recipients was used, which created a funding crisis in the system.

Changes in eligibility and participation also occurred in this period. The number of participants in AFDC increased from 4.4 million in 1965 to 9.7 million in 1970. This was due, in part, to a decline in the stigma associated with receiving public assistance, which made it more socially acceptable for eligible people to claim benefits from the program. The courts also facilitated increased enrollments in public assistance programs by overturning some government restrictions on eligibility.

The fifth source which expanded social welfare spending in this period was business cycles. Income maintenance spending varies substantially with business cycles and it came to a peak in 1975–76 with the mid-1970s recession. As noted earlier, economic downturn leads to changes in spending without policy changes because more people become eligible for programs. But major recessions also tend to lead to policy change. In particular, Congress often has passed legislation that temporarily extended individuals' eligibility for unemployment benefits. What Congress implies is that it is not the fault of individuals that they are unemployed longer; because the economy is doing poorly, we cannot expect them to cycle back into the economy and get new jobs as quickly as they would under normal economic conditions.

Expansion through policy changes ended when the Carter administration came into office. The last major initiative was in 1977, when the federal government ended the purchase requirement for food stamps. In the past, recipients had to pay 30 percent of their income to get food stamps, which was a major burden for families with little cash income. Now, people draw them without cash payment. This policy change led to a dramatic increase in food stamp program participation.

POLICY CHANGE IN THE REAGAN ERA

The change since 1981 in federal expenditures on programs for individuals has been far from revolutionary, as Table 2 shows. Federal spending on income maintenance programs as a percentage of the GNP has essentially stopped growing since Reagan came into office.

TABLE 2   Payments for individuals in the federal budget

Year	Current dollars (billions)	Constant 1982 dollars (billions)	Percent of total federal outlays	Percent of GNP
1970	64.7	152.2	33.1	6.5
1971	80.4	181.0	38.3	7.6
1972	92.9	200.1	40.3	8.1
1973	104.5	215.7	42.5	8.2
1974	120.1	228.3	44.6	8.5
1975	153.5	265.8	46.2	10.1
1976	180.1	290.1	48.4	10.6
1977	196.3	295.5	48.0	10.2
1978	211.0	296.8	46.0	9.7
1979	232.9	301.6	46.3	9.5
1980	277.5	324.7	47.0	10.4
1981	323.4	344.3	47.7	10.8
1982	356.7	356.7	47.8	11.4
1983	395.3	378.6	48.8	11.9
1984	399.8	368.7	46.9	10.8
1985	425.6	379.3	45.0	10.8
1986	448.0	389.4	44.9	10.8
1987*	465.3	392.2	45.4	10.5

*Estimated

SOURCE: *Historical Tables: Budget of the United States Government,* Fiscal Year 1988, Table 11.1. Transition quarter excluded.

This spending remains responsive to the business cycle, however. Spending on income transfer programs went up in 1982 and 1983 and then declined. Health entitlements have continued to increase their share of the GNP. The problem of growing health expenditures is not unique to the United States.

The basic structure of all the major income maintenance and health programs has remained intact throughout the Reagan era. The pattern of statutory changes has been made primarily through limited cutbacks. Means-tested programs have been cut more than social insurance programs. In particular, many beneficiaries at the higher end of eligibility for these programs have been cut off. Efforts have also been made to stiffen work requirements for means-tested programs and to tighten eligibility. Program changes under President Reagan have generally been at the margins rather than comprehensive reform or dissolution of programs, however. The administration's most sweeping proposals for change, notably the New Federalism proposal to turn AFDC and food stamps over to the states in exchange for full federal control of medicaid, have gone nowhere. Most statutory changes in benefit levels and eligibility standards occurred in the first year of the Reagan administration. By 1983, policy change was a mixed bag. As President Reagan lost control of Congress, Congress started undoing some of the cutbacks in eligibility and benefits.

In social security, as William Niskanen notes in his essay, the Reagan administration made a major initiative in May 1981—proposing several cuts that would have hit early retirees especially hard. The proposal created a firestorm of criticism and President Reagan walked away from it. The 1981 Reconciliation Act, which was the big budget-cutting bill, made minor changes in social security. It eliminated the minimum benefit (for recipients whose contributions entitled them only to a very low benefit), which was later partially restored. Another change was the phasing out of a benefit under social security for the college student survivors of people who had died.

Major changes in social security were not addressed in 1981, but it was clear that a major funding crisis was developing in the system. Politicians do not like to face the issue of cutting social security benefits or raising taxes to pay for the program. President Reagan appointed a nonpartisan commission to investigate social security and report after the November 1982 election—temporarily taking the heat off himself and Congress. After a complicated negotiation process, the commission's proposals were adopted and a number of changes were made in social security in 1983. These changes included taxation of the benefits of high-income social security recipients, a delay in cost-of-living adjustments, and acceleration of previously scheduled social security tax increases. As a way to deal with the long-term funding crisis, the retirement age for receiving full social security benefits will be gradually raised from 65 to 67.

Changes to social security disability, the companion program to social security, began before the Reagan administration, and they were strengthened by the Reagan administration. A 1980 act required that most social security disability cases be reviewed every three years unless recipients were declared permanently disabled. This required that administrative discretion be exercised, and the Reagan administration used this discretion to cut about half a million people from the social security disability rolls. Again, there was major political dissent; many people appealed and over 160,000 were put back on the rolls after the appeal. Reacting to this criticism, Congress, in 1984, changed the statutory guidelines to make it more difficult to cut people off disability rolls. Approximately 2.7 million disabled workers received benefits under the program at the end of 1986—compared to 2.86 million when President Reagan assumed office.

The Unemployment Insurance Program, which is the biggest unemployment program in the United States, also underwent a number of changes. The 1981 Reconciliation Act raised the unemployment level trigger at which extended benefits can be given. Perhaps the most important action regarding unemployment assistance by the Reagan administration was they did not do what past administrations had done during recessions, which was adding supplemental benefits for the long-term unemployed to extended benefits. The result was that fewer people were eligible to receive unemployment insurance. In 1982, only 45 percent of the people who were unemployed received unemployment benefits compared with the 1975 recession— when 78 percent of the unemployed received benefits. Congress eventually did pass legislation easing eligibility—two and a half months before the 1982 elections—just in time to claim the credit with voters.

More substantial changes were made in the smaller Trade Adjustment Assistance program. This program provides either cash benefits or relocation and retraining benefits to workers who are affected by imports. Under the Carter administration, this program had expanded dramatically. In 1979, program expenditures were $269 million. The next year, they increased to $1.5 billion—a 600 percent expansion in one fiscal year. President Carter's administration tried to exercise discretion (the act gives the Department of Labor discretion to decide what workers and firms in specific industries are affected by imports and whether or not they should receive benefits) in handing out more benefits in an election year.

Changes made in 1981 had a major impact on the Trade Adjustment program. The Reagan administration proposed, and Congress accepted, changes that turned the program into a supplement to unemployment insurance. Individuals could not get trade adjustment assistance benefits until their unemployment insurance benefits had run out, and these benefits were focused much more on relocation and retraining. This change was based on criticisms that benefits were so high that they kept people from looking for work. In two years, spending on the program declined by about 80 percent.

Cuts were also made in the means-tested programs. The 1981 Reconciliation Act limited AFDC eligibility in a variety of ways. In addition, it allowed states to require that individuals perform community service work or workfare to qualify for benefits. Food stamp eligibility was also restricted in 1981 and 1982. Food stamp benefits were cut by making COLA adjustments less frequently. Once again, however, changes in means-tested programs were less than revolutionary. The number of recipients of federally administered Supplemental Security Income recipients at the end of 1985, for example, was almost identical to the level at the end of 1980. The number of AFDC recipients declined approximately 3 percent (from 11.1 million to 10.7 million) between the beginning of the Reagan administration and the end of 1984.

In health care programs, both the federal government and (for medicaid) the states, since 1981, have restricted eligibility and benefits largely at the margins. Because medicaid eligibility is tied to AFDC eligibility, in many cases, people who qualify for AFDC automatically qualify for medicaid—taking people off AFDC also removed them from medicaid. Medicare is a much more touchy political issue because it concerns the huge constituency of the elderly. The Reagan administration has attempted to squeeze the providers rather than squeezing the recipients—first by imposing a series of cost controls on hospitals in 1982, which scared hospitals so much that they went along with a 1983 reform that imposed a prospective reimbursements system on hospitals. Under the new system, medicare pays a flat fee for treating a specific diagnosed problem—for example, a broken arm. If the government pays the hospital, say $300, and the hospital can treat the broken arm for $200, it can keep the extra $100. If, however, the treatment cost the hospital $500, it must bear the loss. The idea is to provide incentives for cost control and limit overtreatment. The new reimbursement system appears to be exercising some discipline in health care expenditures.

Trying to compare the effects of these policy changes across programs is extremely difficult. How do you measure what expenditures would have been if the program had not changed? The answer also depends on the period examined. Raising the social security retirement age, for example, will have a major impact on expenditure levels for that program over the next fifty years. But the effect on fiscal year 1988 is zero because the increased retirement age does not take effect until after the turn of the century.

Data is available, however, that allows us to make reasonable estimates of the effects of policy changes made in calendar years 1981–84
on expenditures in fiscal 1985. In other words, if the law had remained as it was at the end of 1980, how would expenditures have
differed than if the laws had not changed over those four years? Cuts
made during the first Reagan administration in both social security
and social security disability cut anticipated expenditures by about
4½ percent (6 percent—if taxation of benefits is included). In Supplemental Security Income (which goes to the poor who are aged, blind,
or disabled), expenditures increased by 9 percent. This is due, in
part, to a benefit increase and, in part, from cutbacks in other programs—notably social security. Individuals who otherwise would receive social security now receive Supplemental Security Income instead. Estimates for the AFDC program are that 1985 expenditures
declined about 10 percent over what they would have been if the
1980–84 changes had not occurred. In the Special Supplemental
Feeding Program for Women, Infants, and Children (WIC), which provides a special food package to women who are pregnant, who have
young children, or whose health is considered at risk, spending increased about 9 percent as a result of changes made in the first Reagan administration. Unemployment insurance went up a little because of the 1982 enactment of the supplemental benefits package.
Trade adjustment assistance went down about 90 percent, and it was
essentially eliminated by changes in the Reagan administration. Medicare hospital insurance spending declined by 6 percent in the period
due to policy changes, and medicare supplementary insurance (which
covers physicians' fees and other services) declined by more than 9
percent.

Most of the big cuts were made in 1981. In 1983, expansionary
policy changes became more evident, such as the extension of unemployment insurance, which actually occurred in late 1982 but took effect primarily in 1983. SSI benefits were increased in 1983, and social
security disability rules were eased in 1984.

The major initiative of the second Reagan administration with implications for social policy was the Gramm-Rudman deficit reduction
act, which called for automatic expenditure cuts if Congress did not
meet specified budget cutting targets. The courts overturned the automatic provisions of the act, but its effects on big social programs
would have been quite limited in any case: most income maintenance
and health programs were excluded from automatic cuts. Under
Gramm-Rudman, social security, food stamps, and many other low-
income programs were protected from cutbacks. Their indexing
mechanisms would have remained intact regardless of what was done
with other federal spending. Some of the other programs (such as
Civil Service Retirement) had a lower degree of protection. Benefits

could not be cut in nominal terms, although COLAs could be eliminated. Other programs (such as medicare) could be cut by only a small percentage below inflation.

The conclusion that emerges is that program retrenchment is not a snowballing process. A more accurate image is that the snowball was rolled uphill in the early years of the Reagan administration, and it started rolling back in later years. Clearly, the Reagan era changes are important, but they have not led to ongoing cutbacks resulting in a substantially transformed welfare state.

A second conclusion is that cuts were generally higher as a percentage in means-tested programs than in social insurance programs with a broader clientele. There were notable exceptions in Supplemental Security Income and the feeding program for women, infants, and children. Within the means-tested programs, high-income recipients were affected more.

A third conclusion is that the program changes made were mostly marginal. Only trade adjustment assistance, among the major income transfer programs, was cut by more than a third over what the no policy change baseline would have been. Also, there has been no elimination of major income transfer programs, and no elimination of indexing has occurred. There have been one-time COLA cuts, freezes, or delays—but no permanent elimination. All of these outcomes reinforce the conclusion that the Reagan administration has produced a modification rather than a revolution in income maintenance and health care policy.

EXPLAINING OUTCOMES

There is complex causation in the pattern of social policy cutbacks produced during the Reagan years. The extent of cutbacks is not simply a function of the political strength of a program's clientele, although that is important. There are three kinds of protections that are available to advocates for income maintenance and health programs. These are: procedural protections, political protections, and ethical protections.

Procedural protections involve items like the indexation of benefit levels and eligibility standards. Unless Congress actually tries to cut automatic increases in spending to keep benefit levels consistent over time, increases in indexed programs will occur automatically. Politicians must go through a time-consuming process to prevent it from occurring; that is a clear procedural protection. A second procedural protection results from the fact that most income maintenance and health programs are entitlements: the law has to be changed if there will be substantial cutbacks in spending. This is different from discretionary programs—where appropriations committees can refuse to

appropriate the money at levels suggested by the authorizing committees—the committees that write the laws governing the programs.
This is important because authorizing committees are often dominated by program advocates. They try to increase program funding:
the appropriations committees and the budget committees act as budget guardians. Everyone understands this little game. But the influence of restraining forces is limited for most income maintenance and
health programs because the appropriations committees do not get a
crack at them.

A second set of protections is political; the bigger and better organized the clientele, the less likely the program will be cut. A program like social security, which has a huge and fairly organized (by
groups like the American Association of Retired Persons) clientele, is
better able to defend itself than food stamp recipients.

The third set of protections concerns politicians' ethical convictions. Policymakers have conceptions of who should be helped and
how much they should be helped that are independent of the political
pressures and that affect outcomes. Ethical factors that affect whether
or not programs will be cut include prevailing notions about the
causes of poverty and the nature of citizen's rights. Perceptions of
program efficiency are also important, as well as notions of a budgetary
fair share. If a program increases its share dramatically within a few
years, it will raise questions in policymakers' minds about whether
the program is out of control or subverted from its original mission.

The pattern of changes in U.S. social policy can best be understood by exploring changes in the role and interaction of each of these
types of protection. There are layers of explanation, beginning with
political protections, which can explain much of the observed policy
change, and procedural and ethical protections explain the remaining
anomalies.

A good way to begin examining the role of political protections is
to imagine legislators and the president facing a difficult electoral cal-
culus. On the one hand, they have pressure to increase benefits to
individuals. On the other hand, they also have pressure to limit taxes
and deficits. Intermittently, they face pressure to support the president's program. How has this pattern of incentives changed over the
last few years? One change is that both slower economic growth since
the mid-1970s and the taxpayer revolt of the late 1970s have made
legislators more aware of the need to present an image of fiscal responsibility—of not being big spenders.

A second change has to do with the president's program. President Reagan, particularly in 1981, made a strong push for cuts in programs. He put his prestige on the line and tried to make it politically
costly for legislators who did not support the president's program. He

backed away from social security cuts, but on most income and health programs the push was there.

A third kind of change in incentives was that the 1981 tax cut and military budget increase squeezed the federal budget. There has been little room for program expansion, and there has been tremendous pressure to cut programs to reduce the deficit.

Overall, these changes made cuts in income maintenance and health programs more necessary and more palatable to politicians. But programs' clientele are not powerless, nor are all clientele equally powerful. Programs that have a large clientele, such as social security, and programs that are well organized, like veterans, are more likely to protect their benefits than a clientele that is either poorly organized and has a low electoral turnout (such as AFDC and food stamp recipients) or limited in geographical scope (such as beneficiaries of the coal miners' disability program). This will be true unless the beneficiaries of these programs can form coalitions with other programs. The food stamps program is a good example of how this has worked in the past. Urban legislators supported agricultural programs in exchange for rural legislators' support for food stamps. Programs can also be protected by monopolizing control over policy in a sympathetic forum: the authorizing committees that created and generally favor the programs.

Options to shield programs have declined over the last several years. The way legislators' electoral incentives are distributed, means-tested programs are likely to get cut more because the political strength of their clientele is generally weaker.

Advocates of reduced social spending have attempted to make cuts more politically acceptable by focusing policy changes on relatively weak clientele. An example is the elimination of college student survivor benefits under social security. Few people think that they will die and that their children will need this benefit; the potential recipients are poorly organized. Potential opposition is minimized further by continuing the benefit for current recipients.

Many of the cuts in benefits that were made were disguised to cut down on the political effects. One of the major ways that benefit cuts were made was by delays in cost-of-living adjustments so that real benefits were cut. But easy-to-observe nominal benefits were not cut. Another manifestation of this strategy was the delay of several important cuts—minimizing their political impact. In social security, the gradual increase in the retirement age begins in the year 2000 and ends in 2021—the bulk of today's voters will not be affected by it, and voters who are affected will not focus on a change occurring so far in the future.

Using this analysis of the political incentive structure for legislators and the president explains a lot about the pattern of cuts in income maintenance and health that have occurred under the Reagan administration. But some questions remain unanswered. Why, for example, do some programs with similar clientele fare differently from one another? Food stamps and WIC have overlapping clientele, and they are similar programs: both hand out stamps enabling recipients to get food. But the food stamps program was cut while WIC was expanded. Unemployment insurance and trade adjustment assistance also have similar clientele. But trade adjustment assistance has been devastated while unemployment insurance has not been devastated.

A second outcome that is difficult to explain looking only at clientele strength is why the cuts in the means-tested programs have occurred mostly in the upper-end of eligibility. One might think those people are more likely to be politically active and more willing and able to defend their interests.

A third outcome that is hard to explain is why, given that most of these programs are entitlements, the alleged influence of program supporters on committees that have a monopoly of power was ineffective in preventing cuts.

To explain these outcomes, it is helpful to look first at procedural protections. One item that helped make the cutbacks possible was the odd placement of most of these programs in Congress. Most of the major income and health programs are under the jurisdiction of the Senate Finance and the House Ways and Means committees, which are concerned primarily with tax legislation. This occurred because most of these programs were funded by a special tax mechanism or created as adjuncts to social security. Similarly, the House and Senate Agriculture committees have jurisdiction over food stamps. In both cases, the major policy interest of people on these committees is something other than preserving benefit levels for these programs. Most of the people on the agriculture committee care primarily about farm programs; their major interest in food stamps is as a vote-trading item. As a result, most committee members were not necessarily willing to protect these programs when the momentum for cutbacks occurred in 1981. A more important procedural change is how the budget act was changed in 1980 and, most importantly, manifested in 1981. It was used by presidents and coalitions supporting them to convert a series of unpopular votes that cut income programs into one vote that had substantial political appeal in supporting the president. Most program cuts in 1981 were not considered one by one. Most of the changes were made in one big package that was voted up or down; the major political message in the vote concerned support for the president. There was strong pressure to do so.

Ethical protections are important as a last layer of explanation. Policymakers have ethical notions of who deserves help and who does not. There is never a consensus, but there is a balance of opinion that has shifted due to the turnover among officeholders, officeholders changing their minds, and shifting pressures from the electorate.

Clientele of public assistance programs in the United States have suffered from a widespread belief that poverty is due to individual failings; many policymakers support these programs because they see no acceptable alternative—despite qualms about the need of some recipients. The Reagan administration has also taken a strong stand that government assistance should be limited to people unable to provide for themselves. Aid to the working poor is seen as fostering a dependency on welfare that will hurt recipients in the long run. While many legislators do not share this view, the more morally ambiguous claim of the working poor to benefits made it politically easier to cut their eligibility and benefits.

Both food stamps and AFDC have also suffered from the perception that there is fraud and that there are high error rates in the state administration of these programs. Policymakers have not cut programs blindly. They have concentrated much of their efforts on lessening error rates in state administration of programs. Notions of program efficiency and effectiveness were manifested in other ways as well. Coal miners disability, for example, was cut following recommendations that the General Accounting Office had made for several years. The presumptions—whereby recipients were granted benefits —had become so broad that people who had worked in mining offices and smoked or who had been killed in mining accidents received this benefit even if there was little or no evidence that they had the black lung disease that the benefit was designed to compensate. This is a notion of a problem in a program that cannot be reduced to political implications. It is a notion of deserving and program effectiveness.

At the same time, WIC, the feeding program for women, infants, and children, has benefited from evaluations arguing that the program saves the government more in medicaid expenditures in the long run than it costs because there are fewer low birth weight babies and fewer children who suffer from malnutrition in their infancy. This logic was used by Democrats in Congress in 1981–82 to attack President Reagan's proposed WIC cuts. Finally, legislators have notions about fair budget share. Here is where trade adjustment assistance received initial scrutiny. There was a feeling that a 600 percent expenditure increase in one year reflected a serious problem in the program.

FUTURE DIRECTIONS

The politics explaining the pattern of social policy cutbacks in the Reagan era is complex—involving ethical and procedural protections as well as strength of the clientele. To understand what will happen in these programs in the future, it is necessary to understand what will happen to the three kinds of protections. Are they likely to erode further or be fairly stable? My argument is that changes in protection for the programs will be marginal over the next few years.

Political protections are unlikely to erode further. The social security lobby remains one of the strongest ones in Washington, and politicians of both parties compete to declare their support for the program in the strongest terms. The recovery of a Senate majority by Democrats in the 1986 election makes it even more difficult to cut social programs. The Republican-controlled Senate was the congressional launching pad for most of the Reagan-era cuts in social programs. Without this forum, many cuts will not make the congressional agenda.

Existing procedural protections will also remain intact. The height of a more centralized budget process was reached in 1981. The special protective conditions for many social programs written into the Gramm-Rudman deficit reduction act show that Congress has little interest in eliminating indexation mechanisms that protect the clientele of these programs.

Ethical support for entitlement programs is also unlikely to weaken in the future. Public support for social security spending remains strong. Support for public assistance spending has actually risen in the Reagan era, in part because horror stories about the homeless and starving grandmothers have become more common than stories about welfare mothers with Cadillacs, and that affects public perceptions about too much or too little being spent on social policy. These perceptions filter through to policymakers.

Clearly, the prospects for complete dismantling of programs in either income maintenance or health is minimal for the next few years. The social policy agenda has been altered substantially in the Reagan years. With the country facing huge budget deficits, there is limited fiscal room for new social policy initiatives. Thus, issues like comprehensive national health insurance—modeled on the Canadian pattern—are off the national agenda for the foreseeable future. But three leading items on the social policy agenda for the last two years of the Reagan presidency probably will lead to increased expenditures. A first item is increased protection against the costs of catastrophic illnesses—illnesses that exceed the coverage limits of medicare or private insurance or that require treatment not covered by those insurance plans (such as long-term care in a nursing home). The Reagan administration has proposed expanded catastrophic coverage for medicare recipients, while leading legislators have proposed plans that would cover people under age sixty five as well.

The second major item on the social policy agenda is welfare reform—in particular, an increased emphasis on training and work requirements for the Aid to Families with Dependent Children program. Stiffer work requirements have become more acceptable politically as working mothers of young children have become the norm rather than the exception in the general population, and as concern has grown that an underclass is growing up in America with little education, skills, and job experience. But, it is unlikely that such a plan would save money given the high costs of training, commuting, and day care. It is more doubtful that appropriate jobs could be found for all recipients who want to work—even if the federal government and the states pick up a large part of the bill.

The third major item on the agenda is some sort of aid for the nation's homeless. Homelessness has many causes, including long-term unemployment, cuts in existing income programs, and the release of mentally ill patients from hospitals, and there are no easy solutions. But the 100th Congress, elected in 1986, has already passed legislation to provide increased funding for emergency food and shelter. Additional legislation is certain to follow.

BIBLIOGRAPHY

Bawden, D. Lee, ed. *The Social Contract Revisited: Aims and Outcomes of President Reagan's Social Welfare Policy*. Washington, D.C.: Urban Institute Press, 1984.

Levitan, Sar A. *Programs in Aid of the Poor*. Baltimore: Johns Hopkins University Press, 1985.

Light, Paul. *Artful Work: The Politics of Social Security Reform*. New York: Random House, 1985.

Murray, Charles. *Losing Ground: American Social Policy 1950–1980*. New York: Basic Books, 1984.

Rogers, Joe, Tom Rogers, and Cheryl Rogers. *By the Few for the Few: The Reagan Welfare Legacy*. Lexington, Mass.: D.C. Heath, 1985.

Part VII

THE REAGAN REVOLUTION IN FOREIGN POLICY

The nation which indulges towards another an habitual hatred, or an habitual fondness, is in some degree a slave. It is a slave to its animosity or to its affection, either of which is sufficient to lead it astray from its duty and its interest.
GEORGE WASHINGTON

The following two essays are very different, yet they share at least one important observation: They portray the impact of President Reagan's determination to make the United States stand tall in the world again. This may lead to what John Holmes calls American "unilateralism." In the case of the Strategic Defense Initiative (SDI), we see the American need for "an element of faith" in a millennial approach. Both, of course, may result in a serious rearrangement not only of the United States' relations with the Soviet Union, but with its allies as well.

The decision to pursue SDI was made by the President[1] but its origins go back much further. As Sayre Stevens notes, technological and military developments since SALT I intensified the problem of the relationship between offense and defense. Mutually assured destruction (MAD) presupposed that defensive policies and capabilities will match the offensive policies and capabilities of the opponent. To some, it appeared that the United States was falling behind in defensive capabilities. New technology offered a way out of this dilemma; it also appealed to the optimistic side of President Reagan. Here was a way to break the

---

[1]Reagan is reported to have said that he thought up the SDI "all by himself." See Philip Geyelin, "The Reagan Crisis,"*Foreign Affairs* 65, no. 3 (1987) pp. 447−57.

163

madness of MAD and to demonstrate America's superiority in science and industry.

The reaction of allies has not been wholly enthusiastic. Apart from scientific and technical objections to SDI, they are also concerned about the impact of SDI on the strategic principles underlying the Western alliance. MAD assumed that the United States would defend Western Europe because Americans are as exposed to Soviet missiles as Europeans. With the umbrella of the SDI, however, that assumption may be more difficult to sustain.

How realistic are these fears, and how realistic is the prospect of a functioning SDI? Stevens provides a knowledgeable background to these questions, and he offers instructive insights into the American debate on them. There is more at stake than scientific or even military considerations: the political framework and consequences are just as important. Moreover, as appropriate for a major strategic policy, it is also necessary to evaluate the possible reaction of the Soviet Union—an uncertain enterprise full of new dangers.

The tendency of the United States to focus on its own strength is also raised by John Holmes. Concurrent with American unilateralism is a danger of ignoring other multilateral—and especially international—organizations. In the United States, there is an impatience with the tardiness, confusion, and occasional corruption of international organizations. Yet, the alternative to the United Nations or NATO is not necessarily more advantageous to the United States. These are the costs of unilateralism and the lack of vision in American leadership. Standing tall should not always mean beating up the smaller guy.

The world is not always Manichaean: there are more issues in the world than the struggle between the two empires—the United States and the Soviet Union. It is argued here by a Canadian diplomat and scholar that by ignoring such possibilities, and a possible role for Canada as the United States' closest ally, that the United States denies itself a valuable opportunity to protect its own interests.

SUGGESTIONS FOR FURTHER READING

Bowman, Robert. *Star Wars: A Defense Insider's Case Against the Strategic Defense Initiative*. New York: St. Martin's Press, 1986.

Chalfont, A. G. J. *Star Wars: Suicide or Survival?* London: Werdenfeld & Nicholson, 1985.

Clarkson, Stephen. *Canada and the Reagan Challenge: Crisis and Adjustment, 1981–1985*. Toronto: J. Lorimer, 1985.

Dallek, Robert. *The American Style of Foreign Policy: Cultural Politics and Foreign Affairs*. New York: Alfred A. Knopf, 1983.

Dallmeyer, Dorinda G., and Daniel S. Papp. *The Strategic Defense Initiative: New Perspectives on Deterrence.* Boulder, Colo.: Westview Press, 1986.

Doran, Charles F. *Forgotten Partnership: U.S.-Canada Relations Today.* Baltimore: Johns Hopkins University Press, 1984.

Holmes, John W. *Life with Uncle: The Canadian-American Relationship.* Toronto: University of Toronto Press, 1981.

Pressler, Larry. *Star Wars: The Strategic Defense Initiative Debates in Congress.* New York: Praeger Publishers, 1986.

Stares, Paul B. *The Militarization of Space: U.S. Policy 1945–1984.* Ithaca, N.Y.: Cornell University Press, 1985.

Chapter Eleven

The Star Wars Challenge

SAYRE STEVENS

The Strategic Defense Initiative (SDI), or Star Wars, is an appropriate topic in this series of essays on the Reagan Revolution. It is revolutionary in terms of military and strategic thinking about the ways to shape the confrontation between the Soviet Union and the United States. It also has distinct Reaganesque features: it is optimistic in the extreme, built on faith in American accomplishments, and it looks to the future and a better world in rather imprecise ways that are often shrouded in uncertainty. But the SDI remains an intriguing idea and a product of Ronald Reagan; it would not have emerged in its initial, hortatory form from any other source.

There are a number of centers of enthusiasm in the United States for ballistic missile defense, and SDI reflects the outcome of a resurgence of an earlier antiballistic missile (ABM) debate that occurred in the United States in the late 1960s. There was, and still is, a serious dispute about whether or not ABM defenses are worth the money and if they can contribute to the national security of the United States. The view, even among its proponents in the 1960s, was that there were serious questions about whether or not the technology was adequate to justify the widespread deployment of the system. At that time, Congress was leaning heavily on Lyndon Johnson—insisting that it be deployed. Robert McNamara, then Secretary of Defense, was resistant. Each time the pressure for deploying ABM grew too high, he would demand that another study be performed to see whether or not it made sense. These studies went on and became more complex and difficult to deal with, but they always left the efficacy of ABM defense in doubt. Finally, Johnson gave way to Senate pressure and ordered McNamara to do something about ABM.

So, the Sentinel System, which later became the Safeguard System, began. The system was not to defend United States' cities against the Soviet Union, a mission judged infeasible at the time, but to protect parts of the United States against a Chinese threat that was believed to be emerging. While the Chinese threat never reached the proportions that the Safeguard System was built to handle in those early days, it provided a rationale for continuing the program despite the results of McNamara's studies. But, the uncertainties they generated about the technological promise of ABM systems in general led the United States to propose and seriously pursue negotiations with the Soviets that led to the SALT I ABM treaty.

With existing technology, ABM defenses could not prevent an offensive attack, and they would not be less costly than offensive forces. That is, if an ABM defense was installed, the offense could add more offensive ballistic missiles at less cost. The effect of these two features made the ABM destabilizing in a couple of ways. It was destabilizing in crisis because it presented targets to the adversary, such as large surveillance radars that he had high incentive to kill early and with little warning. Secondly, it was arms-race destabilizing because it produced incentives for the other side to add to its offensive forces. Therefore, we pursued an ABM treaty believing that the deployment of ineffective ABM systems was destabilizing and would not benefit the strategic balance between the United States and the Soviet Union.

There was also a belief that if we concluded a treaty on ballistic missile defense, it might set the stage for restraints on offensive ballistic missiles—particularly in reducing numbers. In SALT I, the ABM treaty and restraints on offensive weapon systems were jointly addressed; a treaty was negotiated on ABM defenses and an interim agreement was reached on constraining strategic offensive weapon systems.

The interim agreement was to be changed, improved, strengthened, and ultimately lead to a treaty. That never happened. In any event, in the aftermath of SALT I, we lived in a world where the United States and the Soviet Union relied on mutually assured destruction—the ability to retaliate against one another in the event of a nuclear attack by the other party. It was this standoff of terror that maintained stability and strategic military balance throughout these years. This was the MAD world, relying on mutually assured destruction for the preservation of peace. Since 1972, when the ABM treaty was signed, a number of occurrences have affected some segments of the American political spectrum more than others. People who were concerned about the strength of the United States and worried about the Soviet threat tended to be the conservative, right-wing element; it has become increasingly aggravated about U.S. policy since 1972.

Clearly, by 1980, the strategic balance was worrisome. Even people who were unenthusiastic about investing in defenses recognized that the state of balance was not only parity—which is what we patronizingly declared it to be when the SALT I negotiations were completed—but many people felt that the United States was unequipped to deal with the emerging Soviet military threat. Our intercontinental ballistic missiles (ICBMs) were vulnerable because the Soviets had improved their strategic ballistic missile forces. The number of individual weapons they carried had increased by a factor of four since the ABM treaty was concluded; their ICBMs were more reliable and more accurate; moreover, they had been MIRVed, that is, the Soviets put more than a single weapon on their ICBMs. Some ICBMs had ten or fourteen weapons, and they were each independently targetable with high accuracy. Consequently, the United States found that critical elements of its nuclear forces needed to assure retaliation—the ICBM force in particular—were vulnerable to a first strike by the Soviets.

Secondly, huge defensive disparities had developed. The United States was more affected by the 1972 ABM treaty than the Soviet Union, not because the treaty required it, but because the United States had chosen to act that way. When the treaty was signed, both countries said they would pursue a vigorous R&D program to investigate ballistic missile defense and make sure that they were not caught unaware of new possibilities based on advanced technology. But with the signing of the ABM treaty, interest in ABM declined in the United States. There was a small element in the U.S. Army that was responsible for ABM R&D, but that was not the place to be assigned. It was not a good career choice because it was not an activity in which a career could be made; it was unlikely that any program could succeed to the point of deployment, it lacked money, and it was forever constrained by a Congress that feared it might produce a threat to the ABM treaty. The U.S. ABM program became stultified. The Soviets, on the other hand, maintained substantial momentum in their program.

While the Soviets, for the most part, observed the ABM Treaty, they implemented a vigorous R&D program apparently intended to develop an ABM system that would be good enough for widespread deployment. It was not unreasonable; it is compatible with Soviet thinking about treaties as temporary accommodations in a continual process rather than ultimate solutions of basic problems—as is often the case in the United States.

The Soviets had an ABM system. The United States had none (it had completed defenses protecting the one site allowed by the treaty and subsequent protocols, declared them operational, and then deactivated them immediately because they were too expensive to maintain). The Soviet system was deployed around Moscow, it became operational shortly after the ABM treaty went into effect, and it has been maintained since then. It is now being improved. The Soviet Union had a formidable air defense system; the United States, after the beginning of the 1960s, had chosen to dismantle its air defenses because there was little point in maintaining them with their vulnerability to ballistic missile attack. The Soviets had massive air defenses, plans for passive defense, plans for protection of key population segments, and plans for the dispersion of industry. There was nothing comparable in the United States. When wars are fought on a computer—which is where nuclear wars are fought and hopefully will continue to be fought—unbalanced defenses have extreme effects on the outcome. They have destabilizing effects that upset the apparent strategic balance—particularly when one looks at the effects of a first strike by the defended side so that the other side can only retaliate with a ragged attack by remaining forces.

The situation continued to be worrisome. It was unbearable for many people that we had chosen not to do anything about ballistic missile defense while the Soviets apparently were pursuing it to be able to deploy a nationwide system. There was a growing conviction that the source of trouble was the existence of the ABM treaty. Some serious looks were taken at new possibilities of ballistic missile defense, but with available technology, there was not much to do. One could defend very hard targets where attacking reentry vehicles (RVs) could be intercepted deep in the atmosphere so that the atmosphere could be used to discriminate RVs from decoys. Ballistic missile silos, for example, could withstand the nuclear detonation associated with intercepts at short ranges, but a city could not survive under those conditions. In short, only a very narrow set of targets, really very hard ballistic missile silos, could survive the kind of defense that could be provided with available technology.

A big problem in all ballistic missile defense considerations is the relationship between offense and defense. The offense always has the option of including countermeasures that vastly complicate the defensive problem, and in looking at the technology available to the defense, it appeared that earlier conclusions about the offense dominating nuclear war would hold true. Defense simply could not keep pace with it. But the situation appeared to change: tremendous advances in technology became available. New sensors, new opportunities to process huge amounts of data, new nonnuclear kill mechanisms, and the possibility of deploying defensive elements in space made it possible to do what had not been done before.

Behind this new technology was a strong lobby for doing something about ballistic missile defense. If a truly revolutionary ballistic missile defense could be developed that freed itself from the limitations of old technology, one could leapfrog many of the offense's advantages, such as penetration aids, MIRVs, and so on. It would change the entire nature of the confrontation. This had particular appeal to people who were dismayed at the growth in Soviet military power, an element in sync with President Reagan. There was a lot of pressure for a move in this direction. It ultimately led to a reaction by the president. His reaction was based on a deepening concern about the confrontation with the Soviets derived from the deteriorating strategic balance. He faced the problem of what to do about increasingly vulnerable ICBMs without any good options. His concerns were heightened by a doctrinaire perception of the Soviet Union as the principal enemy and problem—a genuine military threat that had to be dealt with militarily. All these factors drove him to take a significant and revolutionary step to improve the military situation.

He reacted to the idea of living under the circumstances of mutually assured destruction. I think he really felt, as many people do, that being able to survive, being able to count on peace only because of a balance of terror, was an inappropriate way to live—however effective it may have been for all these years. It was just not right. There were better, more ethical foundations available for avoiding nuclear war than mutual threats of nuclear destruction. Reliance on strategic defenses good enough to prevent the arrival of ballistic missiles carrying nuclear weapons seemed a far better way to keep control. Such thinking was a very personal, Reaganesque reaction that is fundamental to understanding his remarkable commitment to the SDI.

The whole technology challenge appealed to President Reagan. It was going to the moon again, but bigger. It captured the enthusiasm of an optimist, someone who had faith in the future and who believed that we could do anything if we put our minds to it. This is a very Reaganesque line. If we just really knuckle down and think right, we can do it; the technological challenge was just that. He clearly was helped by a close association with Edward Teller, the so-called father of the hydrogen bomb, an outstanding physicist by any standards who had been moved by the opportunities emerging in technology to press for another look at ballistic missile defense.

Reagan produced the kind of plaintive hope that underlies the SDI: that free people could live secure knowing that their security would not rest on the threat of instant retaliation; that, instead, we could deter a Soviet attack—that we could intercept and destroy strategic ballistic missiles before they reached the soil of the United States or our allies. This seemed to him to be the basis for looking at a new world and a substantially better situation for the future. Thus, he announced that he was directing a comprehensive effort to define a long-range R&D program to achieve the ultimate goal of limiting the threat posed by strategic missiles. This could pave the way for arms control measures that would eliminate the weapons. The theory was that if one could produce defenses that were good enough to prevent ICBMs from getting through, then one could convince the other side that the better course was to develop and use those defenses and do away with strategic ballistic missiles altogether. Such are the basic underpinnings of the SDI; whether they constitute an adequate foundation is another question, but they served to define the program and give it an air of technological millenarianism that set it apart from normal weapons acquisition programs.

Shortly after the president's announcement, the Defense Technology Study was undertaken to look at what could be done. It was the first attempt to look at the whole problem in an integrated fashion to see what technological advances were required. It identified the technologies that needed to be pursued and what appeared most promising. It identified the specific uncertainties associated with the major challenge of SDI: developing absolutely new weapons that were a gleam in somebody's eye; such as the nuclear-driven X ray laser, which uses a nuclear bomb to put the energy into a laser generating X rays of sufficient intensity to destroy an incoming reentry vehicle, and establishing command and control over a huge array of individual platforms, sensors, and decision making mechanisms to produce a system that would make the decision about whether or not the time to go to war had come. It was a tremendous challenge.

The other item that came out of the Defense Technology Study was the concept of layered defenses. No single ballistic missile defense is good enough to intercept all incoming ICBMs. One has to have layers of defenses to do it. If there are 1,000 ICBMs carrying 10,000 individual weapons being deployed, all 10,000 weapons will not be destroyed in one layer; you get 90 percent; then 90 percent of the 10 percent that get through; and so on until you winnow the weapons down to where a final mop-up job of conventional ABM defenses can be made. But this assumes that the defense system can catch and destroy boosters just coming off the pad or postboost vehicles before they disperse individual weapons; it has to begin to kill the weapons that survive and are dispersed in midflight (if there is time) and it has to have defenses in the target area that would intercept the weapons that survived. The study characterized the challenge as formidable, but it saw promise in the contribution of new technologies and it sketched out a program to start meeting the challenge.

In the aftermath, the Strategic Defense Initiative Organization (SDIO)has been formed. It is separate from all regular lines of command over military R&D. The SDIO operates its own shop; it now has about 200 people and will grow somewhat larger. In 1985, it spent $1.5 billion, and this year it is expected to spend $2.75 billion. Ultimately, the SDI'S cost over the first five years has been estimated to be $26 billion. This is a research program trying to determine whether or not new technology will really make ballistic missile defense possible. It is a tremendous undertaking working in the face of great uncertainty and difficulty. One of the more important things that the SDI organization has done is to create a number of horse-race contracts. A number of contractors are trying to put together architectures for the entire system. They are inventing the way in which the entire SDI system can be put together so that the various parts will work to produce the protection.

Work is underway across a range of technology areas. Sensors able to detect, track, and discriminate incoming reentry vehicles are being investigated, as are laser technology and particle-beam weapons that can discriminate, track, and kill attacking reentry vehicles. Kinetic energy weapons, normal interceptors that are terminally guided missiles or dartlike weapons that can be fired from electro-magnetic launchers at unbelievable speeds are being developed. Underlying such efforts is a range of basic research dealing with materials, power sources, and so on.

In short, a huge program is underway. One of the early efforts enlisted the participation of U.S. allies in the program. The effort was pursued through the established relationships for joint participation in military R&D, and it involved government relationships as well as national laboratories, universities, and companies working with the SDI organization. There are no special programs set aside for the allies; they must, under U.S. law, compete with American companies or team with them in competitive proposals to win SDI contracts.

There are many concerns about allied perceptions of the SDI. There is widespread debate about whether it is a good idea or not. The debate involves a number of issues. What are the appropriate goals for the SDI? President Reagan has said that we will have a system good enough to defend people and cities and eliminate the threat of ballistic missiles. There is skepticism about that goal, and there are doubts, particularly in the scientific community, that the technology is good enough to achieve it. People who are not enthusiastic about the SDI argue that it must fulfill the president's promise and insist that if it won't do so, its utility is questionable. They also argue that as the visionary goals begin to crumble, the whole program will only be justified as a source of new jobs.

The Defense Department has taken a less ambitious view—saying that the SDI will look, in the short term, at opportunities to improve the strategic balance and to exploit technology until it is possible to develop defensive weapons that are attractive economically at the margin; to develop a broader based deterrent; and ultimately, to find greater reliance in defensive capability. Such a view softens substantially the ultimate goal of the SDI. First because it asks for economic consideration and proven technology. Only then, hopefully in the early 1990s, would a decision on deployment be made. If it appears that significant payoffs will result from deployment, we will negotiate it with the Soviets. People who object to the SDI characterize this scenario as unrealistic.

Much of the debate involves disagreement about feasibility. People who favor the SDI argue that the United States can complete the SDI if the country is willing, and others argue that the technology is inadequate for the job. There are serious questions about the ability of SDI elements to meet necessary technical performance requirements, whether or not the system will survive, and whether it can deal with countermeasures that the other side will employ. The old offense/defense confrontation still cannot be settled.

Another big issue is arms control. The ABM treaty is the remaining anchor in the arms control situation; it is the one accomplishment that has held firm to date. If the SDI dislodges the treaty and leads to its demise, there is fear that the whole arms control picture will fall apart. Proponents of the SDI contend, instead, that it will give the United States better leverage for arms control discussions. The short term appears to be a good time to achieve arms control agreements, but the agreements may come at the expense of the SDI. There is some indication that Soviet objections to the SDI are strong enough that they will move in arms control directions that they have not wanted to pursue previously. SDI proponents say that the Soviets will do whatever they want, so there is no reason to worry about their reaction. People who oppose it express fears that the Soviets will react violently. The Soviets have made threats about ominous consequences if the United States persists in pursuing the SDI. Proponents say the cost of the SDI is worth it; opponents say it costs too much. Nobody knows what it would cost. The minimum is in the hundreds of billions of dollars, but the exact cost is uncertain because no one knows what the system will comprise.

There is also the question of how the allies will react to a deployment decision. Opponents say the allies hate it, and that more trouble will be caused by tearing up NATO and our allied relationships than will be offset by the SDI's benefits. People who favor the SDI insist that the allies should like it because it benefits them, too. In fact, there is a lot of allied concern about the SDI; much of it concerns upsetting the status quo, particularly in the arms control arena. The allies tend to see the ABM treaty as an important element that must be preserved. The SDI has also upset expectations of a stable relationship between the United States and the Soviet Union, and it is uncertain how that will develop. The British and French are concerned that if the United States deploys ballistic missile defenses, the Soviets will respond, and the result will be that their strategic weapons and ability to deter the Soviets will lose value. There is also a concern that if there is a standoff in the nuclear world, it will free the Soviets for nonnuclear, conventional military ventures. That is a worrisome possibility because of the imbalance of conventional forces in Europe. There are people who believe, on the other hand, that if the Soviet Union and the United States achieve SDI defenses, nuclear war may still erupt in Europe, which lacks such protection.

Canadians share some of those views, and they have rejected government-to-government participation in SDI without really rejecting SDI itself. The Canadian government has made it possible for private institutions to play in the game; it is important to Canada because of

NORAD and the thirty years of cooperation that we have had in providing North American defense. The nature of that defense will change
with the SDI. Cruise missiles and bombers will become more of a
problem. There is a good deal of skepticism in Canada about technology
transfer and the readiness of the United States to transfer technology as
part of an SDI relationship. Allied concerns present a problem to Americans enlisting support and participation in the SDI.

Three features of the SDI are particularly radical and worrisome.
One is the technological millenarianism that strongly flavors it, a belief
that come the millennium and the deployment of a full blown SDI
system, we will have a new world where the most salient sources of
today's anguish will be eliminated. If we can implement the SDI through
the mysterious workings of science and technology, we will be out of an
unacceptable situation and have produced a new and better one. That is
a remarkable expectation for the normally pragmatic United States to
pursue. Secondly, it is a commitment to strategic defense that is revolutionary for the United States. Finally, it is a long-term program facing
uncertain returns. The United States may be a good sprinter, but it has
never been a good long-distance runner, and the tournaments that one
must enter to preserve any defense program in the United States are
formidable. The belief that the program manager, even if it is the
president, can survive all of the procedural hurdles needed to pull off
the SDI is questionable.

The United States has embraced the SDI enthusiastically. The Soviet
Union, with a whole set of different predilections and characteristics,
has reacted in horror at the suggestion. Such behavior constitutes a role
reversal between the United States and the Soviet Union in addressing
the questions of strategic defense and distant defense goals. In the
defense arena, the United States deals with pragmatic engineering; it is
not heavily committed to the mysterious workings of science. It likes
pragmatic decisions based on determinations of military need, cost, and
effectiveness. These determinations must be made repeatedly as the
acquisition process posits new challenges when each budget or development milestone is reached.

Remarkably, the United States has never made a commitment to
strategic defense. In the aftermath of World War II, attention was given
to finding a defense against bombers; the Soviets were building them in
large numbers—or at least we believed they were—and we responded
by producing and deploying several thousand surface-to-air missiles.
But with the appearance of Soviet ICBMs, the enthusiasm for air defenses in the absence of ballistic missile defenses waned, and through
the 1960s and 1970s, we effectively dismantled them. We did the same
thing with civil defenses. We chose not to pursue ballistic missile defense except grudgingly, and when we finally deployed the initial elements of a system, we chose not to maintain them after negotiating an

ABM treaty that allowed them. The cost of maintaining and operating so expensive a system cannot be justified by an assessment of its benefits.

Finally, the scope of our defenses has remained limited. Even if we get an SDI that is effective against strategic ballistic missiles, we still face the problem of dealing with cruise missiles and bomber aircraft; we have no air defenses. We have no civil defenses, no real protection for selected population segments that would be required if the SDI became a reality. We do a poor job of sustaining defenses with limited capabilities; we insist on total effectiveness against a threat that is expected to respond to our every defensive move.

The Soviets have a different approach to these matters. Glorification of science was a basic tenet of early Russian revolutionaries; they relied on science to get out of problems in the early years—that occurred in Lenin's time and in the early days of the Bolshevik revolution, when there was a tremendous effort to get the commitment of science for service to the state in solving critical problems. Betting on science and what it can do in the future is not foreign to the Soviet Union. True, if there are any orthodox Soviet dialectical materialists left, they might have dialectical problems with an SDI or a defense-dominated world as the ultimate stopping place. It is not dialectically satisfying. Soviet military doctrine has had a temporal flavor in establishing doctrine appropriate for the historical situation, although it has been slow to change.

Nevertheless, the Soviets are used to pursuing long-distance goals that they never quite reach; but they continue to believe the goals will ultimately provide a better life. This faith has persisted even in the absence of obvious indications that the goals are attainable. Soviet commitment to developing strategic defense is an example. They have built a tremendous air defense, starting immediately after World War II to build the greatest collection of interceptor aircraft in the world. Through the years, they have deployed approximately ten surface-to-air missile defense systems, which they continually improve over the years in making them responsive to changes in the threat. They have about 12,000 missiles on launchers placed in the Soviet Union. They have one ABM system deployed, and another ABM system ready to be deployed —some six years before the United States could begin to deploy any kind of an ABM system. They have passive defenses and extensive countermeasures, and they have made provisions for protecting selected parts of the country's population. None of these systems is entirely satisfactory individually, and the total set of strategic defenses will not protect the Soviet Union fully. But through accretion, the systems have continually been improved.

More importantly, their development of new strategic defenses apparently includes all the basic elements in the SDI. Research on appropriate technology and exploratory development of SDI-like systems has been undertaken in the Soviet Union for a long time. But, it is done with a low profile, without all the hoopla of the SDI, and little is said about it. The Soviets have a high-energy laser program that is substantially larger than the U.S. program; it involves 10,000 scientists and engineers; they work at six R&D facilities and test ranges. There are ground-based lasers with an antisatellite capability, and they have an R&D program using ground-based lasers for ballistic missile defense that could be tested in the 1990s. There are several types of air defense lasers reportedly under development, and they are developing airborne lasers. There are both space-based and ground-based particle-beam weapon programs; they are working on kinetic energy weapons of the sort mentioned earlier as part of the SDI. A whole range of antisatellite systems are under development, and a vigorous military space program is in the offing. In short, a substantial program heading in the same direction as the SDI is underway.

The Soviets have the ability to sustain such a program for a long time. Their doctrine gives the military the responsibility of coping with war if it occurs. While war is not sought, the military is responsible for developing and maintaining the capability to deal with it. Important to fulfilling that role is a concept of damage limiting that is entirely different from the U.S. preoccupation with achieving complete effectiveness. Damage limiting is sought in the belief that, should war occur, every bit of defense helps. It will not prevent widespread destruction, but it enables the Soviet military to better pursue a war if required. Thus, what they get out of a limited ballistic missile defense system is important. Their air defenses are important and passive defenses play a role. They will go a long way in mitigating the damage of a nuclear war. Many of the systems we snickered about when they first debuted have been improved until they have become truly formidable and effective defenses; the Soviets have inched their way into effectiveness rather than achieving it in one large program. Rather than making an investment in a super system expected to be highly effective from the start, the Soviets invest in a standing capability to develop, deploy, and improve weapon systems continually. If a weapon system is cancelled, existing capabilities develop another system.

Who is outfitted better to pursue the SDI, the United States or the Soviet Union? The Soviet Union is far better equipped to do so than the United States. But, the Soviet reaction to the SDI is fear and loathing. They have reacted strongly to the SDI, and they have taken steps to counter it. Reasons for this fear and loathing are basic mistrust and the belief that it is a U.S. attempt to get a first-strike capability. The contention that the United States will provide SDI technology to the Soviet Union is met with skepticism, just as we would receive similar offers made by the Soviet Union. It particularly aggravates the Soviets that every time they get somewhere in the strategic confrontation, the

United States tries to change the rules of the game. The SDI is another attempt by the United States at strategic theology intended to disadvantage them. The Soviets are concerned about an U.S. attempt to render obsolete their military accomplishments of the past twenty years. Soviet achievement of the status of great power was derived from their accomplishments in developing strategic and tactical military forces. They have become a military force on the world scene. But, they are less a moral force than in the past, and they are neither an economic nor a cultural force. The SDI threatens the area in which they have to be taken seriously.

Most importantly, however, the technological challenge posed by SDI is one they do not want. They would prefer to pursue their SDI-like program without competing with the United States. The Soviets would much rather quietly do their own thing, and stick to the rules of the ABM treaty for as long as possible by not challenging the treaty rather than getting into head-to-head competition with U.S. technology. They are not mistaken in that preference; they are substantially behind the West in many areas of technology that are important to SDI—such as computers, data processing capabilities, spacecraft technology, and so forth.

The Soviets are trying to stop the SDI fast. It is characterized in orchestrated propaganda as destabilizing, threatening, and destructive to arms control. An association of Soviet scientists has said that the SDI is technically impossible and will not work. There have been many arms control initiatives, all promising progress in arms control, but all have abandoned the SDI. Clearly, there will be military measures taken. Offensive countermeasures will be developed, although it is hard to determine what they will entail because the SDI is not well-defined. The number of ballistic missile RVs is not likely to decline. The Soviets, however, will push their cruise missile program even more vigorously and introduce new bombers and associated weapons.

One of the more intriguing and likely effects of the SDI has been its boosting of the Soviets' SDI program. As noted above, there are many scientists and engineers who are working on systems based on "other physical principles" that must appear crazy to many people in the Soviet Union. All of a sudden, their questionable efforts gained cachet as the United States announced its belief in the promise of such work. If the SDI has done anything, it has pumped energy into the Soviets' own form of the SDI. We need to worry about that because of the much greater compatibility of the SDI with the Soviet way of operating.

The arms control problem is serious. The people who wrote the ABM treaty had the prescience to recognize that we would deal with questions when ABM systems employing "other physical principles" were conceived, and they made provisions in the treaty for accommodations. They hoped that provisions could be made in technical terms by a group like the Standing Consultative Commission, which has met regularly to deal with the questions, uncertainties, and complaints that arise about the ABM treaty between the two sides. It will no longer be possible to do that. With the SDI, the problem of dealing with new ABM systems has such a high profile that its resolution has assumed great political significance. The SDI has raised hopes and concerns about these new systems in both countries to a level where the ABM treaty will become meaningless if it does not deal with them through some sort of accommodation, which has become very hard to do.

It is disturbingly easy to envision that the United States will work at the SDI for a few years and then decide that it really is too hard, that it costs too much, and that it will not be effective if the Soviets respond in appropriate ways. It may provide some protection, but some missiles will still get through. If we can't really protect ourselves against all possibilities, why blow $100 billion on this crazy system? It was a noble idea, but it is time to give up. We have all too frequently abandoned programs in such a fashion. The Soviets will not abandon their program. They are more apt to relentlessly pursue the program, deploy pieces of it, and accept that it does not do the whole job but it helps. Then, they will make improvements in the system until we are faced with something that looks like the SDI. The Soviet SDI may not be perfect, but we are sure to overrate its capabilities and then find that we face an imbalance in defenses that affects our strategic situation. We must find a way to deal with that possibility—either by putting the SDI under arms control constraints or, having started on this path, being tough, rigorous, and disciplined enough to stick with it.

There is an element of faith in this chiliastic approach. One has to believe that it will work, and one has to make commitments based on that faith; one has to be constant in that faith and live through the hard times along the way. We are not in a position where we can stop before we really know what the SDI's possibilities are because the threat of Soviet development and the hopes of our development are too great. Our allies are becoming involved and making a commitment to the whole approach of defense emphasis. Their hopes and concerns are tied to the SDI, and we cannot let them down by failing to stick with it until we know enough to make a good decision about whether or not to pursue it.

Many people believe that the SDI is the product of President Reagan's naivete about ABM systems and ballistic missile defense. That may be right, but Reagan's behavior after creating the SDI has been precisely right; he has been tough, unwilling to give an inch despite tremendous pressures, and he has never blinked in insisting that he will pursue the SDI to the bitter end. If one is to play in the SDI game, that is precisely the kind of behavior required.

Chapter Twelve

The United States and International Organizations: A Canadian Perspective

JOHN W. HOLMES

The common and shared purposes of the United States and Canada are elemental. They are the product of geography and history, and they are not deeply affected by changes of government. Nevertheless, in spite of the cult of the shamrock and the easy assumption that the foreign policies of the Mulroney government and the Reagan administration are in tune, there is a considerable divergence in our attitudes to international institutions. This divergence has existed in one way or another since we were both present at the creation of the United Nations in the 1940s. So long as we both regarded ourselves as active in the creation, each according to its status, the differences were healthy. Variant perspectives of a greater and a lesser power are natural, and the conflict between them produced a far more workable UN. (When I speak of the UN I am not talking about the General Assembly but about the wide system of agencies from the International Monetary Fund [IMF] to the UN Conference of Trade and Development that are integral parts of the unsystematic system.) Although one may not see the system as workable, the great power hegemony that Roosevelt, Churchill, and Stalin had planned before lesser-power intervention would have lasted six months at most. The system we shaped is ambiguous, flexible, and has been capable of organic growth—in wise and unwise directions. (Would we be better off with a free world UN—with the Second and Third Worlds still raging against us as outlaws?)

With its drift towards unilateralism and its scorn for the UN, however, the Reagan administration has turned away from its role as a creator—and far from being, as it was in the early days, a surrogate UN.

The Mulroney government, on the other hand, has reaffirmed the traditional Canadian belief in the essentiality of international institutions. The first speech from the throne stated: "Canada's opportunity to influence the course of world events lies primarily in sound multilateral institutions. That is as true of economics as it is of defense, of development, and disarmament." That note has been sounded consistently ever since.

It is too much to say that our actions have always matched our words, but the profession of faith is not mere hypocrisy. It is a gut recognition of national interest, more clearly seen when a party is in power and forced to survey the means available to guard our interests and exercise our due influence in a contentious world. Unilateralism may be—or seem to be—a possibility for the United States, the Soviet Union, and a perpetual illusion for France, Albania, or Burma, but it is not for us. The argument is functionalist rather than idealist. Weaker powers are more dependent on internationally agreed rules. It was, for instance, only by an appeal to the International Court that we reasonably settled our east coast maritime boundary dispute with the United States.

The Mulroney government has not been confrontational about these differences and, on the whole, that is good. We go about our own way in UNESCO, in the General Assembly, and over the Law of the Sea. We plan to be active in the UN session on disarmament and development, which the United States is boycotting. In practice, the foreign policies of a lesser or middle power are intrinsically different from a superpower. The ends may be compatible, but the ways and means have to be so different that the *weltanschauungen* are bound to diverge. The biggest difference is that Canada, unlike the United States, lives in the shadow of two superpowers. This is a fact of life—not a cause for resentment. International institutions extend our power rather than restrain it. One reason the practitioners of Canadian foreign policy enjoy international institutions is that they float more freely among the powers in international gatherings. There is a constant opportunity for coalition either to oppose or influence the superpowers.

Neither the United States nor Canada has any greater interest than the slow development of international regulation and order in the face of daunting odds. Many Americans—and a few Canadians—seem to have lost the vision, but we are wise in assuming that this is a temporary aberration. Denunciation is counterproductive. There are rifts within the UN and NATO that ought not to be widened by strong language. Countries prefer to change their policies without admitting that they were wrong. Allies do not normally engage in what could be called the denunciation of each other. In foreign offices, distinct from editorial offices, the prime minister's comments on the Tripoli raid would be recognized as less than a full endorsement. Stephen Lewis, the Canadian ambassador to the UN, used vivid language in criticizing the attitudes of the Heritage Foundation, which is close to powerful people in the Reagan administration, when he addressed the UN. The point, however, was made indirectly.

In spite of my unfashionable argument for quiet diplomacy in long-range interests, I am worried about the trend of American thinking on international institutions. Unilateral action by a great power can, at times, be justified. Likewise, unilateral action by a middle power was justified when, in the case of the Arctic Waters Pollution Prevention Act of 1970, Canada deliberately sought reform of international law. This should be rare. We can never ignore the consequences of precedents that weaken a fabric that has taken centuries to weave. So much more is expected of the United States (or Canada) than of the Soviet Union or Iran. That is why Americans are more bitterly criticized than other peoples. There are arguments for U.S. action against UNESCO, Libya, or for its somewhat arrogant positions in the IMF or the International Bank for Reconstruction and Development (IBRD). They look ominous, however, in the context of the contempt so often displayed for the UN General Assembly, the International Court, and the Law of the Sea, not to mention disloyal allies who fail to recognize that Uncle Sam knows best—or in that invitation to the UN, from a member of the U.S. mission several years ago, to sail off into the sunset from New York. I take comfort in the fact that anyone who could contrive sailing off into the sunset from New York would shortly land in New Jersey.

After that regrettable suggestion, President Reagan came to the General Assembly and affirmed the U.S. belief in the UN with reservations. There are now indications that some American policymakers have concluded that treating the General Assembly with aloof disdain has not paid, and that it would be better to go in and play the game. The game would be hardball, but the UN would at least be taken seriously. The greatest danger to the UN system is the cynical shrug.

In any case, the actions of the Reagan administration have not been in accordance with its harsh words. The administration is now the chief advocate of that great multilateral, if not necessarily egalitarian, UN structure known as GATT—more multilaterally minded in this case than Canada has been of late. The UN International Monetary Fund (IMF) was the only resort when the banking system was threatened by Latin American debts. Other UN agencies are called upon when there are problems of famine, refugees, or when the International Civil Aviation Organization (ICAO) can quietly work out regulations to prevent another KAL disaster. In spite of protests about politicization, there has been no desertion of the most essential elements of the UN system: the World Meteorological Organization (WMO), the World Health Organization (WHO), and the Universal Postal Union (UPU)—indispensable parts of the international infrastructure so successful that we take them for granted. These are UN bodies that are not dominated by the tyranny of the majority. In fact, however, the power of a majority in the General Assembly or even in UNESCO to do more than make gestures is greatly exaggerated by the Heritage Foundation and its ilk. We are moving, in practice, to a closer association of power and responsibility in international institutions of all kinds within and without the UN system. It is in the Canadian tradition to work for reform from the inside rather than by copping out. By no means are all UN bodies sacred, and we badly need a sunset law, but there is fear of a domino effect.

It is the corrosive cynicism about international institutions, the UN in particular, that poses the greatest threat to international order. The alternatives—the United States as world policeman, dual management by the superpowers, or rapid descent from strategic and economic protectionism to international anarchy and unrestrained global pollution, are rarely given the same critical attention as the less-than-utopian systems we have been building. There are international order arguments for and against the swift U.S. action on Grenada—as there were for the British action in the Falklands, but in both cases, the causes were diminished by the anachronistic and adolescent heroics that accompanied them. (In these dangerously unstable times, perhaps we could persuade our two historic friends to toss their favorite ballads, the "Battle Hymn of the Republic" and "Land of Hope and Glory" into the dustbin with "Deutschland uber Alles." Both, unfortunately, have splendid tunes, but the dreadful words are habit-forming—like what the French aptly call *stupéfiants*. For those whose eyes have seen the glory of the coming of the Lord, unilateralism may be a divinely endorsed foreign policy. As for "Wider still and wider shall thy bounds be set," it is surely a recipe for total bankruptcy. Today the Falklands, tomorrow St. Helena).

John Adams wrote ironically to Thomas Jefferson that "our pure, virtuous, public-spirited federative republic, will last forever, govern the globe, and introduce the perfection of man." The objection to that kind of unilateralism is not that it is ill-intentioned, but that it is quite impossible. It is the messianic streak in Americans that has led them astray—to unilateral excess at the Bay of Pigs, in Vietnam, and in Lebanon—not to mention Queenston Heights in the War of 1812. Still, the American enthusiasm is useful in helping us win a world war or constructing a viable world order. It is dangerous when it carries a chip on its shoulder. Canadians cannot have similar temptations, but we have our own issues. We have people who see Canada as a medium messiah with a divine mission to mediate. We must avoid the pious delusion that the weak are *ipso facto* more virtuous than the strong and recognize that our diplomatic hand is in some circumstances strengthened because we are not strong enough to intimidate.

When we look at the NATO alliance as an international institution, we argue that the sharing of decision making is essential if there will be burden sharing. We have to realize, however, that there is no hard and fast formula for policy sharing when there is such a disproportion of military, economic, and technological might. The issue is laden with paradox and the record is mixed. It is best not to struggle for precision. What matters is all-around sensitivity. The U.S. administration has been, on the whole, conscientious in consulting its allies on arms control strategy, but to change the whole game unilaterally by moving to the SDI is not easy to defend. Incidentally, the Canadian response to the SDI is a model of what I am advocating—to say simply and unprovocatively that the SDI does not fit our program.

It would be easier to be a loyal ally if the strategic thought and conscience of the Reagan administration were not so volatile and susceptible to Congressional whims. Not long ago, the allies were scourged for not joining in total ostracism of the Soviet Union, but when the president saw the light in Geneva, trade and cultural cooperation became the way to peaceful coexistence (and presumably the conversion of Russians to the true faith). Of late, we have been told that if we had all enforced tough economic sanctions against Libya, the Tripoli strike would not have been necessary. One is puzzled, therefore, to read about Washington's recent decision to sell bargain-basement grain to the Syrians, contrary to the International Wheat Agreement. I thought we had been told that Syria was as guilty as Libya of supporting terrorists. Who is it moral to starve this month? In more rational times, these contradictions might have been straightened out, but the moods of the moment are not rational.

When it comes to the sins of the UN, we are by no means entirely at cross-purposes. When I was stationed in Moscow, I sometimes thought that the Americans and the British overreacted to constant Soviet criticism. Then, one day *Pravda* attacked the Canadian Prime Minister, Louis St. Laurent, and I threw the bloody journal across the room. It is easier for Canadians than for Americans to view General Assembly debates with equanimity; we are rarely clobbered. We should be suitably modest about our ability to be clear headed in these circumstances, but we must remain clearheaded nevertheless. The United States has been unfairly abused and inadequately appreciated in many UN bodies. We both agree that in these bodies there are too many ridiculous schemes, gross extravagance, patronage, and inefficiency in international civil service— venal sins that we would never tolerate in free-world governments. The amount of money wasted, furthermore, would probably buy one good bomber—in the interest of international discipline.

A degree of firm resistance was required not only from the United States but from all the developed countries—within reason. My impression, after a month at the General Assembly last November, was that the threat of U.S. defection played a part in inducing a mood of sobriety.

There was impressive leadership by some intelligent and responsible Third World spokesmen who have realized that piling up majorities for raucous resolutions achieves nothing. They know that they can further their aims and make the UN function effectively only by building a consensus. That trend was strongly supported by Canada and many other western powers, but it was viewed sourly by the United States and its satellite, Margaret Thatcher. The financial crisis posed by the American withholding of funds has galvanized a new sense of responsibility on the part of both traditional middle powers like Canada, Australia, and the Scandinavians and major middle powers like Japan and Germany. The United States should welcome this shift, but it should also remember the somber warning by the deputy chairman of the delegation sent by Reagan to the final session of the Law of the Sea conference. Distressed by the administration's unwillingness to compromise, he wrote in *Foreign Affairs* that, "Our senior foreign policy makers should understand that once leadership is abdicated and the world finds that it can proceed without us, it will not be easy for the United States to reclaim its influence."

Whatever value there has been in the American tactic will be forfeited by continuing intransigence and sullenness. It encourages anarchical anti-Americanism and the alienation of friends. At the last General Assembly, the United States delegation did not just oppose the Soviets and the Third World. It all too frequently pressed the red button in isolation. Its instructions were so rigid that friends and allies would not go along. It is significant that on arms control resolutions, Canada's voting was close to Germany, Japan, the Netherlands, and Australia, but we were in the same column as the United States on only forty-nine resolutions out of seventy-one.

To align or not to align. That is *not* the question. Canadians are obsessively preoccupied with the relationship of our foreign policy to the United States. For some people, that seems to be the only criterion. For people in charge of foreign policy and new governments coming to power, this simple approach is beside the point. The whole world crowds in on them. We stand with the United States on the basics, but there are thousands of items on the agenda. There is no black or white choice. Even on issues such as Arctic sovereignty, where we oppose each other, neither can ignore certain underlying common interests of security and world law. (The use of absolute terms diverts us from shaping a wholesome Canadian policy. Neither independence nor loyalty is a sensible aim for Canadian foreign policy, although they are always considerations.) On most issues, it is not a matter of being for or against the United States. When we have the same view, we usually reach our own conclusions. It would be helpful if journalists could say at least occasionally that the United States supports the Canadian position. There are situations in which we and other allies voluntarily adjust to an

American position in the interests of solidarity for bargaining. We preserve, nevertheless, our right to judge when solidarity is required. The more enthusiastic Reaganities in Canada should realize that we cannot have a joint North American foreign policy. Even if we wanted to tie our policy to the United States, the United States could not tie its policy to a medium power, especially one that, for most Americans, is not so much a foreign state as a mirage.

Also, Canadians are obsessed with the risk of economic sanctions from the United States administration if we move out of step. Developing countries have been told bluntly by the Reagan administration that their votes in the General Assembly will be noted when decisions on aid are taken. As an ally, Canada would probably suffer if it consistently joined the hornet states that make life miserable in the UN for Americans. There are obvious incentives for tact on the eve, for example, of a crucial vote in the Finance Committee of the Senate. Allies, however, are by no means as defenseless as poor countries. The United States needs our support and our trade. Our condition is not just dependence but intervulnerability. Canada has had a long history of firm but rarely raucous differences with, or deviations from, the United States in all UN forums—including the last session of the General Assembly, but this has not affected the sale of our gas and lobsters. Relations with Canada are too important for the United States to be deterred by irritation over our position on UNESCO. Those who make policy in Washington, usually at cross-purposes with each other, are rarely aware of what Canada thinks about Nicaragua or the SDI. Our opponents on lumber or fish could exploit our deviant behavior in their own cause, but I am not aware of cases where they have done so. In any case, when the Wall Street press implements a scorched earth policy, as they did over National Energy Policy (NEP) and Foreign Investment Review Agency (FIRA), they do not worry about mere facts.

Canadians also have a tendency to demand bold initiatives on Canada's part. That is what attracts media attention—along with controversy. Only Stephen Lewis's more combative speeches against the Heritage Foundation, the Russians over Afghanistan, or male chauvinism in the UN are reported—not Lewis's tireless and by no means ineffective efforts to reconcile North and South and to organize a responsible group of leaders from the various camps to meet financial and other challenges in the UN. Canada has pursued a policy of damage limitation in UN bodies ever since Jeane Kirkpatrick came to New York to alienate as many people as possible and diminish the strength of the United States's arm. Ours is a pro-American policy. If I say that our continuing role is to lead the United States back to a saner approach toward multilateral institutions and to resume its leadership, I am aware that kind of claim makes Americans apoplectic. Americans would rather be hated than patronized. It has always been their task to guide other nations in the true path. It is now said in Washington that Americans should seek respect rather than love. We are in a good position to remind them of the reasons that they have been respected for over two centuries.

I hope Mulroney and Clark agree with what I say about the healing mission of Canada in the face of American waywardness; they have certainly sanctioned it. I hope, however, that they will not say so out loud—particularly with the prime minister's tendency to exaggerate. If I seem to be striking the middle messianic note I have just criticized, let me add that we are working in common with many other friends of the United States who share our worries about the exponential increase of irrational anti-Americanism in the world.

I wish there was room to be more specific about the useful things we have been doing and can do. A notable example witnessed at the recent General Assembly was the skillful effort of the Canadian delegation in making a resolution on the importance of techniques of verification for arms control. The Americans, the Russians, and the Indians were not happy about this, but they were put in a position they could not oppose. I draw attention to this because it is a cause, certainly compatible with NATO interest, to which Canada has devoted, over the years, a great deal of national effort from political strategists, seismologists, and other scientists.

According to press reports, the United States wants more action by NATO on terrorism, but Canada, along with other European countries, will try to turn the attention of Americans to the UN for this purpose. For the first time, last December, the General Assembly voted unanimously to denounce terrorism. There is now a universal will to cope with a universal scourge. That provides no miracle cure, but it is a consensus we can try to build upon. It cannot be done, however, if we assume that there is one international terrorist network. We are in a good position to make the point because last year far more Canadians than Americans or Israelis were killed by terrorist action—over 300. They were murdered in one dreadful crash by terrorists who could certainly not be blessed by Moscow or Tripoli. The chief suspect of the Air India crash was trained not in Libya but in Alabama, where good terrorists, known as mercenaries, improve their skills. The Russians are obviously concerned about terrorism, but their cooperation will not be engaged in an obviously American or Western crusade. Perhaps Canada and India, as last year's principal victims, could take the lead. We need a universal campaign if we are to cope with Libyans, Sikhs, and Armenians, who give us the most trouble, with the Red Brigades and the neofascists, state terrorism in Chile or Kampuchea, and the Animal Liberation Front. There is no easy formula within the United Nations, but I doubt if there is one outside it.

My role was probably supposed to be that of an analyst, but I couldn't resist the chance to preach. What I suggest is a way of approaching what could, if we are not prudent, be a major rift between Canada and the United States—the deep-seated reasons of which we are rarely conscious. I hope that Canadians will not be beguiled or intimidated into abandoning our faith and our hope for international institutions and our functional—rather than utopian—way of looking at them. To do so, we have to think like world citizens rather than neurotic nephews. We have to see our role as functionally—rather than morally—distinct. Above all, we have to overcome our national and continental parochialism and accept our own responsibility for helping to keep the world in equilibrium. We must also recognize the terrible burden on a superpower and the paradoxes of its position. It is not good enough just to tell the Americans what they ought to do. If we do all of this, we will have more than enough solid work ahead of us to satisfy our national craving for gratification, identification, and congratulation.

Part VIII

CONCLUSIONS: AN IMPRINT BUT NOT A REVOLUTION

Chapter Thirteen

Conclusions: An Imprint but Not a Revolution

BERT A. ROCKMAN

At this writing, the Reagan presidency is dealing with its deepest crisis. The recently released Tower Commission report portrays a rudderless presidency and, at best, an absent-minded president. Despite the salvaging efforts being undertaken—most importantly, the replacement of Donald Regan by Howard Baker as chief of staff—the political momentum of the Reagan administration appears to have been exhausted. This exhaustion of political momentum probably would have occurred even without the emergence of the Iran-contra escapades. The 1986 elections took the Senate from Republican hands, while the forthcoming 1988 elections have refocused attention, as they naturally tend to, from the present occupant of the White House to speculation regarding his successor.

Still, the unflattering portrait of the Reagan presidency that has been compiled over the last several months undoubtedly has reinforced the lame-duck status of the Reagan presidency. It is probably fair to say, therefore, that what we now see as its accomplishments are about the full story. If Reagan has brought forth a revolution, chances are that we have seen its farthest edge.

What do we make of the Reagan presidency as it winds down its tenure in Washington? Has it left marks that will long exceed its physical and direct political presence? Will it, in turn, be reversed? Will its definitions guide policy alternatives, institutional relationships, and norms, or will they have played out their special moment in the oscillations of historical political circumstance? The answer to all of these broad questions is affirmative. The impact of the Reagan presidency is both profound *and* passing—but in different respects. Identifying the different areas is what we need to do.

It is useful to focus on four arenas of presidential impact. The first of these arenas is institutions; the second is policies and agendas; the third is norms of governance (which links to institutions); and the fourth is presidential style. While the most profound impact of the Reagan presidency may lie in the policy agenda that its fiscal policies have provoked, especially the massive deepening of the federal deficit, perhaps the most immediately significant feature of the Reagan presidency has been to politicize institutions while polarizing politics.[1] The Reagan administration has made unusual efforts to imprint its philosophy and outlook in its stated policies and in governing institutions. Thus, it has tried to use to the fullest all available tools for shaping other institutions—notably the federal bureaucracy and the judiciary (and to some degree, state and local governments) to its perspective. Despite the general popularity enjoyed until recently by President Reagan, the sharply sculpted ideology of the Reagan presidency also has induced a degree of political polarization that is quite remarkable by recent standards.

THE REAGAN PRESIDENCY AND AMERICAN GOVERNING INSTITUTIONS

How has the Reagan presidency affected American governing institutions? The answer to this question ranges from a lot to a little and, in some respects, it has caused resistance—especially in Congress. The following discussion shows the Reagan administration's impact on four institutional structures: the judiciary; the executive system—including the bureaucracy and the institutional presidency; the Congress; and the federal system.

Effects on the Judiciary

Despite the status of the federal judiciary as a coequal branch of government, its composition is completely dependent on the other branches of government. The judiciary is appointed by the president with the approval of the Senate. Typically, appointments to the federal judiciary follow partisan lines. Democratic presidents overwhelmingly select Democrats to the bench; Republican presidents select Republicans. Many of these appointments, however, are only nominally partisan. Moreover, over time, the expectation is that a mix of presidential administrations will produce a blend of judicial ideologies in the federal court system.

Probably because the Reagan administration has staked out strong

---

[1]Bert A. Rockman, "Government under President Reagan," in *Jahrbuch zur Staats und Verwaltungswissenschaft—1986*, ed. Thomas Ellwein, Joachim-Jens Hesse, Renate Mayntz, and Fritz Scharpf (Nomos Verlag, 1987).

claims on many social positions and has an important constituency pressing for those claims, this administration has subjected candidates for nomination to the federal bench to an exceptional degree of political and ideological scrutiny. A special assistant to the attorney general has organized prenomination interviews with potential nominees to evaluate their willingness to meet Reagan administration guidelines of judicial philosophy and, even more concretely, to meet its positions on some key issues.[2]

Beyond the extent to which the Reagan White House has scrutinized judicial candidates for their conformity to its political philosophy, it also has made a special effort to recruit young candidates whose tenure on the bench will be lengthy. The idea is to ensure that the Reagan imprint on the federal bench will be as durable as possible. The fact that the Senate, which must approve nominations to the bench, has passed into Democratic hands and that the president's political glitter has begun to tarnish means more obstacles will be thrown in the path of purely ideological appointments. But the controversial case of Daniel Manion, appointed to the Court of Appeals in the Seventh Circuit after an exceedingly close vote on the Senate floor, actually shows that only issues of extreme incompetency (or in some instances, racist or sexist indiscretions) provide a basis for opposition to ideologically controversial nominees. Ironically, by making as many nominees as possible adhere to the administration's standards of judicial ideology, fewer cases stand out as ideologically extreme.

Since the Reagan administration apparently will appoint more than half of all sitting judges on the federal bench by the end of its term, the administration's strategies are designed to ensure a fundamental and reasonably durable conservative redirection of the federal judiciary.[3] From an institutional stand, the Reagan revolution can stake its largest claims here—especially if one more of the currently sitting Supreme Court Justices can be replaced by the president's candidate.

Effects on the Federal Executive

The Reagan administration came to Washington with a fundamental commitment to achieve a redirection of American government. One important strategic element in the long-run achievement of its vision has been saturating the judiciary with judges who share the administration's judicial philosophy—particularly in regard to arresting the expansion of constitutionally interpreted rights. That, of course, is for the

---

[2]Ronald Cohen, "Conservatives Step up Efforts to Promote Reagan-Minded Judges to U.S. Bench," *National Journal* 17 (1985), pp. 1560–63.

[3]Ronald Brownstein, "With or without Supreme Court Changes, Reagan Will Reshape the Federal Bench," *National Journal* 16 (1984), pp. 2338–2441.

long-run. More immediately, however, another critical strategic element in the Reagan administration's efforts to get government to respond to its agenda has been to politicize and centralize the White House relationship to the federal bureaucracy.[4]

These developments—politicization and centralization—have happened for some time now, although they have manifested somewhat differently during different presidencies. American presidents, unlike many European prime ministers, do not rub elbows with senior career officials. In Europe and Japan, leading political officials often have been civil servants; they have virtually always headed ministries; and almost always have had, and remain in, close and continuous contact with senior civil servants. Not since Eisenhower has an American president had some of this experience. Among twentieth century presidents, only Franklin Roosevelt's administrative role in the Navy and especially Herbert Hoover's role as Secretary of Commerce gave them experience as the civilian heads of administrative units. Like other political leaders, American presidents crave responsiveness. Unlike other countries' political leaders, senior civil servants rarely play a direct role in shaping policy because of their insulation from both White House and departmental sources of policy. In the United States, the senior servants of the state are regarded merely as government employees.

For many reasons, bureaucrats and bureaucracy are negative symbols in the United States. The last two presidencies—Carter and Reagan —especially pounded hard on this negative symbolism. In a querulous populist gesture, each president complained about how unresponsive and inefficient the government they were to lead had become.

But aside from the symbolic beating to which bureaucrats have been subjected, concrete manifestations of greater political control over the executive are obvious. More and more politically appointed officials have been layered between the top political leadership of departments and the senior civil service. For some time, the Office of Management and Budget (OMB) has become a president's post for central command to the departments rather than a simple clearinghouse for legislative proposals and budgets. Increasingly, also, presidents (or members of their staffs) have done endruns around the departments both making and implementing policy on the sly. This is most evident in foreign affairs. Former Secretary of State Kissinger and Nixon, for example, brewed foreign policy from the White House, and in the recent Iran-contra affair, policy and diplomatic initiatives were concocted quite removed from normal channels.

---

[4]Terry Moe, "The Politicized Presidency" in *The New Direction in American Politics*, ed. John E. Chubb and Paul E. Peterson (Washington, D.C.: Brookings Institution, 1985).

Like the Nixon administration in its later stages, the Reagan administration came to the White House convinced that command of the administrative apparatus was essential. Like the Nixon White House before it, the bureaucracy and career officials were seen by the Reagan entourage as politically unsympathetic and linked more closely to congressional sources of authority than to the presidential administration. The objective of the Reagan administration, therefore, was to cut the career bureaucracy off from as many alternative outlets of authority as possible.

One way to do this was ensuring, as with its nominees to the courts, that persons appointed by the administration—especially in the critical subcabinet regions of the department, possessed the right stuff. Additionally, by making use of the more liberal provisions of rules governing the Senior Executive Service, under the Civil Service Reform Act passed during the Carter administration, the Reagan administration has concentrated additional political appointments in organizational units of special policy or political salience.

Another way of controlling the executive was to concentrate highly active review processes at the center of the executive. In particular, external regulatory behavior of agencies toward society was diminished while internal regulatory behavior from the Executive Office of the Presidency (EOP) was expanded. Processes of centralizing decision making while decentralizing programs were key elements of the Reagan White House strategy for gaining greater control over the executive branch.

On the whole, the Reagan strategy was to politicize and to deinstitutionalize—since many of the prevailing institutions were biased toward programs and governmental interventions that the Reagan administration opposed or wished to redirect. A presidency of radical aims is not compatible with a high degree of institutionalization. By definition, of course, politicization means that personnel and mechanisms of control are reversible and, as some advocates of this process have argued, when political fortunes change, the opportunities for the other side to do the same also will be enlarged.

The impermanent aspect, therefore, of the Reagan presidency's relation to the executive branch lies in the ideological imprimatur that it has bestowed. The more durable aspect of this relationship, however, is the intensive fortification of the processes of politicization and centralization. The Reagan White House did not invent these processes; it has, however, strongly reinforced the acceptability of their underlying norms.

Effects on Congress

Since presidents don't directly influence congressional operations or organization, their impact is likely to be derived from broader political forces—the extent, for example, to which they are perceived to be at the head of an emerging dominant coalition, the degree to which they are perceived as expressing strong popular sentiments, the extent to which a president is viewed as a leader of significant repute in Washington circles (which, in turn, derives from standing among broader public circles), and the degree to which presidential legislative strategies and capacities to mobilize political support are respected.

During the first year of the Reagan presidency, many of these elements came together in a positive way for the administration's legislative program. The Democratic opposition, having lost the Senate and having been severely weakened in the House, was dispirited and confused by the political tide that was perceived as overtaking it. A president claiming a new agenda, endowed with increased popularity following the attempt on his life in late March, possessing excellent oratorical abilities, and equipped with a highly professional legislative liaison and political staff took advantage of these assets within the context of the electoral upheaval of 1980 and the resulting loss of the Democratic opposition's moorings. Reagan enjoyed phenomenal success in quantitative terms during the 1981 congressional session—a success rate of 82.4 percent, the highest rate since Lyndon Johnson's storied successes in 1965. But his special success was in the long-term influence of the legislative program passed in that year.[5]

This momentum, however, was soon arrested, in part a consequence of the budgetary stalemate produced by the successes of 1981. Reagan's success scores began to slip to normal levels after this first, but profound, round of successes. Particularly on fiscal and tax matters, the nature of this stalemate seemed to bring forth strong collective leadership within Congress—especially among the Republican Chairs of the Budget and Finance Committees, Pete Domenici and Bob Dole, and the Republican Floor Leader, Howard Baker. The initiative on these matters increasingly passed from the White House to key Republican leaders in the Senate. The bargains reached with their Democratic counterparts in the House produced a tax increase in 1983, known euphemistically as revenue enhancement. At least on the tax side, Congress reacted with strong collective leadership in spite of the conventional wisdom that targets Congress as a source of little fiscal discipline.

Like other presidencies, the Reagan administration has enjoyed sporadic major successes with Congress since the first flush of success in 1981. Most notable has been the tax reform legislation of 1986, which Congress greatly shaped in the final process. But, for the most part, the revolution stalled in Congress probably because, as former OMB direc-

[5]Joel D. Aberbach and Bert A. Rockman, "Government Responses to Budget Scarcity: The United States," *Policy Studies Journal* 13 (1985), pp. 494–505.

tor David Stockman astutely observed, this was a revolution more desirable in rhetoric than in operation.

In an important respect, however, even before the Democrats won back the Senate in the 1986 elections, the Reagan administration's substantial efforts to legislate (as all administrations inevitably do, to a degree) through administrative regulation or regulatory review elicited strong congressional reaction when it rubbed sharply against congressional intent. Congressional reactions to perceived abuses of executive discretion, consequently, have become more frequent and restrictive. The use of administrative implementation to pursue White House objectives inevitably runs the risk of strong congressional response. Increased micromanagement of the bureaucracy, therefore, has come both from within the central executive (the EOP) *and* from Congress. Prior to the Iran-contra affair, with full Democratic control of the Congress again established, it appeared as though more of this institutional dueling would occur. That, however, appears less likely now since the administration has lost political leverage—and under the new management of Howard Baker, it probably also has fewer predilections—to govern exclusively through executive processes.

Effects on Federalism

Part of the first-year legislative success of the Reagan presidency involved a dramatic reconstruction of recent intergovernmental patterns of relationships in the American federal system. A number of categorical grant programs, especially in health, were folded into less munificently funded block programs that granted greater discretion to the states. In addition, because of the revenue shortfalls and pressure on the federal budget, numerous federal subsidy programs to states (revenue sharing, for example), local communities, or authorities (mass transit subsidies, for instance) were either ended or sharply curtailed. Between fiscal 1980 and 1985, for example, federal grants in aid to states and localities decreased in absolute terms by $10 billion, and as a percentage of state and local expenditures, they decreased from 26.3 to 21.0 percent.[6]

It was anticipated at the time that once responsibility for expenditures was placed on the states, they would be less likely to be sustained. As one might expect from a federal system, though, there was a good deal of variation among the states in the extent to which they were willing to finance new or heavier burdens. In fact, the extent to which a good many states increased taxes to pay for additional obligations created an ironic set of circumstances for the Reagan administration.

---

[6]Paul E. Peterson, Barry G. Rabe, and Kenneth K. Wong, *When Federalism Works* (Washington, D.C.: Brookings Institution, 1986), p. 2.

As with most Republican administrations, the Reagan presidency was in favor, at least theoretically, of more devolution of discretion at the state level. In the American federal system that typically means variety—an outcome displeasing to national Democrats who favor programs with standards manufactured in Washington. This particular Republican administration, however, has been imbued with a strong flavor about what types of policies are good for the country overall. Some of these policy objectives conflict with the idea of greater discretion at other levels of government.

Thus, while the Reagan administration promoted the supply-side economics of lowering tax rates at the federal level and lopping off expenditures—at which it only modestly succeeded—many states increased taxes and took on additional responsibilities. While the federal deficit climbed at a dizzying pace through the first term of Reagan's presidency, the states, overall, ran a fiscal surplus—although much of this was apparently the result of pension fund investments. Since a national economy does not obey political jurisdictions, the fiscal and tax policies of the federal government possibly were countered at other levels of government.

The commitment of the Reagan administration to a diminished public sphere and a lower taxing federal government undoubtedly was reflected in its initial 1985 proposals to eliminate state and local tax deductions from the federal income tax. In his early reactions to criticism of this aspect of the tax reform proposal, President Reagan indicated that individuals facing this penalty either would be better off moving to lower tax states or pressuring their state governments to reduce taxes. One could infer that the objective behind this sort of proposal was to create a national policy rather than enhance state and local discretion. That also seems to be the reason why the administration went to court seeking to overturn some local affirmative action agreements that failed to reflect the Reagan administration's strongly expressed opposition to quotas based on race or gender.

Federal relations will continue to undergo transformation, but at least for the immediate future, any considerable increase of either federal government grant-in-aid burdens to other levels of government or revival of categorical programs from eliminated programs appears unlikely. The federal government owes too much money to consider giving more money back to states, counties, and cities. This legacy will outlive the Reagan presidency for some time. To that extent, the Reagan administration has achieved its goals. Local units of government no longer beat a path to Washington as frequently. Diversity among states and localities appears to reign—in some respects, to a greater degree than some of the policy missionaries in the Reagan administration might prefer.

POLICIES AND AGENDAS

Most policies are reversible. That is why we hold elections. Carter's efforts to develop alternative sources of energy through government subsidy, for example, have passed into oblivion—as did the policy emphasis on human rights in America's international diplomacy.

Not all policies are equal, however; some have the effect of setting agendas in the future and of setting constraints on succeeding leaders. Strictly speaking, almost nothing is irreversible, but the amount of political will needed to redirect a prior course of action can be extraordinary once that course has been institutionalized, accepted, and expected. That is true even in the Soviet Union where, in theory, democratic centrism prevails; it certainly is true in the United States—where a system of competing and sometimes cooperating institutions dominates.

Policies that have received icon status, for example Old Age Survivors Pension Benefits (social security), can be chipped at only incrementally, syndicating decision making, and diverting costs (including benefits reductions) into the future. The older a program and the more people it directly affects, the more likely that it will have attained icon status. The more it is institutionalized, the less likely it will change, and, consequently, the more it will constrain a succeeding leader's freedom. John Chubb observes that contemporary political change tends to be blunted by the growing extent of policy institutionalization. Richard Polenberg notes the same thing—that the Reagan administration attacked the less firmly accepted programs of the Great Society rather than the more established New Deal programs.

In most respects, the specific policies of the Reagan administration can be reversed with relative ease. Yet, the unusual characteristic of the Reagan administration is that, along with the Johnson and Roosevelt administrations, it has set an agenda that will be reversed only with considerable political costs.

Many of the Reagan administration policy directions actually preceded it. Deregulation, increased defense expenditures, and decreased growth in nondefense expenditures were policy lines promoted in the later years of the Carter administration—illustrating that some strong political currents already were moving in these directions.

There is no doubt, however, that the Reagan administration has put its distinctive stamp on accelerating some of the directions generated by the Carter administration, and it has redirected other Carter administration priorities. More important than cutting expenditures—which, in the aggregate, has not happened to a significant degree—was the Reagan administration's lowering of taxes (a bait that Democrats in Congress took so blatantly that they began a bidding war with the Reagan administration). More important than lowering taxes was the approval of indexation which, again, was initially proposed in a Democratic package organized by the House Ways and Means Committee Chair, Daniel Rostenkowski.

The massive budget deficits left in the wake of this venture into supply-side economics, in essence, have defined the federal agenda ever since. President Reagan adamantly has opposed tax increases although some revenue enhancements have slipped by with final presidential approval. The passage of the Gramm-Rudman legislation in 1986 mandates deficit reduction into law. Whether or not the Congress will pass—and the president will sign—a tax increase bill during the remainder of the Reagan presidency, such a bill will be on the agenda of Reagan's successor unless his successor is Republican Jack Kemp, a supply-side enthusiast. It is much less clear that indexation will be repealed. It is clear that pressures to cap or reduce expenditures of continuing programs will be great, and the likelihood of new spending programs will be remote. While Reagan's policies clearly have accelerated a budget-constraint agenda, these directions began under Carter.

The major reason that the deficit is so large is because the tax cuts and indexation were not followed by equivalent levels of expenditure reduction—for two reasons. First, after the initial reductions were packaged with the reconciliation legislation in 1981, most additional spending cuts were politically unpopular. The president shied away from touching social security benefits in the short run when this possibility raised strong reactions. Second, defense expenditures increased more rapidly and with greater impact than cuts in other spending, which produced a net increase in expenditures. Here, again, a direction set under Carter gained rapid momentum under Reagan.

As total budget pressure grew and Reagan administration budgets were rejected on Capitol Hill, the size of budget defense increases came under close scrutiny. Predictably, because these are discretionary expenditures, the part of the defense budget that took considerable cuts was operations and maintenance or readiness. Since weapons procurement is a long-term process and less easy to cut, its share of the defense budget grew larger, as did the R&D activities associated with the opulently funded Strategic Defense Initiative (SDI). An enlarged naval fleet formed a major part of the Defense Department's budgetary growth. Such a commitment, of course, is both expensive and long-term. As with any capital expenditure of this sort, large associated costs in logistics and personnel necessarily follow. The next administration may slow this process, but it will face the commitments that an enlarged fleet entails.

In matters of foreign policy, the Reagan administration struck a posture sharply different from the Carter administration—especially in its palmier early days. The shift can be characterized in many ways— from Carter's human rights to Reagan's *realpolitik*; from North-South issues to East-West ones; from diplomatic response to military response.

Yet, there have been two Reagan foreign policies under one rhetorical roof. Despite its lavish cold war rhetoric, the core East-West relationship with the Soviet Union has followed relatively cautious lines. If detente policies have not been at the American forefront of this relationship, prudence has dictated avoidance of any potential for direct engagement with the Soviets. It even has dictated some engagement with the normal symbols of the relationship—such as summitry and continuing bilateral negotiations which, however, have been marked by an unusual degree of internal conflict among the American decision-makers. At the same time, in peripheral Third-World zones, the Reagan policy has been to engage with direct or proxy military force in areas regarded as under Soviet influence—most directly, the mini-invasion of Grenada and less directly, the proxy wars in Afghanistan, Nicaragua, El Salvador, and Angola reflect the Reagan doctrine.

Foreign policy changes by words spoken, emphases given, and personalities involved at the top. In the peripheral domains of foreign policy, change that reverses the policies of the Reagan administration as completely as these policies reversed Carter administration policies is quite possible. Foreign policy has especially pliable properties. In the more enduring and central matter of direct relations with the Soviet Union, however, prudence and caution have become the durable by-products of nuclear deterrence.

In sum, Reagan's policies are inherited and heritable. Both the New Deal fundamentals and the prudence of great power relations in the nuclear era have been followed, although lacking special enthusiasm. On some matters where the Reagan administration has held a special passion, such as military support for insurgents in Nicaragua and Angola, reversibility is likely even within the remainder of the Reagan term. Yet, on other matters, such as the immense operating costs of managing a dramatically enlarged federal deficit, the Reagan administration has left its mark. In domestic policy, this means the extensive restriction of expenditures and programs, while in defense, it means coping with the expenditures and logistics committed to present conceptions of strategic force structures. This latter problem will be of special relevance, of course, when the defense budget's readiness is cut to the bone. Already, Congress has resorted to cutting growth in the defense budget to plug the federal deficit.

NORMS OF GOVERNANCE

The design of American government inspires institutional competition. Yet, except for rare circumstances, what makes it work—when it does—is cooperation. The complexity of the system provides strong incentives to maximize adversarial behavior. More generally, political incentives at work in the society also seem to endow presidents with the conception that, in the end, they are the supreme governors of an otherwise cantankerous system.

The conception that the presidency is the sun around which other political bodies orbit is part of the modern idea of the American presidency. When this idea is vigorously held by presidents, strained relations with Congress often result. Presidents adopt, sometimes with good reason, hostile attitudes toward what they regard as the small-mindedness and parochial nature of members of Congress. The contempt that Nixon and his entourage had for Congress was legendary. Carter felt that Congress represented an irrational impediment to good public policy. Despite Reagan's first-year success with Congress, his tendency, in spite of Republican control of the Senate for the first six years of his administration, was to treat it as an opposition institution. It is not surprising that by 1985, one year after his remarkable forty-nine-state electoral sweep, his record with Congress, according to *Congressional Quarterly's* presidential support scores index was only the equivalent of the Nixon-Ford level of success in 1974—the year of Nixon's resignation over the Watergate scandal. This meant a decline of about 23 percent in Reagan's success rate with Congress from his lustrous first-year record.

Despite their different styles, three of the last four presidents (excluding the reconciliation presidency of Gerald Ford) have tended to see themselves as the legitimate possessors of political authority against opposition and status quo institutions. Nixon, Carter, Reagan, and, in some respects, Kennedy all had dim regard for Washington institutions —seeing themselves as the single dynamic element in the governing equation. Stylistic manifestations, of course, differed. Nixon and Carter lacked a fondness for politicians as a class. Reagan and Kennedy, in many respects, were quintessential politicians, but they lacked regard for established and, as they saw them, stagnant institutions.

One institution that all of these presidents disliked was the Washington bureaucracy. The bureaucracy embodies the status quo, continuity, and institutionalization. It reflects skepticism toward new directions, and it often represents the link between special interests and government. To presidents who believe that their plans are blessed with a popular mandate for invigorating government, established institutions present obstacles rather than opportunities. None of the established institutions is so expendable to presidents as the bureaucracy; that is, the stratum of senior career civil servants and the organizational apparatus that houses them.

Reagan is an anti-institutional president—more a radical than a conservative. Yet, in this respect, the Reagan administration hardly has been unique in its anti-institutional bias. Its preoccupations with governing through the executive with secrecy, and with centralization from the White House (even if not directly from the Oval Office), have vigorously reinforced a set of norms that are becoming firmly established in the American system of government. These norms include the following presumptions: (1) the president is essentially the head of government rather than chief of a part of it; (2) the president, unlike a prime minister, need be accountable only to popular standing and not to other elites; (3) only the president is capable of discerning and, above all, acting in the national interest—even when this must be done without consulting other constituted authorities or acting through normal executive channels.

The development of these norms of governance certainly received a powerful boost in the Nixon presidency. Despite Carter's care to stay firmly within the bounds of legal behavior, there was no shortage of contempt in the Carter White House toward what it perceived as establishment Washington. Reagan, above all, came to town determined to root out the past. In fact, his administration seems to have affirmed, especially in the light of the recent Iran-contra scandal, a strengthened commitment to its own norms of governing. Here, we witness evolution rather than revolution. Nevertheless, the methods and approaches of the Reagan administration in governing have reinforced the evolution of these norms with particular vigor.

LEADERSHIP STYLES

Of all the features of a presidency, the most ephemeral qualities focus on the president's style of leadership. If, however, a president's style is a vital factor in his success—or if the style vividly contrasts with less fortunate predecessors—much effort may be expended in using it as a model. Thus, in his book *Presidential Power*, Richard Neustadt immortalized the leadership style of Franklin Roosevelt as an engaged president astutely sensitive to his political levers. Consequently, Neustadt also immortalized bargaining as the medium of presidential power.[7]

In some respects, the style of the Reagan presidency is puzzling. Here is an activist presidency without a highly active and involved president. Here is a president committed to considerable change—yet detached from its management. It is a style best described as *commitment with detachment*.

The commitment aspect of the Reagan presidency is what has produced the politicization of institutions and the polarization of politics. A commitment to new directions has brought with it a strategy to put as much of that direction in institutions as possible for now and the future. The Reagan administration also has brought an ideological political style that has induced polarization. The key votes on the Reagan legislative agenda have met more sharp party differences during roll-call votes—

---

[7]Richard Neustadt, *Presidential Power* (New York: John Wiley & Sons, 1960).

Republicans voting for and Democrats against—than any administration's proposals through Eisenhower.[8] Furthermore, despite President
Reagan's high degree of popularity until the Iran-contra affair, he was
also, in 1984, the most unpopular candidate among opposition voters in
any presidential election through the Eisenhower years.[9] Yet, the commitment side of the Reagan administration appears blunted since the
disclosure of the Iran-contra affair and the Democratic takeover of the
Senate. The new White House staff operation under former Senator
Howard Baker will defuse some of the more incendiary proposals of the
administration during the remainder of its term in office.

While the detached operating style of President Reagan has become
a concern, it was not long ago that, as a model for presidential success, it
threatened to become *de rigueur*. Before it became the butt of jokes in the
wake of the Iran-contra affair, the detached management style was the
object of praise from *Fortune* magazine. The classic conception expressed by Neustadt of how presidents ought to manage their presidencies—interventionist and involved—seemed in need of substantial
revision in viewing the apparent success of the detached Reagan style.
This adulation ended with the uncovering of the Iran-contra affair, and
it is no longer regarded as a style worthy of emulation.

One feature of President Reagan's detachment from operations that
may have a lasting effect is the distancing of the president from the
print media, news conferences, and other settings where uncomfortable
questions can be asked of him. Reagan's news conferences have been
scarce; exceeded in this regard only by Nixon. On a per month basis, for
example, Carter held twice as many news conferences as Reagan. Rop-
ing off an inquiring press from close contact with the president has been
an effective strategy for a president whose forte is public outreach and
whose trouble spot is specific knowledge of policy. Keeping the press
away minimizes the need to rationalize actions, and it allows the White
House to stage more carefully its own public relations opportunities.
The strategy is not foolproof, but on many matters of lesser public
salience it works well. Pressures for an immediate and potentially em-
barrassing response can be avoided while time is bought to hatch response strategies from the White House or to allow controversies to
wither away due to neglect.

[8]See George C. Edwards III, "The Two Presidencies: A Reevaluation,"
American Politics Quarterly 14 (1986) pp. 247–63.

[9]Martin P. Wattenberg, "The Reagan Polarization Phenomenon and the
Continuing downward Slide in Presidential Candidate Popularity," *American
Politics Quarterly* 14 (1986), pp. 219–45.

FINAL COMMENTS

To speak of a Reagan Revolution is an overstatement. Politicians in democracies do not make revolutions even when they are seized by radical purpose. They can, however, leave greater or lesser footprints. Assessing the depth and durability of those marks is hazardous while the administration under evaluation is still in power. The real answers will come later—much later. We can offer only educated speculations for now. In any event, more policy is reversible than hoped for by leaders such as Reagan.

Nevertheless, the Reagan presidency has made significant strides in influencing future events. By the end of its tenure in the White House, the federal judiciary will reflect more of the values of the Reagan presidency than the preceding judiciary. It is likely that a majority of federal judges will have been appointed during the Reagan years. The Reagan administration's imprint will be large—reflecting its eight-year tenure and its persistence in searching for nominees who hold shared values. Although many presidents have been disappointed at the independent views that their nominees on the bench develop, the Reagan administration has striven to keep those disappointments to a bare minimum.

In its philosophy of governance, which is that of executive command and dominance over other institutions, the Reagan presidency has not done anything new, but it has vigorously strengthened this norm. In so doing, it has contributed greatly to a further erosion of the institutionalization of government in the executive branch and, with that, a loss of memory and continuity—values, in any event, hardly prized by radicals. The drift toward executive centrism and politicization of the administrative apparatus is not new, but until the Iran-contra episode, the Reagan presidency's ability to do this was applauded, if not for its ultimate effects, at least for its ability to enhance presidential power. Until the Iran-contra episode, the Reagan presidency achieved, with remarkable facility, what the Nixon presidency, only in its later stages, struggled rather awkwardly to do—create a system of exclusive executive command headquartered ultimately in the White House. This norm is firmly embedded, and it also has become increasingly fashionable in intellectual circles.[10]

The single largest contribution that the Reagan administration has made to the future, however, is in policy—especially tax policy and its impact on the magnitude of the federal deficit. The magnitude of the deficit clearly constrains budgetary growth for a successor, and it creates budgetary pressures on existing programs. Whether this constraint was

---

[10]For instance, see Richard P. Nathan, *The Administrative Presidency* (New York: John Wiley & Sons, 1983), and Moe, "The Politicized Presidency."

intentional is unknown, but it is certainly compatible with Reagan's political philosophy of smaller government in the nondefense sector. Still, these budget pressures interact with demands made on presidents to act as spokespersons of the national interest. If drugs, for instance, are regarded as a national problem worthy of presidential attention, that creates a demand for a program, and a program creates demand for funding.

The pendulum has begun to swing again toward more activist, less extravagant conceptions of government. This, no doubt, has been enhanced by Democrats gaining full control of Congress in the 1986 elections, which provides them with a greater voice in setting the tone for future agendas.

How significant the constraint of the budget deficit will be cannot be foretold; much depends on the shifting of the political sands. A powerful Democratic victory in the 1988 elections could be interpreted as a mandate to increase taxes *and* spending. The perceived outcome of those elections will influence the nature and magnitude of future tax increases and spending redirections. The state of the economy also will play a strong role. It may be that once Reagan leaves office, the Democrats, minus a political target to strike at, will again learn to love deficits.

Although Reagan's impact on policy is significant, its significance is less powerful than a presidency such as Franklin Roosevelt's. Unlike Roosevelt, Reagan has left behind no programs to sustain long-standing and broad constituencies. Indeed, his objective has been to cut these dependencies. Yet, modern democracies, for better or worse, have institutionalized them.[11] Reagan clearly realized that and, in the end, took no risks to reverse the most significant of these institutionalized dependencies. In this context, both the Reagan administration and the Carter administration, in a more modest manner before Reagan, have slowed and even reversed some of the tendencies of the modern welfare-regulatory-interventionist state. A more profound and durable influence, though, will depend upon fundamental political changes in the country that, for now, are not momentously visible.

The politics of democracies balance a tacit and permanent ratification of past policies and the accommodation of short-run to medium-run agenda changes that reflect the impermanence of preferences and priorities. What democracies do not do well, however, is generate revolutions. So, if there is no Reagan Revolution as such, the Reagan presidency, like other presidencies, has left a legacy for its successors. In strictly comparative terms, this legacy is more durable and tenacious than most.

---

[11]For a positive view of this institutionalization, see Douglas E. Ashford, *The Emergence of the Welfare States* (Oxford: Basil Blackwell, 1986). For a negative view, see Benjamin Ginsberg, *The Captive Public: How Mass Opinion Promotes State Power* (New York: Basic Books, 1986).

Index

ABOUT THE AUTHORS

B. B. Kymlicka is a Professor of Political Science at the University of Western Ontario, where he has also served as Chairman of the Department of Political Science and Dean of the Faculty of Social Science. He has a degree from the University of British Columbia and a Ph.D. from Columbia University. He has published studies on the politics of higher education and prepared a number of reports for governments.

Jean Matthews is an Associate Professor of History at the University of Western Ontario. She has degrees from the University of London and Smith College and received the Ph.D. from Harvard University in 1977. She is the author of *Rufus Choate; the Law and Civic Virtue* (Temple University Press, 1980) and several articles in American intellectual history and women's history.

A NOTE ON THE TYPE

The text of this book was set in 10/12 Palatino using a film version of the face designed by Hermann Zapf that was first released in 1950 by Germany's Stempel Foundry. The face is named after Giovanni Battista Palatino, a famous penman of the 16th century. In its calligraphic quality, Palatino is reminiscent of the Italian Renaissance type designs, yet with its wide, open letters and unique proportions it still retains a modern feel. Palatino is considered one of the most important faces from one of Europe's most influential type designers.

Composed by The Saybrook Press, Old Saybrook, Connecticut.